Chasing Religion in the Caribbean

Peter Marina

Chasing Religion in the Caribbean

Ethnographic Journeys from Antigua to Trinidad

Peter Marina
University of Wisconsin - La Crosse
La Crosse, Wisconsin, USA

ISBN 978-1-137-56099-5 (hardcover)   ISBN 978-1-137-56100-8   (eBook)
ISBN 978-1-349-93421-8 (softcover)
DOI 10.1057/978-1-137-56100-8

Library of Congress Control Number: 2016949584

Cover image © Sergi Reboredo / Alamy Stock Photo

Printed on acid-free paper

This Palgrave Macmillan imprint is published by Springer Nature
The registered company is Nature America Inc. New York

To Mom and Pop, respectively, Elena Perez Lopez Marina and Pedro Carlos Marina, and is written in loving memory of Silvia Lopez Ventura de Perez, aka Gagi.

"Foreword to the Chase"

Allan Anderson[1] has categorized the growth of Pentecostalism in Latin America and the Caribbean as "one of the most remarkable stories in the history of Christianity." More recently, Anderson noted that while it is difficult to attribute a single place of origin to Pentecostalism, it is clear that Pentecostalism has become global in outlook. By 2010, over 600 million people from all over the world identified themselves as Pentecostal, which amounts to over a quarter of all Christians.[2] Most studies of Pentecostalism in the Caribbean were conducted by anthropologists, historians, and Religious Studies scholars. Marina's study offers a most welcome sociological perspective on Pentecostal leadership and organizations in the English-speaking Caribbean and Haiti.

Peter Marina does high-quality research. I say this because I reviewed his last book *Getting the Holy Ghost* and because our research interests are much the same. In this "Foreword," I will contextualize Marina's contributions to the study of Pentecostalism with attention to the research of Allan Anderson, Felicitas D. Goodman, Simon Coleman, Margaret Poloma, Stephen D. Glazier, Maurice Godelier, and Maarit Forde.

In some respects, *Chasing Religion in the Caribbean* follows Margaret M. Poloma's sociological study of the largest Pentecostal denomination in America—Assemblies of God—but with a distinct Caribbean slant.[3] Like Poloma, Marina addresses problems faced by leaders of Pentecostal congregations and explores the tensions between Charismatic authority and bureaucratic authority as played out in multiple Pentecostal settings. Both Poloma and Marina underscore the pitfalls of Pentecostal leadership and myriad ways in which charisma-based practices—such as glossolalia, healing, and demon exorcism—have fostered and hindered denominational growth.

Of Max Weber's formulations, "charisma"[4] is perhaps his most slippery. When compared to his more rigorous categorizations ("ideal type") of organizational principles like bureaucracy, "charisma" lacks precision, but Weber's formulation of "charisma" makes up for it with its universal applicability. If Weber had not proposed the idea of charisma, social scientists would have had to invent something else like it in order to fully encompass religious experiences.[5]

When I began my research in Trinidad, it would not have been feasible to look at Spiritual Baptist leadership in terms of the "institutionalization of charisma" as Marina has done. The Spiritual Baptists had not yet attained a sufficient level of bureaucratic organization. There were, as now, numerous competing Spiritual Baptist denominations, but membership in these organizations was entirely voluntary and compliance almost non-existent. At that time, no Spiritual Baptist denominations were effective in influencing church policy. Instead of utilizing the Weberian concept of charisma, I opted—following Fredrick Barth's[6] approach to Swat Pathan politics—to focus on individual leaders and leadership decisions as they impacted church growth and decline. Things changed rapidly. By the 1990s, a focus on the institutionalization of Charismatic leadership among Spiritual Baptists would have been more fruitful.

Today, it is appropriate to focus on Pentecostal leadership because Caribbean Pentecostals themselves see their organizations in terms of leadership. Pastors are strongly identified with their churches, and all members are assigned church duties. Most Pentecostals aspire to leadership roles within their churches.

Marina's chase began several years ago. My chase began in 1976. Unlike Marina, I did not go to the Caribbean in pursuit of Pentecostalism. Pentecostalism, it would seem, pursued me. I traveled to Trinidad to begin research for my PhD dissertation focusing on leadership and decision-making among Trinidad's Spiritual Baptists.[7] I rented a small room on Harris Street in Curepe, a suburb off the Eastern Main Road and near the University of the West Indies. On the way to interview my first Spiritual Baptist leader, I crossed McDonnel Street, which is the location of Curepe's Pentecostal Church, then, as now, one of the largest buildings in Curepe. It was a Wednesday afternoon and the church was bustling with activity. Levi Duncan (who served as pastor of the Curepe church since

1962 and would remain pastor there until 1986) and his five assistants were conducting four exorcisms simultaneously. Another six victims of demon attack had been confined to the back of the Church. Needless to say, this drama caught my attention. I began taking notes on the proceedings, and extensive quotes from my 1976 field notes on Pentecostal exorcism were included in Felicitas D. Goodman's book *How About Demons?*[8]

"The services are performed twice a week. Wednesday exorcisms begin at nine o'clock in the morning and last most of the day, while Friday service begins in the evening and goes well into the night. During the first two hours of service, recorded music is played and those who desire to receive the Holy Spirit are organized into one long line to pass before the altar. The pastor blesses each person practicing the laying on of hands. At this time, those possessed by demons began to quake and shout; they must be restrained and returned to their seats. Of the hundreds who pass before the altar only a few (five or six) are found to be victims of obeah attack. [The rest are understood to have medical problems and are encouraged to consult the nurse of the congregation or a physician]. Rites of exorcism are not performed until the final hours of the service. ... [The pastor] turns to the congregation and tells them that they must praise the Lord for what they have heard here today [during testimonies]. The congregation responds by standing, raising their hands in the air, and chanting "Praise the Lord ... Jesus ... Jesus ... Praise the Lord ... Jesus ... Jesus!" The emotion builds as the pastor reminds the congregation that demons cannot bear to hear the holy name of Jesus. ... The possessed jump from their seats screaming. Church helpers rush to wherever they are and carry them to the front of the church. Usually one or two new victims are discovered at this time.

The pastor approaches each victim individually. He brings the hand microphone down from the altar so that all may hear the possessed. This adds considerably to the dramatic impact of exorcism. He asks four questions of each victim: (1) Who sent you? (2) How many are you? (3) Why are you in him/her? (4) How long have you been in him/her? The response is a series of shrieks and curses.

After five or ten minutes of banter with the demons, the pastor grabs the victim by the throat and commands the demon to leave "In the name of Jesus!" The victim gags; this is taken as a sign of the demon's departure. Some victims are found to be possessed by twenty demons or more.[9]

As Keith E. McNeal[10] points out, the vitality of possession arises from intensified uses of both mind and body. He posits that ritualized possession (and other trance forms as well) should be understood as alter-culture practices reflecting a deeply playful relationship to experience and existence. Play is paramount in Pentecostal ritual. In *How About Demons*, Goodman[11] contrasted what she interpreted as "positive" Pentecostal possession and what she saw as "negative" possession by African spirits in Haitian *vodu*. But as Marina (who includes a vivid description of voodoo ceremonies in this book) emphasizes, members of these religions would not accept Goodman's categorization. Pentecostal possession and possession by African spirits can be seen as both positive and negative. While many Spiritual Baptists are also devotees of African spirits (Orisa), Orisa possession in the midst of Baptist worship is considered demonic as is possession by any spirit excepting the Holy Ghost. "One man's demon is another man's god." Context determines the interpretation.

Demonic possession differs dramatically from Caribbean island to Caribbean island, with the greatest variation occurring in Trinidad, which also serves as headquarters of the Pentecostal Assembly of the West Indies (PAWI). Demons in Trinidad might be African Orisa, Hindu deities, Obeah duppies, and/or Kali Mai. Perhaps this is why so much attention is paid to the origins of demons in Trinidad exorcisms and why so little attention is paid to identifying the origins of demons on other Caribbean islands. Another consideration may be that a majority of PAWI pastors were trained in Trinidad. On the other hand, demon possession is rare even in some Trinidad churches, and in these churches, pastors must be brought in from other villages to perform exorcisms.

The Curepe church I first studied now calls itself "The Curepe Pentecostal Empowerment Ministries International." The current pastor (since 2014) is Rev. Dr. Melch A. Pope, originally from Chaguanas, Trinidad, who graduated from the West Indies School of Theology in 1980. Pope was assigned to the Cedros, Trinidad, Pentecostal Church where he served as Pastor/Evangelist. He also served as a pastor on the island of St. Vincent. The PAWI is very much an international organization and its pastors are routinely assigned to different Caribbean islands during the course of their religious careers.

The major differences between Pentecostal Trinidad services in 1976 and those attended by Marina are: (1) exorcisms are now conducted on Wednesday mornings only; (2) many exorcisms are performed privately (Rev. Pope's preference); and (3) Rev. Pope seldom engages demons in conversations as did Levi Duncan, so exorcisms are far less entertaining. In Curepe, questions for demons remain much the same (Who sent you?

How many are you? How long have you been in him/her? Why are you in him/her?), but the pastor rarely waits for a response before grabbing the victim by the throat. Exorcisms have been greatly abbreviated and are no longer the main church event. And in many Trinidad churches, services do not include exorcisms at all.

Meanwhile exorcism is taking on greater significance in churches throughout the Caribbean and in other religions around the world. For example, the Vatican has begun training a new generation of exorcists. A team of practicing exorcists was convened by the Vatican in 2015 to equip doctors, psychologists, and teachers with the skills needed to recognize and deal with demonic possession. Like Pentecostal pastors in the Caribbean, Vatican spokespersons cited a need to distinguish demonic possession from psychological and medical illnesses. And like the Caribbean Pentecostal pastors studied by Marina, Vatican spokespersons—including Pope Francis—assert that the devil exists. In 2015, the Pope performed an exorcism of a wheelchair-bound male who is said to have shaken violently when Pope Francis laid hands on him and issued a blessing.

In addition to a focus on exorcism, Pentecostal leaders worldwide have gained attention for their stance against gay marriage and for their condemnations of homosexuality. In the Caribbean, the PAWI has criticized the recent decision by the US Supreme Court to legalize same-sex marriages, saying it endangers the belief of the church and violates the law of God. PAWI pamphlets make it clear that Pentecostal opposition to same-sex marriage in no way shows resentment or hatred for individuals who are in support of gay marriage and homosexuality, "as this will be in stark contradiction to the very word of God which we uphold as the supreme authority governing our lives." While—like Marina—I find Pentecostal teachings on homosexuality inconsistent and cruel, Pentecostals claim that their teachings are biblically based and consistent with select Old Testament teachings.

Pentecostal positions on gay marriage have been consistent over time; for example, in 1985, Felicitas D. Goodman[12] attended the opening session at the "Christian Center for Information about the Occult" in Santa Fe, New Mexico, where a Pentecostal minister advocated exorcism as a cure for gays. This pastor's explanation is nearly identical to the explanation given to Professor Marina more than 30 years later.

Marina also examines gender inequality and the place of women within Pentecostal churches. Women perform valuable church duties and constitute the overwhelming majority of Pentecostal church members, but they are not well represented in church hierarchies. Marina gives an example of the eminent historian, PAWI executive officer, and sometimes Acting Governor of Monserrat, Sir Howard Fergus OBE, who advocates higher status for Pentecostal women, but has been ineffective in implementing change. Fergus's opinions are shared by almost every Pentecostal I have met, but gender inequality remains an issue. By contrast, the status of women in Spiritual Baptist churches, Orisa gatherings, and Rastafarian communities has changed dramatically. This is largely because women own many religious buildings outright. Males attend ceremonies by invitation.

Marina underscores special difficulties in conducting research with pastors, particularly in establishing rapport while at the same time maintaining distance. As Simon Coleman[13] observed, prolonged proximity can foster ambivalence, and geographical distances are often much easier to transcend than social distances. Isolation, Marina notes, is a common plight for both religious leaders and for those who would study them.

In her now-famous 1987 essay, Susan Harding[14] describes how scholars of the 1980s often categorized American Pentecostals and fundamentalists as "repugnant cultural others." Harding ultimately committed herself as an anthropologist to the project of designing effective strategies to oppose the positions and policies advocated by conservative Christians; yet, at the same time, she recognized that social scientists needed to develop more nuanced, local, and partial accounts to describe who they are, thus "deconstructing the totalizing opposition between us and them." In 2000, Vincent Crapanzano[15] recounted an equally disconcerting encounter with an evangelical in Los Angeles who relentlessly questioned him about his personal religious beliefs for over four hours.

Simon Coleman asserts that there are two routes of ethical practice for anthropologists in relation to conservative and evangelical Christianity, although these routes do not necessarily lead in the same direction. One route is an ethic of overt political action, a hardening of attitudes, and a fight for what is perceived as the morally good beyond the academic world—a kind of engagement as opposition as espoused by Harding. A second route advocates a disciplinary stance that is a form of academic self-cultivation constituted precisely by seeing aspects of the self in the conventionally "repugnant Other." Elaine Lawless[16] talks of how the language of conversion nearly catches her in its narrative hooks. One question is: How might acceptance of the need for politically articulated opposition relate to the ethnographic project of self-deconstruction on behalf of the other? Is the Other repugnant in the first modality but not the second? Another question not addressed by Coleman: Who is the repugnant Other? Is it the informant or the social scientist?

As one who has spent the past 30-plus years interviewing Trinidad religious leaders—Pentecostal, Spiritual Baptist, Orisa, and Rastafarians—I have never found Caribbean religious leaders to be repugnant—or at least as they were encountered by Harding and Crapanzano. A number of factors account for this. The primary factor is that Caribbean religious leaders lack the resource base to engage in the large-scale corruption that Margaret Poloma recorded in her study of the Assemblies of God in the USA. The Caribbean has not yet produced a Jimmy Swaggart or a Jim Bakker. As Gordon K. Lewis[17] pointed out, Jim Jones may have taken his followers to Guyana, but Guyana could never produce a Jim Jones. Another factor is that Caribbean people are more respectful of the religious beliefs of others and assume that everyone is a believer of some sort. Caribbean people take belief statements seriously. They believe that people really believe what they profess to believe; for example, Caribbean Pentecostals assume (perhaps incorrectly) that all who attend their worship services are religious seekers. This is because they too first entered the Pentecostal religion as skeptics.[18]

Wilfred Cantwell Smith[19] cogently argued that statements of personal belief are strong statements and are almost impossible to refute. There are few avowed atheists in the Caribbean, and nonbelievers generally keep their antireligious opinions to themselves. As Spiritual Baptist Leader Albert DeBique told me 20 years ago, "Trinis don't believe in atheism."

Marina correctly contends that the Caribbean is an area where secularization has not yet taken hold. And unlike American politicians and academics, Caribbean leaders gain legitimacy through their religious ties. People expect politicians to act in support of religion. Religious leaders of all persuasions were shocked when Trinidad's Prime Minister (herself a Hindu and a Spiritual Baptist) did not stop the demolition of a Spiritual Baptist Church that stood in the way of a real estate development.

The status of Caribbean scholars and political leaders is greatly enhanced by their religious affiliations; for example, when Marina interviewed Sir Howard Fergus OBE, Fergus stated that his status as a Pentecostal believer enhanced his political and academic reputation in the Caribbean, while Marina contended that a believer/scholar would experience a lesser status in the USA. In his book *Tongues on Fire*, Fergus contends that "there are more Pentecostal Christians from Monserrat or of Montserratian parentage living abroad than living at home. ... Monserrat can boast a significant

Pentecostal diaspora. Echoing the apostles in the book of Acts, as they went, they spread the word."[20] But he also acknowledges that Pentecostal believers in Montserrat are accorded lesser status than Monserrat-born Pentecostals living abroad.

Marina is not shy about expressing his opinions, but he exercises considerable skill and diplomacy in expressing his own ideas without giving rise to acrimonious debate. This is never an easy task. As noted previously, Susan Harding's encounter with a Baptist pastor, Rev. Cantrell, in his church office very quickly turned into an unsettling denouncement of her and her research objectives.[21]

Marina's access to pastors varied from place to place—even on the same island. Generally, I find that when informants are unwilling to talk with researchers, it indicates that they may have little to offer. Like Marina, I found the most prominent Caribbean religious leaders to be the most generous with their time. Perhaps they associated researchers with seminary faculty they had known (many of whom hold doctorates). Marina enjoyed unprecedented access to many of the most powerful Pentecostal leaders. At the same time, lesser, rural pastors did not have as much direct access to the most powerful leaders of PAWI. Of course, a number of leaders refused to talk with Marina at all. This is true for ethnographic research in general.

Theological education has a considerable impact on denominational politics. Most high profile PAWI Pentecostals enroll in continuing education classes at the West Indies School of Theology in Trinidad in order to build and maintain support networks. Marina depicts the confidence and theological sophistication of "Bishop" and "Apostle" of Trinidad who engaged Marina in academic (abstract) discussions about religious leadership while having breakfast at the Trinidad Hilton, an elite setting that also reflects the elevated social and economic standing of these religious leaders. Education is highly valued in the Caribbean. For an entire generation of Caribbean people, "Dr. Politics" was the norm (e.g. Dr. Eric Williams, Dr. Edward Seaga, "Papa Doc" Duvalier—who studied folklore and ethnography in addition to medicine).

George Marcus[22] has suggested that the agency and organizing power of the researcher is made explicit through strategic decisions to "follow" people, things, and metaphors. Marcus mediates between images of fixity and flow, openness and closure, accepting the contingency of the research subject while retaining emphasis on the need to explore the everyday consciousness of informants, including their "system awareness" and their knowledge of other sites and agents.

As Marina emphasizes, Pentecostal leaders act within an extensive network of other pastors and other churches. In many respects, Marina experienced the Pentecostal religion like an itinerant pastor—he traveled from island to island. This is the same way Pentecostal pastors experience their religion. Prominent pastors travel extensively. Clifford Geertz once asserted that ethnographic authority comes from "being there," but in Caribbean islands there is also considerable prestige in "being away." Pentecostal leaders illustrate Maurice Godelier's[23] astute observation that power is not centered in any one group but is accumulated as one moves from one group to another. Social power, according to Godelier, exists primarily between groups—not within a single group. Marina's multi-site research agenda conforms to local expectations for leadership. Religious travel (pilgrimage) is an important component of Caribbean religious leadership.[24] Leaders, too, chase their religion from one island to the next. Movement gave Marina an insider's perspective on leadership and also afforded him a degree of prestige unavailable to previous generations of researchers—like myself—who were encouraged to stay in one place.

To reiterate, Marina has done compelling research. This book constitutes a welcome blend of theoretical sophistication and sensitive participant-observation. As noted, the author's focus on leadership is entirely appropriate because a large percentage of Pentecostals seek leadership positions themselves. And Max Weber's ideas concerning the "institutionalization of charisma" are apt because Weber's ideas about charisma—while less amenable to empirical measurement—are easily grasped by believers and social scientists. Moreover, many of Marina's informants would appear to articulate their leadership problems in Weberian terms. Additionally, Marina provides insight into his methodology and candidly recounts some of his difficulties in establishing rapport with Caribbean religious leaders well as some of the difficulties in establishing and maintaining distance.

Stephen D. Glazier

Stephen D. Glazier is a Graduate Professor of Anthropology at the University of Nebraska-Lincoln. He is general editor of *The Encyclopedia of African and African American Religions* (Routledge, 2001) and a founding member of the editorial board of the journal *PentecoStudies*.

ACKNOWLEDGMENTS

The conception of this book originated in New York's great borough of Brooklyn and became an ethnographic odyssey throughout the Caribbean region involving research in the countries of Antigua and Barbuda, Montserrat, St. Kitts and Nevis, Trinidad and Tobago, Barbados, St. Martin, St. Lucia, Dominica, and Haiti. Antigua, especially, will always have a special place in my heart, especially the capital of St. John's and the delightful village of English Harbour.

The writing of this book took place at Fair Grinds coffee shop in my home city of New Orleans, Root Note Café in the small town of La Crosse along the Mississippi River, Nina's Café in St. Paul of the Twin Cities, Antigua's capital of St. John's, La Cafetera in the Dominican Republic capital of Santo Domingo, and ended in the Zócalo of Oaxaca and at Café La Habana in Mexico City, where it is believed Ché and Castro plotted their rebellion against imperialism in Cuba. Few things in life match the joy of writing and travel.

Thanks to the Research and Grants Committee for the Faculty Research Grant that provided financial support for this project as well as the Small Grants Committee in the College of Liberal Studies, the International Development Fund, and the Department of Sociology at the University of Wisconsin—La Crosse. I hope the university continues to fund projects from scholars conducting international research.

Special thanks to Margaret Poloma, Peter Althouse, Michael Wilkinson, and Stephen Glazier for all the great comments and suggestions to help make this book better. Your scholarship continues to influence my work and thinking.

This research would have been much more difficult without some of the most gracious and selfless hosts encountered during the research. Jackie from "Jackie's Place" provided affordable accommodation in her beautiful house in English Harbour, Antigua. The great missionary Papa Johan Smoorenburg selflessly provided me with full transportation and housing throughout my stay in Haiti. Smoorenburg is another example of the capacity of humans to display altruism.

Reverend "Rev" Henry Nigel and his wonderful family offered their gracious hospitality with full accommodations in my trip to Barbuda. The Rev is a genuine man of outstanding character. I will never forget our time together and the conversations we shared.

The research for this book may not have been possible without Apostle Andrews and his secretary Colette Southwell of Antigua. Andrews is a man of integrity and honor. He allowed me to ask direct and, at times, pressing questions that he responded to candidly. Thanks for all your support and trust, and the connections that you provided throughout the Caribbean. Our time in Antigua and Trinidad will stay with me always.

Thanks to Heather Lynn Millett and the miracle story of her adopted son Taj. Although this testimony was beyond the scope of this book, may the world one day know that beautiful forces are at work in this world.

I thank Bishop Lester Bradford of Brooklyn for making all of this research possible. Bishop Bradford is a highly unique man, one of the most sincere and thoughtful men I have ever known. It is a great honor sharing this world with you.

It does not happen often, since friends are so difficult to find, but I consider Pastor Matthew Noyce as my close friend. We shared so many great conversations in Antigua, including Nash's Place over lunch. Noyce is a rare gem in this world; thank you, Breda. May the memory of Brother Dean Tanner live on.

The folks at Palgrave did a wonderful job throughout the research and production process. Thank you to Mireille Yanow, Milan Vernikova, Mara Berkoff, and all the staff at Palgrave Macmillan who helped bring this book to fruition.

Finally, thanks to my immediate family and close friends for enduring with me and tolerating my incessant talk about this research.

Peter Marina
— New Orleans, 2016

NOTES

1. Allan Anderson, *An Introduction to Pentecostalism: Global Charismatic Christianity* (Cambridge: Cambridge University Press, 2004), 63.
2. Allan Anderson, *To the Ends of the Earth: Pentecostalism and the Transformation of World Christianity* (New York: Oxford University Press, 2013), 2.
3. Margaret M. Poloma, *The Assemblies of God at the Crossroads: Charisma and Institutional Dilemmas* (Knoxville: University of Tennessee Press, 1989).
4. Max Weber, *From Max Weber: Essays in Sociology* (New York: Routledge, 2009), 51.
5. Ann Taves, *Religious Experience Reconsidered* (Princeton: Princeton University Press, 2009), 115.
6. Fredrik Barth, *Political Leadership among Swat Pathans* (London: Athlone Press, 1959). I met Professor Barth on a plane and told him I had used his model for a dissertation on Trinidad religious leaders. There was a long pause. He asked me if it worked. I said "Yes." He replied "Lucky man" and continued reading his newspaper. Later, as we were getting off the plane, he confided his concern that his interpretations of Swat Pathan political machinations might not be applicable in non-tribal settings.
7. Stephen D. Glazier, "Leadership Roles, Church Organization and Ritual Change among the Spiritual Baptists of Trinidad," Unpublished Doctoral Dissertation (Storrs: University of Connecticut, 1981). See also Stephen D. Glazier, *Marchin' the Pilgrims Home: Leadership and Decision-Making in an Afro-Caribbean Faith* (Westport, CT: Greenwood Press, 1983).
8. Felicitas D. Goodman, *How About Demons?: Possession and Exorcism in the Modern World* (Bloomington: Indiana University Press, 1988), 93–94.
9. Other field notes on Pentecostal exorcisms were incorporated into a 1977 paper at the American Anthropological Association in Houston and in Stephen D. Glazier, "Pentecostal Exorcism and Modernization in Trinidad," in *Perspectives on Pentecostalism: Case Studies from the Caribbean and Latin America*, ed. Stephen D. Glazier (Lanham, MD: University Press of America, 1980), 67–80.
10. Keith E. McNeal, *Trance and Modernity in the Southern Caribbean: African and Hindu Popular Religions in Trinidad and Tobago* (Gainesville: University Press of Florida, 2011), 20–21.
11. Goodman, 1988, 52. See also William K. Kay and R. Parry, eds., *Deliverance and Exorcism: Interdisciplinary Perspectives* (Chester, UK: Paternoster, 2011).
12. Goodman, 1988, 87.
13. Simon Coleman, "Borderlands: Ethics, Ethnography and 'Repugnant' Christianity," *HAU* 5, no. 2 (2015): 275–300.
14. Susan Harding, "Convicted by the Holy Spirit: The Rhetoric of Fundamental Baptist Conversion," *American Ethnologist* 14 (1987): 167–181. Webb

Keane has also noted that a discourse underscoring sincerity and the transparent use of language is central to Pentecostal communication with outsiders.

15. Vincent Crapanzano, *Serving the Word: Literalism in America from the Pulpit to the Bench* (New York: New Press, 2000), 83.

16. Elaine Lawless, "I was Afraid that Someone Like You, An Outsider, Would Misunderstand," *Journal of American Folklore* 105 (1992): 302–314.

17. Gordon K. Lewis, *Gather With the Saints at the River* (Rio Piedras, PR: Institute of Caribbean Studies, 1979).

18. Andrew S. Buckser and Stephen D. Glazier, eds., *The Anthropology of Religious Conversion* (Lanham, MD: Rowman and Littlefield, 2003).

19. Wilfred Cantwell Smith, *Believing: An Historical Perspective* (Oxford: One World, 1998), 4.

20. Sir Howard Fergus, OBE, *Tongues on Fire: A History of the Pentecostal Movement of Montserrat* (Brades, Monserrat: PAWI, 2011), 71.

21. Susan Harding, "'Convicted by the Holy Spirit: The Rhetoric of Fundamental Baptist Conversion," *American Ethnologist* 14 (1987): 167–181. Webb Keane (1997) noted that a discourse underscoring sincerity and the transparent use of language is central to Pentecostal communication with outsiders.

22. James Clifford, *Routes: Travel and Translation in the Late Twentieth Century* (Cambridge: Harvard University Press, 1997).

23. See William Roseberry's "Review of *The Mental and the Material*, by Maurice Godelier," *American Journal of Sociology* 95, no. 4 (Jan 1990): 1070–1072.

24. Stephen D. Glazier, "Pilgrimages in the Caribbean: A Comparison of Cases from Haiti and Trinidad," in *Religion, Pilgrimage, and Tourism*, eds. Alex Norman and Carole M. Cusack (New York and London: Routledge, 2015).

Contents

LIST OF TABLES

CHAPTER 1

Spiritual Rumblings in the Caribbean

The stifling humidity of the deep Caribbean wrestles in vain to hold down the perceived supernatural forces where God, Satan, demons, and Obeah forces battle to shape the outcome of this night's events.[1] It starts with the usual calm "yah mahn" tranquility of Caribbean culture. Yet, this calm is unusually suspicious. Settled in the eastern arc of the Leeward Islands, the silence of the night makes a foreboding presence as we enter the empty million-dollar church on the outskirts of Antigua's capital, St. John's. The bishop exudes confidence, complete with a military-style wardrobe that includes a Catholic priest-like white collar, dark robe, and brilliant red buttons, as if he is a commander in God's army. Indeed, to many of those who follow the bishop, he *is* a commander in God's army.

And then light illuminates the bishop and his group of fellow travelers. The bishop's entourage traveled from far and away to witness what was later described as an unprecedented event in Caribbean history—a prayer revival intended to unite the historically divisive traditional, evangelical, and independent Christian churches in the Caribbean to become a more powerful force shaping the political, cultural, social, and economic landscape of the region.

For the bishop, the idea of uniting the divided Christian churches began with a vision; believers call it his divine mission from God. Success required strong communication skills and persuasive rhetoric, the stuff of charisma found in the Evangelical movement. He devised strategies, built strong friendships, traveled abroad, and communicated with religious leaders from all over the Caribbean. God may have provided the

© The Author(s) 2016
P. Marina, *Chasing Religion in the Caribbean*,
DOI 10.1057/978-1-137-56100-8_1

1

idea, but humans must bring ideas to fruition. Like most visions, the right amount of patience must balance with the right dosage of persistence. For the bishop, this moment was 15 years in the making. The long road finally returns to his homeland where—many years after immigrating to the USA—his vision to do the nearly impossible now finally becomes an objective reality.

"Let's go, let's go, let's go, let's just pray," he says giving marching orders to his troops as he begins to walk around the church pews. The church musical team takes its place in the perfectly polished elevated wooden platform five steps above the church floor. The bishop and crew of about ten others begin to "prayer walk" around the interior of the church. Though the celebration is now in full progress, no outsiders have yet entered the church. But their being alone does not stop the intensity from building steam, a locomotive determined to reach its end.

Sitting in this church looking at subjective visions unfold to realized objective realities inspires one to think back to "the cradle of the worldwide Pentecostal movement"[2] in 1906 Azusa Street in faraway Los Angeles. It was a leaderless, Charismatic, and spontaneous wave with a raw energy so great that it set in motion a tide that would seemingly never crash. The momentum, the sheer spontaneity, the pure burst of emotion produced one of the greatest religious movements in the contemporary world. There was a sense that all the injustices of the world, all the wrongs, the evildoers, the oppressive institutions, and the trivial rulers of the world, would have to succumb to the great powerful tidal wave of God's cleansing of the world's sins. There was a sense of victory, an inevitable feeling of success, that the wronged world would turn right. It was, as Walt Whitman once said, "nature without check with original energy."[3] They were riding a supernatural crest of what they believed as God's love that would cover the Earth and expose all of humanity to this truth. The Pentecostal movement started as a powerful global force with the weight of the Gods behind it.

Now, over a 100 years later, many scholars argue that, at least in the Western cultures, the once mighty tide is now rolling back, hardening to a bureaucratic and cold institution losing its mojo.[4] But in the Caribbean, and during this night here in Antigua, where 15 years—what I will later call "Charismatic religious networking"—lead to a verbal agreement of Christian leaders to unite as one powerful force; here, there is no high water mark, and there is no rolling back of the tide. Unlike the USA, 1300 miles away, followers continue to ride a towering crest of a high and rising wave with the feeling that they—the soldiers of God—will triumph and prevail over all evil forces and obstacles and continue to flourish. The prayer walk is a ritual that serves as a form of "spiritual warfare" intended to cleanse the church sanctuary of evil spirits and provide a veil of protection to the people of God to bring forth the will of their deity. It is not joyful prayer or a tender worship that describes this scene, but rather, an intense emotionally charged determinism. The bishop shouts, "In the name of God, we carry out your will today" as others shout, "We are not worthy, oh Lord, we are not worthy of the power you befall upon us."

The first outsider eyes, shocked and bewildered, peak through the cracks of the church door to witness this religious decadence. They were expecting to attend a service for "National Prayer Day" as the bishop advertised on ABS radio 90.5 FM earlier that week. There was much more in store than advertised.

The huge church space gradually fills with audience members impressed with the unusually intense beginning of this night of prayer. The service follows the same basic structure of typical Charismatic Christian services with musical performances that blends worship and praise songs, bible readings, testimonies, and tithing leading up to the preaching. Even the preaching remains what one expects in many services with storytelling that reveals the wisdom and power of God. Everything seems relatively normal until the bishop pauses for a moment and then speaks. In prophetic tone he says, "The Lord showed me the principalities over this nation. And principalities, they're prince demons. They are of high rank. They're right under Satan."

He makes connections between the spiritual and material world explaining that the material world is a direct manifestation of the spiritual world where demons and heavenly forces battle for the fate of humanity. These demonic spirits have a devastating impact on the social world of the Caribbean, especially on its political institutions. He declares, "These principalities go after presidents and prime ministers, the leaders of countries, and the highest rank in the nation. ... They are wicked and powerful spirits. ... The system that you have in this world is a satanic system."

While religious worldviews no longer dominate our understanding of politics in today's increasingly secularized late modern world, such views continue to dominate Caribbean life. These demonic spiritual forces are believed to influence the decision of political leaders that leads to institutional political corruption. The bishop explains to his listeners, "That's why the system is so crooked, that's why politicians are crooked. You can't take what politicians say [as reliable], you need to take it with a grain of salt. And to be honest, you need to take it with many bags of salt." Demonic spirits, he continues, have captured Antigua and the rest of the English-speaking Caribbean ushering in decades of poverty, corruption, stagnation, suffering, crime, disease, and social ills of every kind. A new era is dawning, a new time approaching to deliver the islands from these evils, these demonic forces and spirits that cause otherwise good people to carry out the will of evil.

The supernatural forces believed to shape social, political, economic, and cultural life prior to the enlightenment gave way to the principles of science and rationality. If the spirits remain sleeping in the modern Western world, they never slumbered here in the English-speaking Caribbean where they are awake and prospering. Religion permeates every aspect of social life in the region. Most scholarly accounts understand secularization using one or more of the following characteristics: (1) religion as no longer the dominant institution shaping world events; (2) religion as less influential within other institutions, (3) people as less religious today than in the past, and (4) religions themselves as becoming increasingly less religious.[5] It is clear though, that, at least in the English-speaking part of the Caribbean, religion dominates social life. In particular, religion remains a potent force in shaping the economic, political, social, and cultural world of the Caribbean and its people remain, since the days of slavery, religiously minded with strong Christian ties.

If evil is the cause of failed secular society, and if evil exists in spiritual form, then, at least to these believers, only God's forces can combat the worldly wrongs. The bishop preaches, "God is talking to this nation right now about unity. It is for us to be one. This is the reason why you see a Catholic bishop, a Methodist pastor, a bishop from the Anglican church, and another from a Moravian bishop, with us. We have leaders from established churches and leaders from the evangelical churches." The crowd looks around trying to place the location of all the religious leaders throughout the church. He goes on, "Do you know why? Because the Lord has said to me, 'you cannot win the nation when the church is divided.' The Lord said to me, 'Satan has a plan and it is to keep the church divided,' because once we are divided, we have no power."

Power. Power. Power. That is a word that seems to describe, in many ways, Pentecostalism. Its adherents use it as a weapon to combat problems from the personal to the social, while its leaders use it to shape politics and world events. The poor use it to lift themselves out of poverty or use it as a theology of liberation, or as others argue, "Liberation theology opted for the poor, but the poor opted for Pentecostalism."[6] It works well as a strong force to assimilate people into the status quo while it also has the potential to resist the structural forces that weigh heavily on us all. In some ways it simultaneously stifles its adherents while also proves to be a vehicle for agency and resistance. Its seemingly supernatural forces have scholars wondering with fascination about its empirical ability to radically shape politics in Latin America, especially Brazil.[7] While some scholars say its power is diminishing north of the equator, others—like I have pointed out elsewhere—show how it remains a big force in small places, like the small storefronts within our inner-city ghettos.[8] Others show its ebb and flow, succumbing to routinization, only to be jolted back to life with powerful revivals like the Toronto Blessing.[9] Still others, myself included, look at the movement's power to impact the largely ignored (but not for long) Latino congregations, whose members seem to use Pentecostalism as a tool to reinvent themselves in a new and foreign country.[10,11,12] Even during interviews, Pentecostals frequently use the rhetoric of power as common in their vernacular. Power is the discourse of Pentecostals. That one word, power, defines, in part, this Pentecostal movement and its stubborn refusal to fade into obscurity.

The bishop requests, "I want all the pastors and church leaders, I want you to come. The church cannot be one with the world. If you're a leader please come. The church cannot be one with the world." About seventeen males and one female approach the elevated wooden platform and stand looking directly up to the towering bishop, who eyeballs each and every one of them as he tells them of the precarious future. With his piercing eyes glaring down upon the unsuspecting religious leaders, the bishop prophesizes, "The Lord said the principalities in Antigua and Barbuda are suckled spirits over our nation. They are dark sinister spirits … four powerful spirits that have been with us for hundreds of years. … One, the spirit of deception, two, a religious spirit, three, spirit of falsehood and four, the spirit of division. And the Lord said that those spirits have sealed our nation." These spirits, he says, control the political and economic leaders of the country and have led the Caribbean people astray since the days of slavery to present-day poverty.

The bishop uses his body as a "vessel" for supernatural forces to break seals and cast off demons one at a time:

> The seal of deception, religion, falsehood and division, in the name of Jesus, upon thee authority that you have vested in me, you have sent me at this time to do this. This is not something I took upon myself. But it is something that

you have commissioned me to do in the name of Jesus. ... I break the spirit of deception. I break the spirit of religion. I break the spirit of falsehood. I break the spirit of division. Over the spiritual leaders of this nation of Antigua and Barbuda and in the name of Jesus, I declare that the unholy seal is broken. I call upon the fire of God to bring those principalities, bind the principalities right now into the fire, bind them over your leaders, these men of Jesus, bind in Jesus name.

Now only one evil spirit remains. He uses the "Holy Ghost power" to strike this final spirit believed to be responsible for the centuries-long division of the Church. He declares, "Spirit of estrangement, I come against you, in Jesus's name, and I bind you. I cast you off the people of God. We declare that no more will we be strangers, no more will we be separated from one another, but we are bound together by Christ and His blood."

The leaders stare at the preaching bishop looking up to this towering ferocious man fighting the demons believed to be responsible for wreaking havoc in the Caribbean. The seals, he proclaims, are now broken and the demons cast out. A new path is set. Reminiscent of the biblical quote, "It has been written but now I say unto you," the bishop decrees that the Church has been divided, but now, he says unto us, it will be united. This is charisma par excellence.

The first steps of his vision now begin to materialize. In this triumphant moment, he makes a final declaration, "In the name of Jesus, I declare that we are one; we are of the same following, under the same Shepard, the Lord Jesus Christ. ... We have entered into this fellowship. Hear the Holy Ghost say, 'embrace your brothers and your sisters.' Embrace your brothers and your sisters."

The leaders embrace each other and shake hands giving symbolic gesture to their unity. The leaders represent various traditions including the Anglican Church, Pentecostal Church, Moravian Church, Methodist Church, Seventh-Day Adventists, and other mainly Protestant groups. Together, these leaders promise to unite as one unified force to combat the demonically influenced secular political, social, economic, and cultural institutions that are believed to be responsible for a plague that has caused the people misery and ruin. The bishop jumps off the lectern to join the collective embrace. A new era, they believe, has proverbially dawned.

The service ends. The lights turn off as we walk out the church into the large parking lot surrounded by huge walls that make the church building seem like a castle protected by a moat. We jump into the car ready to reminisce on the events that just transpired.

The bishop is now relaxed. The pressure and tension vanished.
  Time to lime.
  Enjoy the victory.

The bishop, I could tell, is pleased that I witnessed this event. After all, it's proof that great things are happening; the Charismatic Christian movement is making headway for social change. It was an impressive feat. The world is all right.

Everything changes as we enter the car.
  First comes the panic.
  "Jesus! Jesus! In the name of Jesus!"
  Then comes the wailing and screams as if someone were just slaughtered.
  "Help, help, oh no."
  "In the name of Jesus!"
  "What's that?"
  "She wants to fight?"
  "Who's that?"
  "Jesus! Jesus!"
  "She wants to fight, the girl."
  "Dear Lord!"
  "Father! Son! Holy spirit! Dear lord! Jesus! Jeeesus! Jesus! Jesus."

A young woman throws wild and fast punches with reckless abandon. "Just swing as hard as possible" seems to be fighting strategy.

The rage shocks us the most, that wild rage. And the noises she makes; horrible, frightful noises as she swings her closed fists at, first, the bishop's son, and then anyone trying to stop her.

She is about 17 and a half-dozen grown men cannot stop her. She moves fast and swings harder. Her physical strength displays much more power than her thin athletic frame would seem capable of producing. Her strength downright deceives.

The bishop runs to the scene startled, bewildered, and shocked. He attempts to break up what automatically registers in his mind as a fight. The young woman delivers a direct blow to his face. The bishop, a strong and athletic man in his own right, is unfazed.

Now about a dozen men surround the flailing woman who shows no signs of relenting. In this commotion, the men plead their case to the bishop arguing that she is attacking them for no apparent reason. I wonder to myself, "Why is this happening? What is going on? What will happen next?"

People interpret reality through numerous theoretical lenses. And there are multiple interpretations of reality from our dreaming to waking state, sober to high, and in to and out of love lives. The lenses people develop relate to their positions of power and ideology within our institutions. The Charismatic Christians at this scene occupy positions within a religious institution that believes spiritual battles in a supernatural world powerfully shape human life in a physical realm. As the Thomas dictum states, "If men define situations as real, they are real in their consequences." And to these men, the reality is that this woman is demonically possessed.

Satan, it is believed, brought his evil spirits to prevent the church from fulfilling the bishop's divine mission to unify the church.

And an exorcism is needed.

Merton's concept of latent and manifest functions[13] provides some insight to understand the complexities of what is about to transpire below. On the surface, the manifest function of the exorcism is to relieve the unfortunate woman of her demonic possession, its effectiveness, of course, beyond the scope of sociological questioning. On the one hand, the ensuing exorcism carries practical implications that serve as an important utility for the group. Merton would call this a latent function. This latent function, within the bounds of sociological inquiry, is to give the mission a sense of urgency and importance. The bishop's 15-year "divine" plan to unify the churches is now coming to fruition. People from faraway places just witnessed God's plan for church unity manifest itself. The attack provides evidence that Satan, now threatened, is on the defensive. The bishop's army just delivered a powerful blow to the enemy. The mission to unify the churches is urgent; they are winning a battle in a much larger war. As one member of the group later states, "Our mission is real. As we continue to unify [the churches] we must protect ourselves from these attacks in Jesus's blood."

If anyone doubted the importance of the mission, that doubt diminishes as all hands are on deck to exorcise the demon possessing the woman believed to be sent from hell to prevent church unity, to prevent the bishop's divine vision from becoming reality. Now the entire group, many of which verbally agreed to unify just moments ago, must actually unite in the physical world right here and now, to face a common and dangerous menacing enemy attempting to destroy their unity. This, in turn, strengthens and solidifies the mission.

Yet, the unfolding scene tells us more about the strong relationship between religion and culture in the English-speaking Caribbean. The immediate interpretation of this woman as demonically possessed and in need of an exorcism also reveals how everyday reality is interpreted from a religious perspective. Here, supernatural forces of good and evil are thought to be powerful forces shaping world events. People in the West might interpret this young woman as a deviant, or perhaps a mischievous youth causing trouble for adults, and dismiss the behavior as youthful angst. Or perhaps she would be considered a mere "psycho" who cracked under the stresses of lower class adolescent life. Not here in the Caribbean, and not among those who share positions of power within their religious institutions. To them, it's a possession steeped in the historical religious practices of the region with roots that date back prior to slavery. This must be an Obeah spirit influencing this young woman's mind. Only the supernatural forces of God, they believe, can exorcise this demon out.

"Tell me your name?"
"Demon, in the name of Jesus, what is your name?"

Panic and confusion quickly transform into solemn determination. Two men subdue the woman grabbing her arms and legs as others roll up their sleeves, find bibles, take out holy oils, and position themselves to begin the exorcism. Meanwhile, people in the background outside of the central activity taking place speak in tongues and offer shouts of "In the name of Jesus, get out of her, get out of her now, fire of God, burn you out of this child, get out of her." The chaos moments ago almost instantly turns to a full-blown organized mass intervention—a real-life exorcism.

"Get out of her. Get out of her now. In the name of Jesus, I command you to get out of this girl at once."

The bishop lays both hands on the woman's forehead while his two sons hold her arms and feet to prevent her from moving or striking anyone and stares in her eyes with determination while a medley of sounds and wails drone in the in the background, "We burn you out, we command you to leave this body in the name of Jesus. Release your diabolical hold."

The bishop removes his excessive garments preparing to get to work. He approaches the immobile woman struggling to get free, places his hands on her head, and forcefully shouts with an echoing thunder, "Fire of God! Bring you out! Bring you out of this woman. Burn you out of this child. Burn you out of this child, in Jesus's name. You have got to get out of her."

The bishop's wife serving a complimentary role shouts, "Get out! In the name of Jesus! Use your Holy name! Fire of God!" The bishop repeats, "In Jesus name" as his wife repeats "Fire of God! Fire of God! In Jesus name, fire of God!"

> Bishop: Loose her now, in the name of Jesus. I command you to get out of her. Now! In Jesus name, come out! You will bow to him now.
>
> Jeanette (bellowing over Bradford): Yes! You shall bow, in the name of Jesus.
>
> Bishop: Your master Satan, he is a loser. This is not your property. (Screaming and shaking her head forcefully with his huge hands over her comparatively small head) Come out of her. The fire burns you, in the name of Jesus. Holy Ghost fire burn you out. ... You are coming out. I break your power. I command you to loose your hold, you wicked spirit, you have no power, you're coming out, you are getting out cause you don't have any power. You diabolical spirit, get out of her now.

The woman, her furor persistent, continues to struggle for freedom as three men hold her down. She remains standing using her feet, body, and arms to release herself from the grasp of these men. Meanwhile two other men, including this bishop and a man with a yellow Mohawk, grasp her head while performing the exorcism while a crowd of about ten others form a complete circle around her shouting various phrases about God and demons, all in hope of assisting in the performance of a successful exorcism.

> Another woman: In Jesus name, we plead the blood of Jesus; we plead the blood of Jesus, in the name of Jesus. In the name of Jesus, we call you out now, in the name of Jesus.
>
> Another man: Come out! Come out!
>
> Another yells out: Get out this woman, demon the blood of Jesus commands you.

This scene continues for almost 30 minutes.

After working to exorcise the demon from the girl, the bishop removes himself from the spiritual onslaught. He seems to be thinking about what to do next. Or perhaps he was simply exhausted. The exorcism is just not working. Yet.

The bishop stares into the quiet empty parking lot, only feet away where this intense scene continues to unfold. It is taking too long, and concerns seem to build. It is a feeling of desperation.

Still, it is obvious that no one in the crowd thinks for a moment that this perceived man of God is about to forfeit this battle. The crowd does not miss a beat as a temporary new "exorcism leader" takes his place.

The others take up his slack.

A renewed energy takes over as an excited man with a yellow Mohawk, a former famous New York deejay with roots in Antigua and recent born-again Christian, revitalizes the crowd jumping into the action with adrenaline filled vigor. This ebb and flow of energy continuously moves back and forth from a waxing thunderous crescendo to a lulling whimper.

As the bishop wipes the sweat from his forehead, his associate pastor removes a heavy gold bishop's chain from around his neck protecting it from damage. Meanwhile, the mohawked man places both hands on the young woman now pressed up against the front of the church to the left of its wooden front doors. She now displays little effort to free herself from the grasp of two men continuing to hold control of her body. The mohawked man shouts, "In the name of Jesus, the fire of the Holy Ghost, in the name of Jesus, come out of her. We gonna get to you! In the name of Jesus!"

The already warm 80-degree night turns feverish. About 15 men and women, many of them pastors and their family members, act like paramedics attempting to save the life of a dying girl struggling for her last breath. It is difficult to discern one voice from the other. The night's stillness is only interrupted with shouts, screams, and bellows of individually produced noises occurring within the collectivity of what resembles a mob.

The man with a Mohawk continues with the enthusiasm of a new firemen recruit rushing into a fire to save the day, "Fire, in the name of Jesus. JESUS! Fire in the name of Jesus. Fire In the name of Jesus. Fire. In the name of Jesus. Hallelujah."

Woman One: Mighty God!

Woman Two: In the name of Jesus (repeated three times). Hallelujah. In the name of Jesus (seven times), loose her, in the name of Jesus.

At this point in the exorcism, *In the name of Jesus* is the collective chant of the crowd, crusaders exorcising demons from a struggling victim.

Sacred utterances and numinous sounds emerge from the stillness of the night, it is almost like a performed mantra.

A woman yells: In the name of rage, we come against you. In the name of Jesus, spirit of rage will come against you in the name of Jesus. In the name of Jesus, in the name of Jesus, come out. Loosen your hold. In the name of Jesus, loose your hold, ...

A man commands: Come out! Come out! Fire of the Holy Ghost! In the name of Jesus! The fire of the Holy Ghost. The fire of the Holy Ghost. In the name of Jeeeesus. We evict this spirit.

Another man shouts: The fire. The fire of the Holy Ghost, in Jesus name, the fire of the Holy Ghost. The Fire! In the name of Jesus! The fire of the Holy Ghost! In the name of Jesus!

They bring her to the ground. She lies there, still, her body seemingly frozen in place. They all chant in synchronicity. Some yell out various commands to accompany the flowing chant.

"Fire in the name of Jesus."
(Shrieking) "Get out! Get out! Get out! Get out! Get out! Rababbab kotah yah yah eeyah na na kota nanana. Hodana nannnanna. Hadana katchen yeh yeh yeh."
"Set free from this binding here, this woman here, from the binding."
"You are coming out, in the name of Jesus. We bind you, in the name of Jesus. Ya robohta ya gayan gay a an kashanda. Bow to the Lord Jesus Christ."
"Yes. Bow in the name of Jesus. Jesus. Yes. Yes."
"Jesus, you have the power."
"We plea the blood of Jesus. Holy ghost fire. Holy ghost fire. The blood of Jesus. Come against you. In the name of Jesus (repeated five times), loose your hold (repeated four times)."
"You are coming out. You are coming out. You are coming out. Roboshakanah. You are coming out."
"You have no power, in the name of Jesus."
"Loose her, Jesus will burn you out."
"The blood of Jesus is all over you. The blood of Jesus is all over you."
"Come out of your hiding place. Make yourself known and get out of this body. You will not be comfortable in this body. We command you to leave now. In the name of Jesus."
"Fire will burn you out. Burn! Get out! Burn!"

The woman begins to twitch.

Her body seems to react to the thundering chants of the exorcism. One arm begins to convulse, then a leg. As the chant heightens her whole body begins to shake with a seemingly uncontrollable agitation. Perhaps a demon really was trying to get out of her burning body.

Her eyes roll to the back of her head. Her body continues to convulse. The chant becomes more ferocious growing increasingly determined the more this young woman shakes and jerks on the ground. A feeling overwhelms the crowd that the exorcism is working. Good is prevailing over evil.

The woman rolls to the left, then to the right. Like a turtle on its back, she rolls left to right, gaining momentum. The crowd is jumping up and down, wailing, shouting, and screaming. She kicks a man in the groin and gets to her feet. She connects another kick to a man's kneecaps, throws a punch to another, and kicks another man right in the stomach. The crowd grabs hold of this woman to restrain her.

She displays a maniacal smile. They restrain her head rendering it immobile. She smiles wider, makes strange noises, sticks her tongue out, laughs "hahahaha," and rolls her eyes back into her head. They begin to rub "holy" oil on her forehead and recite bible quotes. Her grin grows more menacing, as if she is a demon toying with her weak victims. As the group becomes more aggressive in their approach, holding her tighter and commanding the demon to leave, she begins to shout, "I curse you, curse you."

After surrendering to the men who have control of her movements, she now begins to struggle again, and struggle mightily, to get free. At this point, I begin wondering if this is a false arrest. They are holding this woman against her will, and with no apparent plans to call the police or charge her for the attack. After all, no one was injured, save for a bruise or two. It was possible to sense from the participants that they felt uneasy about restraining this woman desperately trying to flee. The mohawked man, one of the main actors in this scene, seems to cast away any blame of his involvement stating "Dear God, it is not by will, it is not by my might, it's not by a physical fight, but by the name of his son, Jesus Christ of Nazareth, sister we are here. Shalaya keeta katop. High sheilabacka aali kop." He too seems to feel guilty that he is restraining and overpowering a girl.

The crowd begins to calm. Everyone talks at the same time, but the volume decreases.

In the tone of a composed parent speaking to an unruly child, the bishop gently commands, "Get out of her. Spirit of witchcraft. Get out.

Spirit of witchcraft. Get out. You manipulative spirit. Get out of her, in Jesus name. GET OUT! Free her from being a captive of Satan. Free her now Father. I command you. I bind you."

The bishop commands the young woman to stand upright and asks her questions, "Young lady, what's your name? What's your name young lady? In the name of Jesus, what's your name?"

The others remain praying and accompanying the bishop's request saying, "Speak in the name of Jesus."

> I command your spirit to loose her now. Release her mind. Mind controlling spirit, release her mind, right now. God bring her into her right mind. I command you to free her. Get out of her now. What is your name, young lady? Yes, I come against the spirit of witchcraft. Get out of her now, in the name of Jesus.

The crowd grows excited as more people begin to yell with a feverish pitch. The young woman begins to make growling noises. The enchanted crowd applauds like a cheering audience in a sports bar.

Slowly enunciating each word, the bishop asks, "What is your name, you disobedient spirit? The fire of God is upon you."

A large woman takes charge holding the head of this young woman with her meaty palms. She stares the woman directly in the eyes inches from her face. She says condescendingly, "You think you can't talk, but your days are numbered. Oh yes they are. Because we're going to close every door, and you'll not going to be able to come back. The house will be vacant and Jesus will enter and remain. In the name of Jesus. Yes. You have no more hold of this body."

Straw man, you have to leave. You have to leave. Because of Jesus Christ. He is gonna get you out and she'll be saved. He is going to evict you, not us. Jesus Christ has more power over you. We have the minute set when you will leave this body. He has the minute set. And you cannot stay any longer than that minute. You can't be comfortable in this body any longer. We tell you to link up with whoever have in here.

The large woman begins to laugh and mix tongue speaking with her native English.

"Ha ha. Hehe heh. Ha hah hahahahahahahahahha, your days are numbered, hahahahahahahhahahahha, get out of her, ken yababarobotahah. I call blazing fire death. I call blazing fire death." She repeatedly intersperses "blazing fire" language with tongue speaking.

Holy spirit reign; confuse the enemy. In the name of Jesus, confuse the enemy now. The Lord's enemies be scattered now. Scatter, scatter, scatter, in the name of Jesus, bring confusion to the pit. Confusion to the pit. Confusion, yes. We render you powerless. In the name of Jesus, we bind you in your work, and we send back to the pit of hell.

As the restrained woman shouts back "I curse you," the large woman responds, "No curse will materialize, in the name of Jesus. We send you back, in the name of Jesus. You are a loser, in Jesus's name. Jesus is the winner man. We break every curse, in the name of Jesus."

After 30 minutes, the crowd quiets once again. They pray softly while still holding the woman. They release her, finally, but not before grabbing the cell phone ringing in her pocket.

"Hello."

It was the young woman's mother. The exorcism failed, as it turned out, for a reason immediately apparent to all but me until it was explained. It is believed that a "hereditary spirit" bound the young woman to a supernatural demon. One needs to look into the history and cultural context of the region in order to understand this widely accepted belief in hereditary spirits and demonic possessions.

Here in the English-speaking Caribbean, Christianity and Obeah form an interesting cocktail of old and new world religious practices that sometimes contradicts, other times complements, and always blurs in fascinating ways. Obeah involves an eclectic mix of practices that derive from the Central and West African religion of slaves and Hindu indentured servants brought to the Caribbean.[14],[15] Obeah, which American pop culture would associate with vodou, is a widely acknowledged term in much of the English-speaking Caribbean and refers to forms of magic, sorcery, animism, witchcraft, and mysticism associated with tapping into malevolent supernatural forces.[16] Though many Charismatic Christians in the region reject its practices, many believe in its utility to harness evil forces. Obeah was once openly practiced in much of the Caribbean and used as a source of resistance against colonial domination. Today, it is considered taboo, a remnant of a colonial past. Perhaps the rejection of Obeah as a religious practice has to do with a symbolic act of moving beyond the history of slavery and colonialism and into a new, modern world following independence. Indeed, Obeah has increasingly become hidden in private places, making it less of an obvious impact on social life. But instead of disappearing altogether, Obeah now blends into the dominant religion in the Caribbean, especially Charismatic Christianity complete with its complimentary beliefs in supernatural forces of good and evil. As a result, Charismatic Christianity and Obeah beliefs and rituals sometimes collapse into each other as they both absorb elements into their practices.

The next day, the Bishop and I spoke with the local pastor, the Apostle, who knows this young woman and her family. In response to my question asking how he can be certain that the young woman was possessed, he explains how the young woman, named Cleona, has been recently texting strange messages.

> Apostle: "The last thing she says is, 'I was assigned to destroy you.' So that tells you that there are demons involved. That's for you, as you're asking, how do I know that she is possessed."

They speculated what "cult" this woman belongs too. Rumor has it that her mother practices Obeah, though she attends a Seventh-Day Adventist Church. After discussing Cleona's biography, the bishop and apostle provide more "evidence" to her dealing with a hereditary demon. The Apostle offers the following story:

> Apostle: It will take a period of time (to relinquish her from demonic influence) because it's deeply rooted in her. Her father is dead. That father died when she was about seven years.
>
> Marina: How'd he die?
>
> Apostle: AIDS. How she got pregnant to her mother is her father just used to lime [spend leisurely time with] with her. ... The father and the mother used to go to Adventist church, and she end up getting pregnant. But her mother is very rude to her mother, which is her [Cleona's] grandmother. The mother was very rude to her, and her mother, at the same age, used to call the pastor and disguise her voice, just like what her daughter is doing to me. That's why I'm telling you it's *hereditary*. It's something she inherited because we also found that if we deal with her, and she gets back home (claps his hands) she just goes right back in to it [demonic influence]. So we see there is a connection here. There is a resident spirit here.

According to "demonic law," it is believed that the children of parents under the influence of demons are also bounded to that same demon. In other words, demons cling to family lines. Based on Exodus

20:5, many Charismatic Christian leaders in the Caribbean believe that families who become involved in the occult, or cult practices, open up demonic doors to their children and grandchildren. This explains the failed attempt to exorcise the child of her demon. In order to cure the child of the spiritual affliction, one must first deal with the parents. To release the young woman from demonic influence, one must first remove the demon's legal right to possess the person before casting out the demon. Pentecostals and other Charismatic Christian leaders are considered legitimate healers to spiritual diseases. In short, they are professional spiritual healthcare professionals.

Returning to the scene, the exhausted crowd begins to dissipate returning to their cars realizing that the midnight hour will soon strike. On the drive back to their villa in Jolly Harbour, the bishop's family and friends try to make sense of the events that just transpired. It was a monumental victory for the pastor to receive verbal support to unify the Christian churches. But with each new battle won, a counter attack is sure to follow. The demonic scene that just transpired provides ample evidence. The group realizes the dangers of performing their God's work, and protection from demons and further attacks are necessary. One member of the group offers a prayer of protection:

> Cover everyone, especially now if they got any kind of an enemy, any assignment that he's sending any of demons. I bind him (Satan) now, in the name Jesus. Please be in our souls and our spirits. Anything that we're attached to God, I ask you to saturate it with your precious blood so that we know that what comes to us. Let there be no nervousness. Let there be a peace that passes all understanding. Even now, may He work for the young lady. Dear God, I pray that you loose any stronghold that is attached to her, that's been granted to her from a child, from her mom, from her grandmother, from her lineage. Lord Jesus in your assignment, I block the demon now, in the name of Jesus. Cover Peter, cover Durie, cover Joanne, cover Danielle, cover Gibson, cover Nadeetha, cover Sister Pauline, cover Craig, cover his wife, cover his children, cover Elder Swindell, cover Andre and cover everyone of our households, cover Lady Bishop, and the Bishop, in the name of Jesus.

It is here in the deep Caribbean world of Antigua, filled with demonic possessions, spiritual demons, and supernatural healers, where the journey begins to understand the spread of the Charismatic movement in the Caribbean as well as gain insights into religion and culture in the region.

NOTES

1. The word "God" and all references to God such as "Holy Ghost" and "Lord" are capitalized throughout this book to follow the expectations of the research participants. In no way does this imply the privileging of the Christian God.
2. Donald E. Miller, Kimon H. Sargeant, and Richard Flory, eds., *Spirit and Power: The Growth and Global Impact of Pentecostalism* (1st ed., Oxford: Oxford University Press, 2013).
3. Walt Whitman, *Leaves of Grass* (1855) "Song of Myself."
4. Wolfgang Vondey, *Beyond Pentecostalism: The Crisis of Global Christianity and the Renewal of the Theological Agenda* (Grand Rapids, MI: William B. Eerdmans Publications, 2010). Margaret Poloma, "The Symbolic Dilemma and the Future of Pentecostalism: Mysticism, Ritual, and Revival," in *The Future of Pentecostalism in the United States*, ed. Eric Patterson and Edmund Rybarczyk (Lanham, MD: Lexington Books, 2007), 105–122.
5. José Casanova, "Religion, the New Millennium, and Globalization," *Sociology of Religion* 62 (2001): 415–441; and José Casanova, *Public Religions in the Modern World* (Chicago and London: The University of Chicago Press, 1994).
6. The exact origin of this quote remains unclear originally deriving from multiple sources. For example, in a panel with the Pew Forum on the Azusa Street revival's 100th anniversary, Pentecostal scholar Donald Miller says, "One interesting comment I received from someone I interviewed in Argentina was that liberation theology, typically associated with the Catholic tradition, opted for the poor, but the poor opted for Pentecostalism." Another scholar, Juan Francisco Martínez, points out in a footnote how numerous versions of this quote come from numerous sources. He says, "The Samuel Escobar quote, which I have personally heard from him was 'Liberation theology opted for the poor, but the poor opted for Pentecostalism.'" Another version, attributed to an anonymous nun in Guatemala, states that "the Catholic Church opted for the poor, but the poor opted for Pentecostalism." This latter version is quoted by Antonio González in *The Gospel of Faith and Justice* (Maryknoll, NY: Orbis Books, 2005), 163, and in Juan Francisco Martínez, *Los Protestantes: An Introduction to Latino Protestantism in the United States* (Santa Barbara: Praeger ABC-CLIO, 2011), 207. I also found references to this quote in "Dealing with the 'Disposable People' of the Globalized Economy: Just Peacemaking in Immigrants, Refugees and Displaced Persons," in *Formation for Life Just Peacemaking and Twenty-First-Century Discipleship*, ed. Glen H. Stassen, Rodney L. Peterson, and Timothy A. Norton

(Eugene, OR: Pickwick Publications, 2013), 215, and in D.E. Miller and T. Yamamori, *Global Pentecostalism: The New Face of Christian Social Engagement* (Berkeley, CA: University of California Press, 2007).

7. Andrew R. Chesnut, *Born Again in Brazil: The Pentecostal Boom and the Pathogens of Poverty* (New Brunswick, NJ/London: Rutgers University Press, 1997). Andrew R. Chesnut, *Competitive Spirits: Latin America's New Religious Economy* (New York: Oxford University Press, 2003).

8. Peter Marina, *Getting the Holy Ghost: Urban Ethnography in a Pentecostal Tongue-Speaking Church* (Lanham, MD: Lexington, 2014).

9. Margaret Poloma, *Main Street Mystics: The 'Toronto Blessing' and Reviving Pentecostalism* (Walnut Creek, CA: Alta Mira Press, 2003).

10. Harold J. Recinos, "Mainline Hispanic Protestantism and Latino Newcomers," in *Protestantes/Protestants: Hispanic Christianity within the Mainline Traditions*, ed. D. Maldonado, Jr. (Nashville, TN: Abingdon Press, 1999), 194–215.

11. Manuel A. Vasquez, "Pentecostalism, Collective Identity, and Transnationalism among Salvadorans and Peruvians in the U.S.," *Journal of the Academy of Religion* 67 (1999): 617–636.

12. Gerardo Martí, "The Diversity-Affirming Latino: Ethnic Options and the Ethnic Transcendent Expression of American Latino Religious Identity," in *Sustaining Faith Tradition: Race, Ethnicity, and Religion Among the Latino and Asian American Second Generation*, ed. Carolyn Chen and Russell Jeung (New York: New York University Press, 2012), 25–45.

13. See Robert K Merton, "Social Structure and Anomie," *American Sociological Review* 3 (1938): 672–682; and Robert K. Merton, *Social Theory and Social Structure* (Glencoe, IL: The Free Press of Glencoe, 1963)

14. Mario Incayawar, Ronald Wintrob, and Lise Bouchard, *Psychiatrist and Traditional Healers: Unwitting Partners in Global Mental Health* (New Jersey: Wiley-Blackwell, 2009).

15. Venetia Newall, "Some Examples of the Practice of Obeah by West Indian Immigrants in London," *Folklore* 89 (1978): 29–51.

16. *Ibid.*

CHAPTER 2

The Study of Charismatic Christianity in the English-Speaking Caribbean

Welcome to the heart of the Charismatic Christian movement in the English-speaking Caribbean. Here, the tidal wave of the Pentecostal movement landed on the shores of the Caribbean and spread throughout its many islands in the region, sweeping into the Caribbean world with its original bursting energy that ignited a uniquely Caribbean fire. It started in the "Cradle of the Worldwide Pentecostal Movement" on Azusa Street in Los Angeles and spread to the Pentecostal Church of God in Trinidad in 1906[1] and finally to the "Cradle of the Pentecostal Movement in the Caribbean"[2] Montserrat. As the exorcism scene above on the small island of Antigua shows, Charismatic Christianity sometimes competes against, at others times simultaneously blends and juxtaposes with, old African religious practices, like Vodou and Obeah, as they have taken shape in the region since slavery. But like the religious practices that in many ways resisted slavery and colonialism, Pentecostalism[3] in the Caribbean continues to act as a form of resistance to various forms of institutional domination. Placing religion, and more specifically Charismatic Christianity, in the realm of culture locates the movement as, in part, a creative cultural response to collectively experienced structural problems.

This book is about the large and explosive global Charismatic movement in the small and tranquil English-speaking Caribbean. It captures the spread of Pentecostalism, which began almost 120 years ago, in a remote and understudied but important region of the world. The chapters that follow will take the reader through ten islands and countries

© The Author(s) 2016   21
P. Marina, *Chasing Religion in the Caribbean*,
DOI 10.1057/978-1-137-56100-8_2

into the places of Charismatic Christian practices where religious leaders expand the movement throughout the Caribbean. The central focus is on (1) how the Charismatic movement spreads throughout the region, (2) the ability of the movement to maintain charisma in the face of modern rationalizing forces, and (3) its potential to become a more powerful force for social change in the region. Rather than looking at the Pentecostal faith and its adherents, the analytical focus is on how religious leaders use various types of transnational religious networking strategies to spread the Charismatic movement throughout the English-speaking Caribbean. This work offers a useful construct that provides a historical and theoretical overview of the Charismatic movement in the Caribbean, explains the networks religious leaders develop to spread across the region, and offers insight into religion in late modernity using the Weberian concept of charisma as a central analytical frame.

While scholars have pointed to the uniqueness of Caribbean Pentecostalism, they are quick to point out that we don't know much about it; it simply hasn't been adequately studied (Yong, 2005). Given the geographic proximity of the Caribbean to the USA, Canada, and South America, and given the vibrant religious landscape of the region, it is surprising that the English-speaking Caribbean has been so ignored in the literature. While little attention has been focused on the English-speaking Caribbean, the influence of the Charismatic Christian movement in the USA and South America is well documented, receiving considerable academic attention in the USA, Asia, and Africa. This book brings into the conversation a small, but culturally and historically rich region of the world just between the Global North and South. The work will venture into the rich and diverse religiously influenced cultures that flourish in this lesser-known part of the Caribbean world beyond tourist walls. Indeed, the time is ripe to bring the, until now, silenced Caribbean into the fold to tell its fascinating story of the global Charismatic Christian movement in a region where religion has long been a major player in the social, political, economic, and cultural arenas. This research takes the reader into the Caribbean world to increase our sociological and scholarly understanding of one of the most powerful religious movements of our time in a place with a historically turbulent and politically divided history that persists today.

Some scholars now use the term "Pentecostalisms" to refer to its many varieties and forms that exist.[4] This suggests that there is little agreement on what exactly constitutes as Pentecostalism or its global movement.[5] While outside observers and interested scholars struggle to agree on what exactly constitutes Pentecostalism, adherents and scholars of the movement also remain divided, often based on doctrinal disputes.[6] Going along with Anderson's[7] adaptation of an inclusive definition of Pentecostalism, this book uses Charismatic Christianity to describe those Caribbean churches and movements that emphasize the born-again experience and receiving gifts of the spirit including speaking in tongues. Unless otherwise noted, Pentecostalism refers to the movement and its churches that can trace their origins to Azusa Street and specifically identify as Pentecostal.

Of course such contested definitions make official data on the number of Pentecostals and Charismatic Christians difficult to ascertain, and efforts in doing so have been inconsistent. The Pew Forum estimates that 279 million Pentecostals[8] and 305 million Charismatic Christians[9] exist in the world. Combined, that's about 584 million adherents, or 27 % of all Christians and 8 % of the world's total population, that are part of the global movement discussed in this book.[10] Other scholars estimate that sometimes the numbers reported are far below the actual count, while other estimates count over 612 million combined Pentecostals and Charismatics in the world today.[11] It is of little dispute that this religious movement is one of the most powerful in the world, with the potential to be a force for social change. And in places like Latin America, especially Brazil, Pentecostalism has been a major source of social change both for the politics and economics of the region.[12] But what is happening in the English-speaking Caribbean? This is a region where religion runs deep within the very fabric of social life as well as into its institutional structures. Looking into some of the hard numbers of the religious demographic landscape of the region offers a starting point.

THE HARD NUMBERS: CHARISMATIC CHRISTIANS IN THE WORLD TODAY

The *Center for the Global Study of Christianity* reports that the Christian population reached somewhere between 2.2 and 2.3 billion in 2010 and is expected to grow to over 2.5 billion, or just over 33 % of the world's population.[13] While the Catholic and Anglican Church continue to experience a decline in numbers, other Protestant groups, mainly those associated with the Charismatic movement, have experienced a large increase in their number of adherents. But who are these Charismatic Christians and how do we define them? Further, how do we distinguish between the various Christian groups who talk about the importance of becoming born again and speaking in tongues? Just as first- and third-world distinctions begin to blur and collapse in late modern society, so do religious categories that separate mainline churches from the various forms of Pentecostal and Charismatic churches.[14] The traditional distinctions between Evangelical, Charismatic, Pentecostal, and Traditional churches seem insufficient to describe these Christian churches today.[15] Some scholars use the more inclusive term Renewalists[16] to include Pentecostal, Charismatic, and Independent Charismatic churches into a single category. The report from the *Center for the Global Study of Christianity* shows that globally Renewalist movements increased to almost four times the growth rates of the Christian population between 1970 and 2010, or one quarter of all Christians.[17] As we head toward 2020, it is expected that Renewalist movements will grow almost twice as fast as all of global Christianity—from 62.7 million in 1970 to a whopping 709.8 million in 2020—and this increase will accelerate as we advance closer to 2020. Although Charismatics have previously been the fastest growing of the Renewalist Christian groups for the past 40 years, specifically it's the Pentecostals that are expected to grow even faster for at least the next decade. As the chart below indicates, while the percentage of Pentecostals decreased between 1970 and 2010, there is an expected percentage increase as we push toward 2020. Charismatics, on the other hand, have dramatically increased between 1970 and 2010, a trend that is expected to continue into the future. Interestingly, while the percentage of Independent Christian decreased between 1970 and 2010, the raw numbers increased from almost 44 million to just over 257 million in that same time period, with a continued 44 % growth heading toward the end of the decade.

Pentecostals (Type 1), 1970–2020[18]

	1970		2010		2020		Rate**	
	Pentecostals	%*	Pentecostals	%*	Pentecostals	%*	1970–2020	2010–2020
Pentecostals (Type 1)	14,475,000	23.1	91,825,000	15.7	115,200,000	16.2	4.7	2.0
Classical	13,537,000	21.6	89,133,000	15.3	112,000,000	15.8	4.8	2.0
Oneness	938,000	1.5	2,692,000	0.5	3,200,000	0.5	2.7	2.0

*% = Percentage of continental population

Center for the Study of Global Christianity, Christianity in its Global Context, June 2013

**Rate = average annual growth rate, percent per year indicated

Charismatics (Type 2), 1970–2020

	1970		2010		2020		Rate**	
	Charismatics	%*	Charismatics	%*	Charismatics	%*	1970–2020	2010–2020
Charismatics (Type 2)	4,334,600	6.9	234,222,000	40.2	281,924,000	39.7	10.5	1.9
Anglican	967,000	1.5	18,648,000	3.2	22,000,000	3.1	7.7	1.7
Catholic	2,001,400	3.2	176,551,000	30.3	215,500,000	30.4	11.9	2.0
Protestant	1,027,000	1.6	34,824,000	6.0	40,000,000	5.6	9.2	1.4
Orthodox	339,000	0.5	4,179,000	0.7	4,400,000	0.6	6.5	0.5
Marginal	200	0.0	20,000	0.0	24,000	0.0	12.2	1.8

*% = Percentage of continental population
Center for the Study of Global Christianity, Christianity in its Global Context, June 2013
**Rate = average annual growth rate, percent per year indicated

Independent Charismatics (Type 3), 1970–2020

| | Independent | | | | | | Rate** | |
	Charismatics	%*	Charismatics	%*	Charismatics	%*	1970–2020	2010–2020
Charismatics (Type 3)	43,875,400	70.0	257,161,000	44.1	312,704,000	44.1	4.5	2.0
Apostolic	4,789,000	7.6	32,834,000	5.6	39,200,000	6.0	4.9	2.0
Charismatic	7,491,000	12.0	70,168,000	12.0	90,000,000	13.0	5.8	3.0
Deliverance	25,000	0.0	515,000	0.1	670,000	0.0	7.9	3.0
Full Gospel	937,000	1.5	6,714,000	1.2	8,300,000	1.2	5.0	2.0
Hidden non-Christian believers in Christ	110,000	0.2	425,000	0.1	484,000	0.1	3.4	1.3
Individuals in non-Charismatic networks	7,836,400	12.5	40,693,000	7.0	51,800,000	7.3	4.2	2.4
Media	2,464,000	3.9	1,042,000	0.2	1,300,000	0.2	-2.1	2.0
Non-traditional, house, cell	537,000	0.9	6,020,000	1.0	7,400,000	1.0	6.2	2.0
Oneness	2,394,000	3.8	11,823,000	2.0	13,500,000	2.0	4.1	1.0
Pentecostal	16,154,000	25.8	75,515,000	12.9	87,150,000	12	3.9	1.0
Word of Faith	104,000	0.2	3,099,000	0.5	3,900,000	0.5	8.9	2.0
Zion	1,034,000	1.6	8,313,000	1.4	9,000,000	1.3	5.3	0.8

*% = Percentage of continental population
Center for the Study of Global Christianity, Christianity in its Global Context, June 2013
**Rate = average annual growth rate, percent per year indicated

The Pew Forum shows that the numbers of Pentecostals and Charismatics have reached almost 600 million people worldwide, or about 27 % of all Christians. This number increases to almost 900 million when putting Evangelicals into the mix. But equally important is where this growth occurs, and all arrows point south.

Christians by Movement[19]

Regions	Estimated number	Percentage of total world population (%)	Percentage of world Christian population (%)
Pentecostal	279,080,000	4.0	12.8
Charismatic	304,990,000	4.4	14.0
Pentecostal and Charismatic together	584,080,000	8.5	26.7
Evangelical	285,480,000	4.1	13.1

Looking at specific regions around the world, most Pentecostals and Charismatics live in the Americas and sub-Saharan Africa. Although sub-Saharan Africa has the highest percentage of the Pentecostal population, the region that makes up the Americas boasts the highest percentage of the Charismatic population in the world.

Pentecostals by Region[20]

Regions	Percentage of region that is Pentecostal (%)	Percentage of world Pentecostal population (%)
Americas	10.9	36.7
Sub-Saharan Africa	14.8	43.7
Asia-Pacific	1.1	15.5
Europe	1.5	4.0
Middle East–North Africa	0.1	0.1
World total	**4.0**	**100.0**

Charismatics by Region

Regions	Percentage of region that is Charismatic (%)	Percentage of world Charismatic population (%)
Americas	15.8	48.5
Sub-Saharan Africa	6.5	17.4

(Continued)

Regions	Percentage of region that is Charismatic (%)	Percentage of world Charismatic population (%)
Asia-Pacific	2.2	29.5
Europe	1.8	4.3
Middle East–North Africa	0.2	0.3
World total	**4.4**	**100.0**

It's Latin America, however, that is experiencing the highest growth. Further, in 2020 Latin America is expected to have the highest percentage of Renewalists in the world, with North America and Africa trailing significantly behind. Although Latin America does not include the English-speaking Caribbean, the region is not far behind, both geographically and statistically.

The Renewalist movement in Latin America has increased from 10 % to over 30 % in Latin America over the past four decades, a trend that continues as we move into the future. Latin America has clearly distanced itself from the others, though Asia is making a sharp increase upward. Scholars acknowledge that Charismatic Christianity is expanding throughout the Caribbean, but we know less about the English-speaking Caribbean.[21] Now let's look as best as we can into this part of the region. While scholars have well documented the extraordinary rise of global Pentecostalism in Latin America,[22] including the Spanish speaking Caribbean, they have largely ignored the numbers of Pentecostals and Charismatic Christians in the English-speaking part of the Caribbean. Although the numbers are less known and understudied, scholars have at least long established that Pentecostals are also growing rapidly in the Caribbean world not considered Latin America.[23] The *Center for the Global Study of Christianity* reports that Christianity in the twentieth century experienced a great shift to the Global South, a trend that will continue well into the twenty-first century.[24] This evidence is backed with decade-long data collection from scholars who have documented the spread of the Charismatic movement to the Global South.[25] As Christianity continues to experience a dramatic decline in the Global North, it experiences an equally dramatic increase in the Global South—from 41.3 % in 1970 to a predicted 64.7 % of all Christians by the year 2020.[26] The Pew Forum offers similar numbers, but going farther back to 1910, to show the dramatic shift in the Christian population for the Global North to South.

Christian Population by Global North/Global South, 1910[27]

	Estimated 1910 Christian population	Total world population	Percentage of population that was Christian (%)	Percentage of world Christian population (%)
Global North	502,900,000	580,210,000	86.7	82.2
Global South	108,910,000	1,178,200,000	9.2	17.8
World total	611,810,000	1,758,410,000	34.8	100.0

Christian Population by Global North/Global South, 2010[28]

	Estimated 2010 Christian population	Total world population	Percentage of population that was Christian (%)	Percentage of world Christian population (%)
Global North	856,360,000	1,240,250,000	69.0	39.2
Global South	1,327,700,000	5,655,640,000	23.5	60.8
World total	2,184,060,000	6,895,890,000	31.7	100.0

The *Center for the Global Study of Christianity* also reports that although a strong Anglican presence remains in the English-speaking Caribbean, its membership has declined giving way to the growing number of Protestants—the largest Christian group in most of the English-speaking Caribbean countries.[29] Meanwhile, Independents are growing faster than Protestants and now represent the third largest Christian group in the region.

The chart below shows the overall growth of Christianity from just over 25 million identified adherents (78.2 %) to an expected 37.5 million people (84.7 %) for the entire Caribbean between 1970 and 2020. Looking at the chart below, every country researched in this book, including Antigua and Barbuda, Barbados, Dominica, Haiti, Montserrat, St. Kitts and Nevis, and St. Lucia are expected to continue having a Christian population rate above 90 %, and in most cases well above 90 %, except for Trinidad and Tobago with a high Indo-Trinidadian Muslim population.

Christianity in the Caribbean, 1970–2020

Country	1970			2020			
	Population	Christians	%	Population	Christians	%	Rate*
Caribbean	25,327,000	19,816,000	78.2	44,321,000	37,529,000	84.7	1.29
Anguilla	6400	6200	96.1	17,500	15,800	90.3	1.91
Antigua and Barbuda	65,600	64,200	97.9	97,400	90,200	92.7	0.68
Aruba	59,100	57,200	96.9	111,000	106,000	95.4	1.24
Bahamas	169,000	164,000	97.1	383,000	355,000	92.7	1.56
Barbados	239,000	235,000	98.2	279,000	264,000	94.5	0.23
British Virgin Islands	9800	8900	91.0	25,400	21,300	84.0	1.76
Cayman Islands	9500	8600	91.0	60,500	48,300	79.8	3.50
Cuba	8,702,000	4,013,000	46.1	11,173,000	6,901,000	61.8	1.09
Dominica	71,100	70,000	98.4	67,900	63,900	94.1	-0.18
Dominican Republic	4,512,000	4,390,000	97.3	11,121,000	10,548,000	94.9	1.77
Grenada	94,400	93,500	99.0	108,000	104,000	96.3	0.21
Guadeloupe	320,000	312,000	97.3	479,000	458,000	95.7	0.78
Haiti	4,710,000	4,552,000	96.7	11,311,000	10,637,000	94.0	1.71
Jamaica	1,869,000	1,708,000	91.4	2,828,000	2,388,000	84.4	0.67
Martinique	326,000	321,000	98.4	414,000	398,000	96.2	0.43
Montserrat	11,600	11,300	97.6	6400	5800	91.3	-1.31
Netherlands Antilles	159,000	154,000	96.8	212,000	197,000	93.0	0.50
Puerto Rico	2,716,000	2,673,000	98.4	3,747,000	3,584,000	95.7	0.59
St. Kitts and Nevis	44,900	44,400	99.0	58,500	55,200	94.4	0.44
St. Lucia	104,000	102,000	98.4	190,000	182,000	95.8	1.16
St. Vincent	90,500	87,700	96.9	110,000	97,300	88.5	0.21
Trinidad and Tobago	968,000	672,000	69.4	1,373,000	870,000	63.3	0.52
Turks and Caicos Islands	5600	5600	99.5	42,600	39,000	91.6	3.97
US Virgin Islands	64,100	63,000	98.3	106,000	99,900	94.3	0.93

*Rate = average annual Christian growth rate, percent per year 1970–2020
Center for the Study of Global Christianity, Christianity in its Global Context, June 2013

This Christian population, which are largely dominated by Catholics or Anglicans, is quickly giving way to Protestantism and, as will be pointed out below, adherents to the Charismatic movement. Suffice it to say, just looking at the raw hard numbers, the Charismatic movements in the English-speaking Caribbean merits investigation.

The Pew Research Center offers a breakdown of the Christian population for almost every country in the world (they seem to have missed St. Martin). Here is a breakdown of some of those numbers specific to the Caribbean countries discussed in the book.

Christian Population in Numbers by Country[30]

Country	Estimated population					
	2010 Christian population	2010 Catholic population	2010 Protestant population	2010 Orthodox population	2010 Other Christian population	2010 Total population
Antigua and Barbuda	80,000	<10,000	70,000	<1000	<10,000	90,000
Barbados	260,000	10,000	240,000	<1000	<10,000	270,000
Dominica	60,000	40,000	20,000	<1000	<1000	70,000
Jamaica	2,110,000	70,000	2,000,000	<10,000	40,000	2,740,000
Montserrat	<10,000	<1000	<10,000	<1000	<1000	<10,000
St. Kitts and Nevis	50,000	<10,000	40,000	<1000	<1000	50,000
St. Lucia	160,000	110,000	50,000	<1000	<10,000	170,000
Trinidad and Tobago	880,000	350,000	510,000	<10,000	20,000	1,340,000

In every case with the exception of Trinidad and Tobago with a large Hindu population, these Caribbean countries have a Christian population close to their total populations. These are some of the hard numbers; let's take a brief look at the soft, but powerful, story of the history of Pentecostalism in the USA before proceeding to its history and development specifically in the Caribbean.

A Brief Pentecostal History

Pentecostalism began with Charles Parham's spiritual revival in 1901 Topeka, Kansas leading to the now-famous Azusa Street Mission in 1906 Los Angeles, California.[31] The story of the Pentecostal movement began with pure charisma, a raw energy so great that one imagines the entire state of California must have rumbled. Either way, the story of the infamous Azusa Street now reigns in the American imagination as a quintessential example of a powerful religious movement that would quite possibly change history. And indeed, for many, it has done exactly that.

The Pentecostal movement is a story of charisma. Indeed, every aspect of Pentecostalism oozes charisma, from its church services to its music. Even the very beginning of the movement, its very first day, relates back to charisma. That first day was April 9, 1906, in a little place called Azusa Street. It may look run down now, right next to Korea town, but it was certainly magical then, at least in the minds of scholars interested in the movement.

AZUSA STREET TODAY

The events leading up to the Azusa Street days began with a Methodist preacher named Charles Fox Parham who held a Bible meeting at Bethel Bible College in Topeka, Kansas. This is where Pentecostal historians believe Agnes Ozman spoke in tongues signifying a spiritual baptism that would usher in what many would later consider a global spiritual awakening. Although most scholars admit that the "First Global Great Awakening" originated with various eruptions from other places around the globe—real or perceived—Azusa Street, and the media attention it received, became the birthplace for the spontaneous combustion of a spiritual flame that would spread to the far reaches of the Earth.[32] Parham, convinced that the spirit awakened from a long incubation, traveled throughout the USA to spread the proverbial good news that times were about to change. "Holy Spirit" baptism and tongue-speaking were the key elements to this process. But the movement had yet to take off; perhaps it lacked that "umph," that fire that burns so bright and intense, you remember that moment, that one definitive moment, when you know nothing will ever be the same again.

That moment came in 1906, a year after a one-eyed Charismatic African American Louisianan named William Seymour met Parham while preaching at a Houston revival. Parham took Seymour under his wing; he especially adopted a belief in the practice of spiritual baptism and speaking in tongues. But this relationship was short-lived, perhaps just because Parham was a racist or a jealous guy, but eventually Seymour refused his teacher's segregationist policies and left Parham's church, taking his message to more fertile pastures on the West Coast. Seymour circulated through churches in Los Angeles preaching about things like divine healing and speaking in tongues, the very stuff of Pentecostalism. He then organized a small group to begin a ten-day fast in hopes of bringing in a new day of Pentecost. That new day started on the third day of the fast.

First it was Edward Lee, one of the group members, who spoke in tongues after briefly falling ill and receiving "spiritual healing." The Charismatic fire erupted that night, and to Seymour's group, it provided evidence that a "second Pentecost" arrived for the still new century. The fire spread like ripples from an earthquake. It was a proliferation that led to a widespread epidemic of spiritual power in the form of tongue-speaking. And in that burning Charismatic group, others spoke in tongues, people fell to their knees, and still others prophesized. Some shouted while others rushed from their houses to witness the birth of a religious movement. And finally, its first Charismatic figure, a man called Seymour, now the stuff of legend, spoke in tongues six days later on April 12, 1906. Eventually, the media were drawn to it like moths to a flame.

As the fire intensified, membership rapidly grew, as did media attention. Seymour's church became known as Azusa Street Apostolic Faith Mission—now thought of as the birthplace of the modern Charismatic movement known as Pentecostalism. People from places far and near descended upon Azusa Street. The movement originally attracted a racially diverse audience, impressive considering the racism of the times. It is believed that thousands of people visited the Azusa Street revival and experienced the "Holy Ghost" baptism and the subsequent gift of speaking in tongues. People from this revival established world missionaries that eventually helped ignite the global Pentecostal movement that would, in time, make its way to the Caribbean.

It's important to note that the Pentecostal movement, at least the movement scholars trace back to Azusa Street, rejected authoritarian control and bureaucratic domination over the congregation. The movement challenged institutional domination and stressed individual empowerment. It opposed pastoral oversight, strong central organization, ministerial education and credentialing, merit promotion, doctrinal disputes, formal missions, and the establishment of church doctrines; the best oppositional qualities that characterize charisma. At least in the early Pentecostal movement, scholars agree that it challenged the institutionalization of the church and its spirit-crushing bureaucratic ways. It was a religious movement of the heart over the mind, both metaphorically and literally as it challenged hierarchical domination and institutional subordination. Perhaps it was all about individual Charismatic power, or a challenge to denominational legitimacy, or, as Harvey Cox[33] puts it, "experiential Christianity" and a "protest against man-made creeds," or perhaps it was the rediscovery of the supernatural[34] that led to the movement's global spread. But whatever the exact ingredients or formula that created the great movement, it was all about individual empowerment and resistance against institutional subordination, and charisma was the fire that fueled the engine. In fact, charisma was that engine. But what has happened to charisma? Some scholars say it has faded into obscurity, others claim that its slumber is temporary; still others argue that its magic is still alive making big changes in places like Latin America, while still others note that a big fire burns large and bright in small places like storefront churches in Brooklyn ghettos. But what do we make of the Charismatic movement in the English-speaking Caribbean?

Though it is now well documented that the Pentecostal movement, and the larger Christian Charismatic movement, attracts both the wealthy and downtrodden, the initial Azusa Street Pentecostals attracted the attention of the poor and dispossessed living in American ghettos and poor rural areas. Some say it was the pure emotion behind the movement that attracted people the most, while others say that it proved particularly attractive to the poor who were dealing with the precariousness of destabilization associated with rapid urbanization and social upheaval.[35] As the movement expanded, it flooded into highly concentrated areas of poverty, like the shantytowns and barrios of Latin American cities and the slums of many European and Asian cities. As Mike Davis explains, "If God died in the cities of the industrial revolution, he has risen again in the postindustrial cities of the developing world."[36] In the Caribbean, the growth of Pentecostalism has been directly linked to urbanization.[37] Scholars point out that Pentecostalism particularly attracts residents in the urban centers of the Caribbean.[38] Sociologist David Martin argues that a major factor for the emergence and growth of the Pentecostal movement was its attraction to the underclass, especially those neglected by or disenchanted with the major Christian denominations that catered mostly to the middle and upper classes.[39] Pentecostalism offered a form of spiritual or religious capital—or what I previously called Holy Ghost Capital—to the excluded classes tired of their material and cultural conditions. In short, it was a popular solution, real or magical, to the spiritual sickness associated with oppression and marginalization.[40]

The spontaneous acts of ecstatic worship and emotional outbursts associated with the "poor" and "barbaric" were unpalatable to middle and upper classes. For the posh religious bourgeoisie, the original Pentecostal movement was too loud, black, emotional, unpredictable, spontaneous, and therefore threatening to orthodoxy and establishment. The Azusa

Street revival became, for many, a clarion call to the underclass throughout the world to create an alternative system through a religious movement, one that offered new forms of status and meaning-making through one's relationship to the divine, a relationship that offered "spiritual gifts" such as tongue-speaking. These gifts worked particularly well in those cultures where spiritual forces of good and evil are still believed to shape human life. Pentecostalism continues to spread around the world especially attracting cultures where religion and spirituality are used as viable tools to combat social ills, and perhaps especially the secular institutions that are believed to cause them. Recent scholarship provides strong evidence that Charismatic Christianity continues to flourish in places where dislocation, inequality, and conflict are most intense.[41] It is here where the dominant features of Charismatic religion—including its challenging of traditional institutions, fluid authority structures, ecstatic and less restrained worship styles, and spiritual empowerment—most attract those living under such conditions.[42] This might explain why Pentecostalism proved so attractive to the English-speaking Caribbean where religion, especially Pentecostalism, has found new forms of legitimacy and power in shaping the region's affairs. In fact, recent events in the Caribbean show that Charismatic religion is now playing a larger role in the political and economic life of the region. In this part of the world, the Charismatic movement is becoming a possible force for change. Before turning to this topic, the next section provides a brief history of the spread of the Pentecostal movement in the English-speaking Caribbean.

Section: The Early Pentecostal Movement in the Caribbean

Although the growth of Pentecostalism varies throughout the Caribbean, the movement is exploding in some parts of the region.[43] And though the movement was introduced to the region from North America, its growth is less a product of missionary work than the work of local Caribbean churches organizing independently from the central headquarters of large foreign religious institutions.[44] In this way, even as Pentecostalism developed in the Caribbean, it kept true to one of its central characteristics of defying modern forces of institutionalization and resisting subordination to North American domination, and thus Pentecostalism was uniquely incorporated into the cultural practices of the region. As Pentecostalism developed in the

Caribbean, it became deeply embedded in the region's culture and used the region's local talents to develop organizational leadership.[45] Pentecostalism proved attractive to the Caribbean particularly with its ability to fight corruption and challenge institutional power and leadership, empower ordinary people and provide them with new forms of upward mobility, while blending with traditional African practices that emphasize community, resistance, and solidarity, provide power to combat spiritual forces that bring mental and physical diseases, and its penchant to relate testimonials through traditional oral modes of communication.[46] As Edmonds and Gonzalez put it, "Pentecostalism is able to negotiate between the modern and the traditional worlds, making it especially appealing in Latin America and the Caribbean. … It also highlights one's individual experience of the sacred, connecting to the modern Western emphasis on the individual. It focuses on healing, testimony, and expressive rituals, all elements that connect with Caribbean worldviews."[47] Perhaps it was exactly because of these traits that the twentieth-century Caribbean experienced an explosive growth in Pentecostal, Neo-Pentecostal, and Charismatic churches.[48] The best way to summarize the English-speaking Caribbean's attraction to Pentecostalism and its exponential growth in the region is as follows:

Christianity in the Caribbean during the twentieth century was marked by the explosive growth of Pentecostalism. Though a late arrival in the history of Christianity, it has become the most significant Christian movement throughout the Caribbean. Pentecostal faiths arrived either through direct work by North American missionaries or through individuals who converted to a Pentecostal faith elsewhere and later returned to their homelands. For many a reflection of religion in the contemporary Caribbean, Pentecostalism "is by and large the new Christianity of black people, which in some measure is refuting the claim of those who speak for traditional European Christianity that divinity can only be perceived through the eye of the people of Europe, interpreted in their mythology and language, and represented visually through the imagery of their culture."[49] Pentecostalism created an indigenous Christianity that appealed greatly to the masses; through its incorporation of a Spirit-based Christianity and local leadership, Pentecostalism offered a religious ethos that appealed to poor Caribbean peoples that resonated with their African aesthetics and religious life. … The complexity of Christianity in the twentieth-century Caribbean and in the Caribbean today reflects global Christianity, which is becoming increasingly supernatural in belief and more localized in terms of leadership and membership.[50]

Yet, the most powerful Pentecostal institution in the English-speaking Caribbean today is the PAWI that began in Montserrat. And its capacity to appeal to the masses and continue its growth as we push toward a postmodern world will depend, in part, upon how the movement is able to balance charisma with the modern forces of rationality as well as how it continues to grow across borders in the region. First, it helps to take a look into the history of the PAWI.

The Origins of Pentecostal Organization in the Caribbean

The English-speaking Caribbean experienced new religious developments in the late nineteenth century that derived from a wide variety of Christian denominations mainly in the USA—from Presbyterians and Methodists to Pentecostals and Jehovah Witnesses. This US religious influence makes sense given the country's increasing political, economic, social, and cultural influence in the Caribbean at the time, prompting some critics to refer to this as a form of religious colonization. As religious revivals developed in the USA throughout the twentieth century, from Evangelical to Pentecostal revivals such as Azusa Street, increased travel to and from the Caribbean as well as new communication technologies brought the influences of these revivals to Caribbean shores. Much of the hot and fiery rhetoric found in US televangelism is clearly found in the impassioned preaching of many local church congregations throughout the Caribbean. As mentioned earlier, new local churches in the Caribbean were initially linked to the larger denominations of their northern neighbor. Eventually, just as they did political domination in the past, local churches became independent from the larger institutional churches in North America.

According to their own history, the PAWI originates from three moments in history: (1) Acts II in the Christian Bible when the Holy Ghost descended on the disciples of the biblical Jesus, (2) eighteenth-century Holiness and Revivalist movements happening around the world, and (3) the 1906 Azusa Street revival in Los Angeles. The three year, or "thousand day" Azusa Street Revival caused a spiritual wave that crossed northern borders into Canada. Scholars trace Pentecostalism in Canada[51] to the Azusa Street revival and 1906 Hebden Mission in Toronto, the very same year as the Los Angeles revival.[52] Ellen Hebden, the British immigrant and first known person in Canada to speak in tongues, ignited

Canada's version of the Azusa Street Revival with the East End Mission, or "Hebden Mission," on May 20, 1906, in a three-story building located on 651 Queen Street East in Toronto.[53] Most scholarly accounts show that the East End Mission started independently from Azusa Street, and that Hebden, who spoke in tongues only about a month following the first tongues spoken on Azusa Street, never reported her experience until after learning about the Azusa Street around November 1906.[54] The Hebden family, what some scholars consider the "first family of Pentecost in Canada,"[55] helped ignite, along with the Azusa Street revival, one of the largest and most important Christian religious movements in modern times.[56] Within months of speaking in tongues for the first time, Hebden's husband followed with his own tongue-speaking experience, and like dominos, the spirit caught on.[57] At the end of the first decade of the twentieth century, that spirit led to the sprouting of over a dozen Pentecostal churches in Canada with connection to the Hebden Mission. And these churches needed to organize, especially as the movement spread throughout Canada, eventually leading to the formation of the Pentecostal Assemblies of Canada (PAOC), the largest Pentecostal denomination in the country today.[58]

While this organization informally existed for a few years, PAOC received official government legitimation in 1919 from a Canadian government issued charter.[59] It is important to note that although the Hebden Mission was composed of a socio-economically wealthier and racially whiter demographic composition than the participants of Azusa Street,[60] both revivals shared some essential characteristics. The Hebden Mission shared Azusa Street's egalitarian and more informal form of organization, with emphasis on religious experience over doctrine, focus on grace and free will over nature and determinism, promotion-based God's will over bureaucratic red tape, and a greater potential for a more gendered equality.[61] Central to arguments made in the chapters below, once PAOC became the very embodiment of religious institutionalization, the movement began losing the original charisma that sparked its birth. Order and dogma replaced the spirit, formal and rigid educational training and institutional procedures determined rank and promotion, and financial control in the hands of formal bureaucracy led to the loss of its original fire.[62] As PAOC institutionalized, it began to lose its potential to empower women,[63] and perhaps diminish its charisma so important for a religious movement to serve as a vehicle for social change.

Although some of the exact details seem lost in history,[64] a Quebec-born American missionary named Reverend Robert Jamieson is tradition-ally credited with the initial founding of a small church in Montserrat that led to what is now the PAWI.[65] According to PAWI's website and self-published book *Ablaze: The Pentecostal Assemblies of the West Indies,*[66] Jamieson's small church spread rapidly throughout Montserrat and the rest of the English-speaking Caribbean. It was in Montserrat where PAWI was born.

THE PENTECOSTAL ASSEMBLIES OF THE WEST INDIES

Although the PAOC was not formally associated with the Caribbean until 1926, PAWI considers 2010 as its first centennial of fellowship; this was when Jamieson—the Canadian appointed director of the of PAOC's West Indies Mission—transitioned from a Holiness orientation to a decidedly Pentecostal one. As much of the Caribbean experienced political, eco-nomic, and social upheaval in the 1930s and 1940s, PAOC created a semi-independent and autonomous PAWI District.[67] According to its website and self-published book *Ablaze*, PAWI held its first Biennial Conference in August of 1946 at Kashmir Villa in Petit Valley, Trinidad, where the move-ment officially became affiliated with the PAOC. The semi-autonomous PAWI district included the islands Montserrat, Trinidad, Barbados, Antigua, and Granada. Soon after in 1946, 22 missionaries were already operating in parts of the Caribbean. Two years later, Bermuda, Grenada, and Dominica joined, and in the late 1950s, Tobago and St. Vincent became part of the organization. Finally, PAOC's West Indies Mission became the PAWI at a 1958 conference held in Trinidad. During what became known as a time of religious decolonization between 1958 and 1966, PAWI became fully independent and autonomous, in control of its own fate. According to PAWI's religious leadership, PAWI owes its origins and development to the four decades of care and nurturing PAOC pro-vided since the beginning of the twentieth century. PAWI, according to its history over a century old, now reports having a "membership of over 33,000, countless thousands of adherents, approximately 227 churches, and around 550 credential workers."[68] PAWI serves as the strong arm of Pentecostalism in the Caribbean and the quintessential example of Pentecostal institutionalization—one that is highly organized into vertical degradations of rank.

PAWI's Formal Organizational Structure[69]

This section explains PAWI's formal organization to showcase how much of the Pentecostal movement in the Caribbean developed into a top-down, vertically arranged, and highly structured institution complete with formal rules, regulations, and procedures. Its constitution and Biennial General Conference proceedings reveal a religious movement that epitomizes Pentecostal institutionalism.

PAWI's constitution includes a mission statement stating "The Pentecostal Assemblies of the West Indies International exists to fulfill the purpose of God by transforming people and communities everywhere, by the gospel of Jesus Christ and through the power and manifestation of the Holy Spirit, for the glory of God" and a preamble with six statements of belief. The 15 articles within the constitution establish bylaws, interpretation of its legal terms, intentions and objectives, functions and powers, a statement of faith, requirements of membership, establishment of districts and assembly bodies, and organizational structure and power hierarchy, among other formalities. Article VII establishes PAWI's formal organization listed below.

(1) *General Conference* (Biennial conference that serves as the highest decision-making body)

(2) *General Executive* (Provides oversight between General Conferences) The General Executive is responsible for:

- Human resource development at all levels of organization (i.e. identifying skills needed and where, skills possessed, and develop training programs for imparting those skills).
- Providing the infrastructure for social ministry on a macro scale.
- Maximizing the use of finances and creating new streams of income.
- Creating a structure for effective communication throughout the organization especially from the head office to all congregation members.
- Encouraging greater real estate development.

(3) *District Conference* (Highest decision-making body in each District held annually)

(4) *District Executive* (Gives oversight to the District between District Conferences).
The District Executive acts as the facilitator and middle manager in ensuring that the directives of the executive body are carried out. Secondly, they will also be responsible for ensuring that the primary objectives of the church are well mapped out and that they are being executed. In their role as the overseer of churches, the District also acts as liaison/communication facilitator between the executive and the pastors and churches, ensuring a two-way flow of information.

(5) *Local Assembly* (The pastor-led local church, in each locale, forms a District).
The responsibilities of the local church are evangelism, missions, counseling, discipling, family growth, and financial stewardship.

According to PAWI International 35th Biennial General Conference held at the Jolly Beach Resort and Spa in St. John's Antigua, the composition of PAWI's internally elected officials, from General Executive Officers to Departmental Directors, include the following in order of rank:

(I) Eleven General Executive Officers (General Bishop, Assistant General Bishop
General Administrator, Executive Director of Church Ministries, and Executive Director of World Missions, Districts' Presiding Bishops, National Bishop of Trinidad and Tobago and Chairman of the Board of Directors of the West Indies School of Theology, and three persons the General Executive nominates and the General Conference approves).

(II) Thirteen Presiding District Bishops—(1) Antigua and Barbuda, St. Kitts and Nevis, (2) Barbados, (3) Dominica and Guadeloupe, (4) Grenada, (5) Montserrat, (6) St. Lucia, (7) St. Vincent and the Grenadines, (8) Tobago, (9) Trinidad and Tobago, (10) South Trinidad, (11) Northwest Trinidad, (12) Northeast Trinidad, and (13) Central Trinidad.

(III) Four Other Executive Members (One Chairman of the Board of Directors and three Members-at-Large).

(IV) Five General Departmental Directors (Men's Ministries, Women's Ministries, Christian Education, Youth Ministries, and Crusaders Regional Commissioner).

(V) They also have a Chairman of the Board of Directors for their West
Indian School of Theology along with eight other members.

PAWI's General Church Ministries Organization includes an Executive
Director for Church Ministries with a General Church Ministries Council
composed of (1) The Executive Director of Church Ministries, (2) A
Secretary/Treasurer, (3) Legal Consultant, (4) Business/Marketing
Consultant, and (5) A minimum of five persons representing the respective departments within the Church Ministries. PAWI establishes districts within its organization geographically, with each district under
the governance of an executive council. Each district's General Church
Ministries Council includes (1) The Director for Church Ministries
(Chair), (2) Assistant Director for Church Ministries, (3) Directors of the
respective District Departments, and (4) Secretary/Treasurer. Districts are
classified into either pioneer or autonomous districts. While autonomous
districts are self-propagating, self-governing, and self-financing, pioneer
districts are working toward those ends.

PAWI serves as a highly centralized organization with a full-fledged
bureaucracy complete with a constitution and bylaws, rules and laws,
formal procedures and regulations, hierarchies and ranking systems, and
formal training schools and conferences. Of course, though the formal
organization of an institution matters, it's the informal organization
that often proves most important. In fact, promotion to many positions
within the organization relies more on one's perceived Charismatic abilities rather than formal qualifications. For example, nomination to become
a member of the General Councils requires having qualities difficult to
quantify that rely more on interpretation rather than any definite qualifica-
tion. According to the requirements set forth in PAWI's 35TH Biennial
General Conference, General Council Members must "Be persons of
mature experience, whose life and ministry are above question, and who
possess such qualities and skills which shall determine their eligibility for
office." Further, personal connections within PAWI go a long way for
social mobility though its ranks. Promotions to most offices require the
recommendations from the superiors of the institution. As the following
chapters will show, it's the Charismatic leaders within the cold, dry institutions such as PAWI that, remarkably, keep charisma alive in a postmodern
world where charisma and institutionalization not only coexist, but make
each other possible.

THE EMERGENCE OF PAWI IN CARIBBEAN POLITICAL AND ECONOMIC AFFAIRS

Let's fast forward to 2013 where great changes have brought Charismatic Christianity within the existing political and economic power structures of the Caribbean Community (CARICOM) in the English-speaking Caribbean. Sometimes big things start with many small steps. Let's take a brief look into the small steps taken ten years prior to the explosive event leading up to the exorcism described in the introduction of this book. These ten years of small steps eventually led to a verbal agreement for the various historically divided Christian churches to unite as a more powerful force to shape social life in the Caribbean. Perhaps related, these churches now seem to play a large and growing role in shaping the economics and politics of the region.

The Charismatic movement in the Caribbean witnessed two major events in the first few years of the second decade in the twenty-first century. First, an Antiguan-born Brooklyn Bishop of a Pentecostal Church finally succeeded, after ten years of networking, in at least verbally uniting the historically divided Traditional, Evangelical, and Independent Churches of Antigua. The CARICOM reached out to the religious leaders of the Caribbean less than two years later, enabling them to become a greater force in the shaping of the political, social, economic, and cultural affairs of the region.

THE CARIBBEAN COMMUNITY (CARICOM)

The CARICOM is an organization established in 1973 composed of 15 mainly English-Speaking nations. The countries of CARICOM designated as "less developed countries" (LDCs) include Antigua and Barbuda, Belize, Dominica, Grenada, Haiti, Montserrat, St. Kitts and Nevis, St. Lucia, and St. Vincent and the Grenadines. CARICOM designated "more developed countries" (MDCs) including the Bahamas, Barbados, Guyana, Jamaica, and Suriname, and Trinidad and Tobago. According to its website, CARICOM seeks to "promote economic integration and cooperation among its members, ensure the equitable sharing of benefits of integration, and coordinate foreign policy." CARICOM coordinates economic policies and development planning, devises and institutes special projects for LDCs within its jurisdiction, operates as a regional single market for many of its members, and handles regional trade disputes.

The first CARICOM Inter-Faith Service and Conference was held on Monday, February 17, 2014, in Antigua and Barbuda following a request from Antigua and Barbuda's Prime Minister Baldwin Spencer, who earlier in 2014 called for religious groups to become involved in the CARICOM change process.

The goal of this Inter-Faith Conference was to unite the Caribbean community's religious leaders and to develop official channels for faith-based organizations (FBOs) to become involved in the Caribbean's decision-making process. Spencer urged that Faith-Based Organizations "have a contribution to make in the future development of the region and that there was agreement for the institutionalization of the CARICOM Inter-Faith Conference." He goes further to explain the importance of the emerging role of religion stating that the church should have an official role within CARICOM that will "reflect the relevance of the church and religion in building a modern Caribbean civilization." Part of this plan establishes official structures for churches, like the Pentecostal Churches that dominate much of the Caribbean, to engage governments in a consultative process with the State. In addressing the Caribbean Community's imbalanced development and unequal resources as well as the structural legacy of colonization, political leaders like Spencer now argue that the governments of the Caribbean must now partner with the religious leaders of the region.

A separate CARICOM caucus held about a month later provided an endorsement for regional leaders to pave the way for the development of FBO to play an important role in the social and political issues of the Caribbean community. Unlike much of the Western world to the North, religion, the Charismatic movement in particular, is becoming a more powerful force in shaping the affairs of the region. And it's the leaders of PAWI that lead the way for providing religious influence in the political and economic affairs in the English-speaking Caribbean.

THE STORY OF A BROOKLYN BISHOP WITH CARIBBEAN ROOTS

Antiguan-born Bishop Lester Bradford of Brooklyn networked for 15 years to unite the historically divided Christian Churches in the Caribbean, starting with his home country of Antigua and Barbuda. His vision is to unite the Established, Evangelical, and Independent churches in the

Caribbean to become a more powerful force shaping the political, cultural, social, and economic landscape of the region. What starts as a vision
became a decade-and-a-half-long dedicated mission to realize this dream.
The Bishop's strategy was to make contacts with religious leaders in the
Caribbean and become a man of influence in the region. He wrote letters,
traveled throughout the region to guest preach in various churches, using
his connections to build more networks, established contacts and formed
genuine friendships within the religious circles of the region, and worked
tirelessly to win the support of important religious people.

The first steps to materializing the vision began with writing letters.
Bradford recalls the long journey just a day after the religious leaders in
Antigua agreed to unite stating, "I started writing letters, letting other
pastors know what the vision is all about. It started 15 years ago. …
There were people who started out, they did not catch the vision; many
of them came out of curiosity. And they dropped off." Bradford traveled
to Antigua renting out a space in the multipurpose center to hold a prayer
luncheon. In Bradford's words, "I invited only pastors and religious leaders to tell them the vision. I told them at that first meeting that I'm in
it for the long haul. I'm going to be here until the Caribbean world is
safe." Bradford continued this yearly visit attempting to unite the religious
leaders, starting in Antigua and eventually spreading through the rest of
the Caribbean region. But annual attendance remained inconsistent and
eventually waned. Something else needed to be done. Bradford turned
to a friend, an older and long-standing pastor in Antigua named Barnes
with a church of almost a thousand members. Pastor Barnes agreed to
hold the annual meeting in his church "Bible Believers Fellowship" that
comes with a ready-made audience. Relying on Pastor Barnes with his
near 1000-member congregation turned out to be both a blessing and
hindrance. The good Bishop got lazy.

Working closely with a big time pastor on the island and holding healthy
looking services with a large attendance made Bradford complacent. As
Bradford admits, "Since I was working there with Pastor Barnes, I was not
reaching out much to the other pastors because all of the services looked
healthy. You had 1000 people, over 1000 people sometimes. He had a large
church; I just went along with that." As a result, nothing changed. Not until
Pastor Barnes died, and was replaced with another pastor who divided the
church congregation and alienated many of Pastor Barnes's friends, including Bradford. He now had to start "from scratch." Cue the letters. Bradford
secured a list of religious leaders and pastors from the consulate general of

Antigua and Barbuda in New York City and sent letters out to pastors at random throughout Antigua. At first he handwrote the letters, and then typed it out for his family to review before sending it out by regular mail. He eventually began sending e-mails too. Success proved elusive.

Like academics, it's difficult to get pastors to agree. His approach was clever; don't start with asking pastors to put aside their differences and unite. That will never work. Rather, take it in small steps. Those small steps were just to pray together. Bradford wrote, "In the first letter, I was telling them that we need to pray for our nation. I outlined some of the ills of the nation. So let's come together and pray for the nation. This is how I was appealing to them." Pastors, while they might be men and women of God, remain unequivocally human and prone to human ways, especially when there is something to lose. As Bradford admits, "Most of them, they didn't respond. One of the most difficult things is to get pastors together, and for different reasons. Some pastors are insecure and believe that if they did fellowship with other churches, they will lose members." He goes on to explain that some pastors fear losing church membership to pastors whose churches boast better singers or choirs, more pristine buildings and sound systems, and modernized equipment. As a result, some pastors are very insecure. As Bradford puts it, "They don't like to do fellowship with others because they're afraid of losing members. That's one of the reasons. There are other reasons too." Perhaps recalling his perceived power in God, or perhaps drawing from his own remarkable biography, going from a poor kid growing up in a small rural area in Antigua (Gray's Farm) to a bishop in New York City, Bradford remained determined to see his vision come to fruition.

Bradford started from the ground up, making connections and establishing contacts with as many people as possible. He explains the process, "So now I am contacting these people, and encouraging them to tell their friends to come and let's talk. Let's have a conversation, that they can catch the vision also." One way to spread the message, now an essential tool pastors throughout the Caribbean use to spread their message—and in turn the Caribbean Charismatic movement—is the medium of media, especially radio and Internet broadcasts. Now, Bradford proudly explains, "We put it on the radio, so everybody can hear it. Every year we've come, we put it on the radio. And now we put it on radio and television." Indeed, I accompanied the pastor to a radio program based in St. John's to spread the message, for religious leaders to unite and pray for the country and entire Caribbean.

Bradford contacted not only pastors throughout the island, but all the radio stations too. He took the bull by the proverbial horns. Bradford lands in Antigua from JFK airport and knocks on radio station doors with a big vision and few funds.

> And there are times when I come down and I would go into certain radio stations. I call them and I said, the national day of prayer is coming up, and I would like to advertise the national day of prayer. Because we do not have a lot funds working with, I tell them that listen, we're coming to pray for the nation. When we come praying for the nation, you benefit. You benefit from it, because as a nation prospers, you prosper. So, we don't have a lot of money right now to pay all this spots that we need. See that we're doing it for the people; I'm asking if you would do it at very minimal costs. In many cases, they said 'No, we'll just do it for free.'

For example, he explains that in the last radio station he attended just the day prior to this conversation, there was no charge. In fact, both the television and radio interview cost nothing; his only expense was a paid advertisement from a local television station. It helps that Bradford is a native son of Antigua, not some outsider with a religious message. It also helps that he was once a bit of a local celebrity on the island with a musical team called Lenny and Libby who once opened up for James Brown. For those who know him, it is quite a surprise that Bradford became a born-again Christian and Bishop of a tongue-speaking Pentecostal Church.

Learning from his mistake of relying on large congregation numbers to do the work for him, Bradford realizes that success depends on keeping focus and ambition. It's not the large crowds that will get religious leaders to unite, but rather a commitment from the religious leaders themselves. His renewed drive the past two years to network directly with religious leaders led to that triumphant moment where these leaders from a variety of denominations verbally agreed to unite.

It's important to note that Bradford accomplished this through his own personal forms of Charismatic networking, grassroots style. He did not rely on belonging to any large institution to bring influence to force his vision to the Caribbean religious leaders. There was no pushing bureaucratic channels and relying on informal networks to bring his mission of religious unity to the Caribbean. He developed personal connections, nurtured them, and created strong networks of support to accomplish his "divine" goals. And as Bradford spreads his vision, others jump on board to use their own personalized forms of networking to bring their respective religious visions to reality. The people he networks with begin to develop connections themselves. As a result, a complex system of networks developed in Antigua and spread to other religious leaders throughout the Caribbean. As Bradford reveals in his most recent experience:

> They will begin to do their own networking. This happens when you bring others in. When we went to Jamaica on Wednesday, there was a new pastor that came on board. He was the one who was sitting next to me in the church the other day. He came and that was the first time that he was meeting with me. And he is very excited about what is going on. He will establish his own networks to make this now shared vision come true.

The scene in the introduction of the book shows the final moments leading to the 15-year vision finally materializing into reality. There they were—religious leaders from the Anglican to various Pentecostal churches, Moravian to the Methodist Church, and Seventh-Day-Adventists to other mainly Protestant groups—standing before the wild bishop talking about God's vision of unity. It was reminiscent of Jesus's famous biblical quote, "It has been written but now I say unto you" as the Bishop decrees "The Church has been divided, but now," he says unto them, "it will be united." These leaders verbally agreed, some I later found out were unsuspecting of the events that transpired, to unite as one unified force to combat the demonically influenced secular political, social, economic, and cultural institutions believed to be responsible for a plague that has caused the Caribbean people misery and ruin. The bishop had to display charisma beyond those derived from his institution through his ability to convince other religious leaders of his exceptional qualities—a man of God on an unstoppable mission. This example is one of many found throughout this research traveling in known and unknown places throughout the Caribbean to see firsthand how religious leaders—some without a church, others part of PAWI, others totally independent—make their impact spreading religious ideas and visions across the region.

Bradford's story is about establishing strong religious networking relationships from the ground up, or what I call Charismatic religious networking, that requires Charismatic transnational Holy Ghost Capital. How Charismatic religion spreads across the Caribbean impacts the success of the movement and its ability to act as a vehicle for social change at both the community, national, and international levels. The facility of the Charismatic movement to maintain functions specific to individualized local communities will heavily impact its emphasis on the inner-worldly to deal with experiences and everyday life, communal orientation, and stubborn resistance to both accommodative forces and its refusal to become fully routinized. Perhaps Charismatic networking like Bradford's will allow for the possibility of the Charismatic movement to impact social life in the region in potentially radical ways. First, a bit of a theoretical overview follows below to place these concepts and ideas within the existing scholarship.

TRANSNATIONALIZATION AND RELIGION: CHARISMATIC CHRISTIANITY CROSSES CARIBBEAN BORDERS

In the late modern world, transnationalism—or the movement of institutions, people, ideas, and goods between and among nation-states with trans-border relationships—rapidly spreads through permeable borders, using new modes of communication, transportation, and networks, shaping local regions on a global scale.[70] Scholarship on transnationalization typically focuses on the political, economic, social, and cultural forces cutting across borders while paying less attention to how religions also engage in creative ways to network across national boundaries, profoundly shaping the regions in which they become embedded.[71] Further, previous scholarship has paid even less attention to the ways various types of transnational religious networks impact how globalizing religions influence local communities.[72] This is surprising given how religion and religious movements continue to impact world affairs, especially in the Caribbean. As the pace of globalization intensifies, transnational religious networks hasten the speed of ideas, information, goods, and services as well as the spread of people and their institutions between and among nation-states. A discussion on transnational religious connections involves analyzing how people, goods, services, and information spread across political boundaries within the context of global capital and nation-states.[73] A look at how the Charismatic movement spreads in the Caribbean by making transnational religious connections is important to understand how the movement spreads globally and how this impacts both the vitality of the movement and influence in the regions where it settles.

Recent scholarship on transnational religious networks shows the importance of how establishing connections through various types of power relationships shape the spread of religion and its potential to make an impact.[74] The distinction between religious transnationalism from "above" and "below" clearly shows that the way religious movements cross boundaries matters.[75] Religious transnationalism from above refers to religious groups receiving the support of large "legitimate" institutions such as the nation-state and wealthy corporations that encourage religious expansion through subsidizing or funding religious festivals, pilgrimages, tourist destinations, and other mainstay religious activities.[76] Religious transnationalism from below refers to religious groups forming at a grassroots level through informal networks established with people developing close personal ties, usually through deep spiritual interests.[77] Although religious groups crossing borders can develop both approaches to transnationalization, most tend to resemble more closely to one or the other. And the way religious groups cross borders matters for both the vitality of the religious group and how it impacts the regions where it settles.

Similarly, recent scholarship on religious groups crossing borders identifies other types, or patterns, of transnational religious organizations that include "extended" and "negotiated" forms.[78] Extended transnational religious organization usually involves highly influential public institutions, like the Catholic Church or Pentecostal Assemblies of God, that transnationalize through establishing highly impersonal international networks from above and incorporating members from local communities from below into powerful networks rich in resources.[79] Such top-heavy forms of religious organization face the challenges of becoming so bureaucratically institutionalized and formal that the original spark that initiated the group and its spread begins to diminish.[80] In other words, when transnational religious networks spread through impersonal and more bureaucratic connections that rely on institutions of power, the vitality of that movement faces possible decline.[81] And let's face it, homogenization, while perhaps comfortable, is boring.

Negotiated transnational religious organizations, on the other hand, develop through personal connections established between individuals and decentralized institutions that transnationalize through informal agreements made between friends or associates who share a vision.[82] For example, finances and administrative decisions happen through friends making informal agreements, writing grants, creating missionary campaigns, guest preaching, making deals with hotels and travel agents, sharing investments, and so on.[83] This form of transnational religious organization from below emerges through grassroots and decentralized forms of organization that are highly localized and flexible to both the members of the religious group and the communities it settles. Characteristics such as spontaneous, adaptable, malleable, flexible, creative, and innovative, while certainly not boring, better respond to the needs of local communities.[84]

This study of the Charismatic movement in the Caribbean, and its spread throughout the region, involves close inspection of religious transnationalization from "above" and "below" as well the similarly related extended and negotiated types. PAWI represents the former type of religious organization with a high degree of institutionalized bureaucracy, formal networking, and impersonal relationships. This research also examines the latter type of religious organizations looking closely at the small but powerful Charismatic churches and how they spread throughout the region. Religious transnationalization from below, or what I call "Charismatic Religious Networking," shows how religious leaders and groups develop informal and highly personalized connections. These informal types of transnational religious groups develop Charismatic leaders with the ability to create personal, informal, and spontaneous global networks—or what I call "transnational holy ghost capital" extending my earlier concept of "Holy Ghost Capital."[85] Transnational Holy Ghost Capital reveals how Charismatic leaders possess a unique type of religious capital based not on their attachment to an institution but rather their ability to create personal, informal, and spontaneous global religious networks.

The questions that guide the following chapters include inquiring about (1) how Charismatic Christianity crosses borders in the English-Speaking Caribbean, (2) how this impacts the vitality of the movement pushing toward the future, and (3) how the different types of religious transnational organization influences the movement's impact on the region. Looking at both types of transnational religious organizations will provide insight into how Charismatic Christianity spreads throughout the Caribbean and what types of impacts it makes in the region. The way the movement networks and spreads across political borders matters for the health of the movement as well as its local and regional influence, and this can have important implications for social change that offer potential challenges to power along with alternatives to modernity in a part of the world that has received relatively little attention.

MAP OF THE BOOK

Chapter 1 described a scene depicting the fulfillment of a Pentecostal bishop's vision to unite, at least verbally, the divided Christian churches to become a stronger force in shaping the affairs of the English-speaking

Caribbean. This led to an explosive confrontation between perceived demonic forces operating to sabotage God's plan to accomplish the goal of church unity, providing further legitimacy to religious leaders and their adherents that they are warriors for Christ combating sinister supernatural forces operating in the physical realm of everyday Caribbean life. This scene highlighted some major themes on Charismatic religious networking, its ability to impact the Caribbean world, and the fate of the Charismatic movement as it pushes toward an uncertain and precarious future.

This chapter introduced the Charismatic movement in the English-speaking Caribbean and provided a religious demographic portrait of the Charismatic movement in the region as well as of the world's Christian population from both the Global North and South. A brief history of the Pentecostal movement was provided from its origins in the USA to its inception in the Caribbean. The early Charismatic movement developed into a large-institutional hierarchy in Montserrat culminating in the massive PAWI that continues to dominate the movement in the Caribbean. Recently, PAWI joined the political and economic elite of the CARICOM taking a larger role in shaping Caribbean affairs.

Chapter 3 explains the methodological approach of the book that requires moving beyond the conventional methods of qualitative research to delve deeper into the fabric of social life in the English-speaking Caribbean. Just as religious leaders develop their own form of networking to move across political borders, this ethnography requires Charismatic ethnographic networking across borders and finding the ethnographic *it*.

Chapter 4 begins with a descriptive scene juxtaposing Apostle Stephen Andrew's large PAWI church with Pastor Matthew Noyce's small, institutionally unaffiliated church to highlight the striking contrasts between Charismatic styles and types of religious networking across borders. An analysis follows on religion and culture in the Caribbean before delving into the personal lives of Apostle Andrews and Pastor Noyce to reveal the types of religious networking strategies religious leaders and pastors use to impact their local communities and the larger Caribbean region. This chapter develops a four-fold typology on the types of transnational religious networking strategies of Charismatic leaders that will be developed throughout the remaining chapters. The chapter ends with a powerful scene while island hopping with the PAWI leader Reverend Henry Nigel.

Chapter 5 discusses religious life in Trinidad beginning with a shocking scene of a demonic possession and exorcism during an afternoon prayer hour. The scene highlights some of the major ideas explored in this chapter including the blending of religion and culture in the Caribbean, charisma in the highly institutionalized PAWI churches, and the informal Charismatic networking strategies of PAWI leaders that somehow defy the iron cage of rationality. This chapter develops new and creative concepts such as the "Bureaucrasaurus" and "Charismaticrats" to understand the various styles and networking strategies of highly Charismatic religious leaders in PAWI. This chapter ends with an analysis of PAWI's emerging voice in shaping Caribbean life as it joins the political and economic elite of the region.

Chapter 6 introduces St. Lucia, Barbados, and Dominica and its Charismatic religious leaders both inside and out of PAWI as well as their various types of religious networking strategies in the Caribbean. This introduction leads to a larger analysis of the Charismatic movement in all three countries developing some of the major themes of this book including (1) the challenges of church growth and power, (2) the dialectical process of external adversity and internal conflict in the Charismatic movement, and (3) the simultaneous process of structural centralization and decentralization as the church continues to grow in numbers and power. The chapter ends with insight on the Charismatic movement's capacity to defy rationality and its potential to make social change while questioning Weber's iron cage.

Chapter 7 introduces St. Kitts before offering insight into the challenges of PAWI religious leaders attempting to enforce institutional control over a Charismatic church that defected from its stronghold. The religious leader must unevenly negotiate between congregational freedom and pastoral authority, or risk losing legitimacy. Another look at Charismatic leaders show how their struggles help facilitate supernatural gifts that leads to a tragic scene of a miraculous healing attempt highlighting how Pentecostal leaders understand worldly and otherworldly diseases. The section on Montserrat provides analysis on the origins of the Pentecostal movement in the Caribbean leading to a discussion on Pentecostalism and gender inequality. The section ends with insights on the emerging leaders of the Charismatic movement and its ideas for the future.

Chapter 8 offers some final thoughts and comments beginning with a discussion involving a high-ranking PAWI official on Bishop Bradford's attempt to unite the previously divided Christian Churches in the English-speaking Caribbean. This chapter continues with a brief summary of some of the book's major themes and findings on topics related to religious networking, church growth, the simultaneous process of centralization and decentralization, balancing charisma and institutionalization, and the internal divisions and external pressures of the Charismatic movement. A discussion ensues that provides deeper insight into some of the more controversial issues within the Charismatic movement. The book concludes with an outlook on the Charismatic movement in the English-speaking Caribbean and its possibilities as it pushes toward the future.

NOTES

1. Bridget Brereton, ed., "Teresita Martínez-Vergne," in *General History of* the Caribbean: The Caribbean in the Twentieth Century, co-eds. René A. Römer and Blanca G. Silvestrini (UNESCO, 2004).
2. Thomas Maginley and Alvin O. Thompson, Ablaze: The Pentecostal Assemblies of the West Indies (Maracas, St. Joseph, Trinidad and Tobago: Pentecostal Assemblies of the West Indies, 2010).
3. Perhaps it might make some Pentecostal scholars cringe, but I use the Pentecostal and Charismatic movement interchangeably knowing that Pentecostalism is one such Charismatic Christian movement among others. I'm interested in the part of the Caribbean Christian world where born-again Christians speak in tongues and believe in the gifts of the spirit, along with ecstatic worship and divine miracles.
4. D. Chiquete, "Latin American Pentecostalism and Western Postmodernism," International Review of Mission 92 (2003): 29–39; M. Vasquez, "The Global Portability of Pneumatic Christianity: Comparing African and Latin American Pentecostalisms," African Studies 68 (2009): 273–286; W.J. Hollenweger, "An Introduction to Pentecostalisms," Journal of Beliefs & Values 25 (2004): 125–137.
5. Hollenweger, 2004.
6. C.M. Robeck Jr., "Pentecostals and Ecumenism in a Pluralistic World," in The Globalization of Pentecostalism: A Religion Made to Travel, ed. Byron D. Klaus and Douglas Petersen (Oxford, UK: Regnum Press, 1999), 338–362; A. Anderson, An Introduction to Pentecostalism: Global Charismatic Christianity (2nd ed., Cambridge, UK: Cambridge University Press, 2013); and S. Hunt, Handbook of Global Contemporary Christianity: Themes and Developments in Culture, Politics, and Society (Boston: Brill, 2015).
7. Anderson, 2013.
8. The Pew Forum defines Pentecostals as "members of distinct Protestant denominations or independent churches that hold the teaching that all Christians should seek a post-conversion religious experience called the baptism of the Holy Spirit. These denominations and churches teach that those who experi-

ence the baptism of the Holy Spirit may receive one or more spiritual gifts, including the abilities to prophesy or utter messages from God, practice physical healing, speak in tongues or spiritual languages (glossolalia), and interpret tongues."

9. The Pew Forum defines Charismatic Christians as "members of non-Pentecostal denominations—including Catholic, Orthodox and some Protestant denominations—who hold at least some Pentecostal beliefs and engage in at least some spiritual practices associated with Pentecostalism, including divine healing, prophecy and speaking in tongues."

10. Pew Research Center Forum on Religion & Public Life, *Global Christianity, A Report on the Size and Distribution of the World's Christian Population* (Washington, DC: Pew Research Center, 2011).

11. A. Anderson, *To the Ends of the Earth: Pentecostalism and the Transformation of World Christianity* (Oxford: Oxford University Press, 2013).

12. N. Street, *Moved by the Spirit: Pentecostal and Global Christianity in the Global South, Center for Religion and Civic Culture* (Los Angeles, CA: University of Southern California, 2013); R.A. Chestnut, *Born Again in Brazil: The Pentecostal Boom and the Pathogens of Poverty* (New Brunswick, NJ: Rutgers University Press, 1997); D. Martin, *Pentecostalism: The World Their Parish* (Oxford: Blackwell Publishers, 2002); and D. Martin, *Tongues of Fire: The Explosion of Protestantism in Latin America* (Oxford, UK: B. Blackwell, 1990).

13. Center for the Study of Global Christianity, *Christianity in its Global Context, 1970–2020: Society, Religion, and Missio* (South Hamilton, MA: Center for the Study of Global Christianity, Gordon-Conwell Theological Seminary, 2013).

14. N. Street, *Moved by the Spirit: Pentecostal and Global Christianity in the Global South, Center for Religion and Civic Culture* (Los Angeles, CA: University of Southern California, 2013).

15. *Ibid.*

16. "Pentecostal and Charismatic churches are best conceptualized as part of a single, interconnected set of movements (together called "Renewalists") of three distinct types (Pentecostals, Charismatics, and Independent Charismatics)."

17. Pentecostals are defined here as those who are associated with denominations that identify themselves in explicitly Pentecostal terms, or with other denominations that as a whole are phenomenologically Pentecostal in teaching and practice. Charismatic movements consist of Pentecostal individuals within the Anglican, Roman Catholic, Orthodox, and Protestant traditions, designating renewal within an existing tradition. Independent Charismatics are found in churches that have emerged from established Pentecostal and Charismatic denominations and are no longer affiliated with their "home"

denomination. Each Renewal movement emphasizes particular gifts of the Spirit to varying degrees, including speaking in tongues and signs and wonders.

18. Center for the Study of Global Christianity, 2013.

19. *Ibid.* Pentecostals and Charismatics are mutually exclusive categories. They overlap, however, with the evangelical category, and the three categories should not be added together. Many Christians do not identify with any of these movements. Population estimates are rounded to the 10,000. Percentages are calculated from unrounded numbers. Pentecostal and Charismatic figures may not add exactly due to rounding. See: Pew Research Center Forum on Religion & Public Life, *Global Christianity, A Report on the Size and Distribution of the World's Christian Population* (Washington, DC: Pew Research Center, 2011).

20. For the next two charts, Pentecostals and Charismatics by region, the data is from the Pew Forum analysis of data from the Center for the Study of Global Christianity. Percentages may not add exactly due to rounding. See: Pew Research Center Forum on Religion & Public Life, 2011.

21. L. Hurbon, "Pentecostalism and Transnationalism in the Caribbean," in *Between Babel and Pentecost: Transnational Pentecostalism in Africa and Latin America*, ed. Andre Corten and Ruth R. Marshall-Fratani (Indianapolis, IN: Indiana University Press, 2001).

22. C.L. Smith, *Pentecostal Power Expressions, Impact, and Faith of Latin American Pentecostalism* (Leiden, Netherlands: Brill, 2011); David Martin, *Pentecostalism: The World Their Parish* (Oxford: Blackwell Publishers, 2002); and David Martin, *Tongues of Fire: The Explosion of Protestantism in Latin America* (Oxford: Blackwell Publishers, 1990).

23. Ennis Edmonds and Michelle Gonzalez, *Caribbean Religious History: An Introduction* (New York: NYU Press, 2010); and Martin, 1990.

24. Center for the Study of Global Christianity, 2013.

25. Street, 2013.

26. In this report, "global North" and "global South" are defined in geopolitical terms according to the United Nations. The Global North includes Europe and Northern America, while the Global South includes Asia, Africa, Latin America, and Oceania.

27. Pew Forum analysis of data from the Center for the Study of Global Christianity, 2011. For the purposes of this report, the Global North is composed of North Arica, Europe, Australia, Japan, and New Zealand. The rest of the world is considered the Global South. Population estimates are rounded to the 10,000. Percentages are calculated from unrounded numbers. Figures may not add exactly due to rounding.

28. Pew Forum analysis of data from the Center for the Study of Global Christianity, 2011 (You can access the report here: http://www.pewforum.

org/files/2011/12/Christianity-fullreport-web.pdf). For the purposes of this report, the Global North is composed of North Arica, Europe, Australia, Japan, and New Zealand. The rest of the world is considered the Global South. Percentages are calculated from unrounded numbers. Figures may not add exactly due to rounding.

29. Center for the Study of Global Christianity, 2013.
30. Pew Research Center, "Table: Christian Population in Numbers by Country,"http://www.pewforum.org/2011/12/19/table-christian-population-in-numbers-by-country/. According to the Pew Forum, "Percentages are calculated from unrounded numbers. Figures may not add exactly due to rounding. Populations of less than 1000 are shown as <1000. Populations of 1000 to 9999 are shown as <10,000. Populations of 10,000 and more are rounded to the 10,000. Estimated 2010 total population figures are based primarily on the 2010 revision of the UN Population Prospects. The estimate for Kosovo is based on the World Religion Database. The estimate for Serbia is based on the UN figures minus the Kosovo figure from the World Religion Database. The Taiwan estimate is based on the UN's regional total, which includes Taiwan's population but does not specifically identify Taiwan. The Sudan and South Sudan estimates are based on the UN figure for Sudan divided using estimates from the World Religion Database."
31. Edmonds and Gonzalez, 2010.
32. Street, 2013.
33. Harvey Cox, *Fire from Heaven: The Rise of Pentecostal Spirituality and the Reshaping of Religion in the Twenty-First Century* (Reading, MA: Addison-Wesley Publishing Company, 1995); Harvey Cox, "'Pentecostalism and Global Market Culture': A Response to Issues Facing Pentecostalsm in a Postmodern World," in *The Globalization of Pentecostalism*, ed. M.W. Dempster, B.D. Klaus, and D. Petersen (Carlisle, CA: Regnum Books (in association with Paternoster Publishing), 1999), 386–395.
34. E. Patterson, *The Future of Pentecostalism in the United States* (Lanham, MD: Lexington Books, 2007).
35. Street, 2013.
36. Mike Davis, *Planet of Slums* (London: Verso, 2007).
37. Edmonds and Gonzalez, 2010.
38. L. Hurbon, "Pentecostalism and Transnationalism in the Caribbean," in *Between Babel and Pentecost: Transnational Pentecostalism in Africa and Latin America*, ed. Andre Corten and Ruth R. Marshall-Fratani (Indianapolis, IN: Indiana University Press, 2001); Edmonds and Gonzalez, 2010.
39. David Martin, 2002 and 1990.
40. Street, 2013.
41. *Ibid.*

42. *Ibid.*
43. Edmonds and Gonzalez, 2010.
44. Edward L. Cleary and Hannah W. Stewart-Gambino, eds., Power, Politics, and Pentecostals in Latin America (Boulder, CO: Westview Press, 1997); Ibid.
45. Ibid., Ibid.
46. Edmonds and Gonzalez, 2010; Martin, 1990.
47. Ibid.
48. Ibid.
49. The authors of this passage quote: Ashley Smith, "Mainline Churches in the Caribbean: Their Relationship to the Cultural and Political Process," Caribbean Journal of Religious Studies 9 (1998): 32.
50. Edmonds and Gonzalez, 2010, 174.
51. For an expert history and analysis on the Pentecostal movement in Canada, see Michael Wilkinson and Peter Althouse. Also see: Michael Wilkinson, ed., Canadian Pentecostalism Transition and Transformation (Montreal: McGill-Queen's University Press, 2009); Michael Wilkinson and Steven Studebaker, eds., A Liberating Spirit: Pentecostals and Social Action in North America (Eugene, OR: Pickwick Publications, 2010); Michael Wilkinson and Peter Althouse, Winds from the North: Canadian Contributions to the Pentecostal Movement (Leiden: Brill, 2010); Michael Wilkinson, The Spirit Said Go: Pentecostal Immigrants in Canada (New York: Peter Lang, 2006).
52. S. Reimer, "Pentecostal Assemblies of Canada's Congregations: Vitality, Diversity, Identity, and Equity," Canadian Journal of Pentecostal-Charismatic Christianity (2012): 41–69.
53. Adam Stewart, "A Canadian Azusa? The Implications of the Hebden Mission for Pentecostal Historiography," in Winds from the North: Canadian Contributions to the Pentecostal Movement, ed. Michael Wilkinson and Peter Althouse (Leiden, Netherlands: Brill, 2010), 17–37; W. Sloos, "The Story of James and Ellen Hebden: The First Family of Pentecost in Canada," Pneuma 32 (2010): 181–202; P. Holmes, "The 'Place' of Women in Pentecostal/Charismatic Ministry Since the AZUSA Street Revival," in The Azusa Street Revival and Its Legacy, ed. Harold D. Hunter and Cecil M. Robeck, Jr. (Eugene, OR: Wipf & Stock Publishers, 2009), 297–316.
54. Stewart, 2010, 17–37; Holmes, 2009.
55. Sloos, 2010, 181–202.
56. Stewart, 2010; Reimer, 2012.
57. M. Wilkinson, The Spirit Said Go: Pentecostal Immigrants in Canada (New York: Peter Lang, 2006) and M. Wilkinson, ed.,Canadian Pentecostalism: Transition and Transformation (Montreal: McGill-Queen's University Press, 2009); Steward, 2010.

58. T. Augustine, Pocket Dictionary of North American Denominations: Over 100 Christian Groups Clearly and Concisely Defined (Downers Grove, IL: InterVarsity Press, 2004).
59. Maginley and Thompson, 2010.
60. Steward, 2010.
61. Holmes, 2009.
62. Ibid.; R. Holm, "Canadian Pentecostal Spirituality: These Boots were Made for Walking," in Canadian Pentecostalism, ed. M. Wilkinson (Montreal: McGill-Queen's University Press, 2009); R. Holm, "A Paradigmatic Analysis of Authority" (PhD diss., Laval University, 1995).
63. Holmes, 2009.
64. Maginley and Thompson, 2010.
65. T. Rommen, "Mek Some Noise" Gospel Music and the Ethics of Style in Trinidad (Berkeley: University of California Press, 2007).
66. Maginley and Thompson, 2010.
67. Ibid.
68. Ibid.
69. This section below borrows heavily from PAWI's official constitution (access:http://pawi-online.org/wp-content/uploads/2015/07/Constitution-July-2015.pdf).
70. H. Andreas and C. Olivier, "Transnational Social Networks: Current Perspectives," Transnational Social Review 2 (2012): 115–119.
71. P. Levitt, "Redefining the Boundaries of Belonging: The Institutional Character of Transnational Religious Life," Sociology of Religion 65 (2004): 1–18; P. Levitt and B.N. Jaworsky, "Transnational Migration Studies: Past Developments and Future Trends," Annual Review of Sociology 33 (2007): 129–156; K. Fjelstad and N. Thi Hien, Spirits without Borders: Vietnamese Spirit Mediums in a Transnational Age (New York: Palgrave Macmillan, 2011).
72. Afe Adogame and Jim Spickard, eds., Religion Crossing Boundaries: Transnational Religion and Social Dynamics in Africa and the New African Diaspora (Netherlands and Boston: Brill, 2010).
73. R. Wuthnow and S. Offutt, "Transnational Religious Connections," Sociology of Religion 69 (2008): 209–232.
74. Fjelstad and Hien, 2011.
75. Ibid.; O. Sheringham, Transnational Religious Spaces Faith and the Brazilian Migration Experience (Basingstoke: Palgrave Macmillan, 2013); Helen Rose Ebaugh and Janet Saltzman Chafetz, eds., Religion Across Borders: Transnational Immigrant Networks (Walnut Creek, CA: AltaMira Press, 2002).
76. Fjelstad and Hien, 2011.
77. Ibid.

78. G.N. Schiller and P. Levitt, "Conceptualizing Simultaneity: A Transnational Social Field Perspective on Society," International Migration Review 38 (2004): 1002–1039; P. Levitt and B.N. Jaworsky, "Transnational Migration Studies: Past Developments and Future Trends," Annual Review of Sociology 33 (2007): 129–156.

79. Levitt, 2004; Adogame and Spickard, 2010.

80. Levitt and Jaworsky, 2007.

81. J. Noret, "On the Inscrutability of the Ways of God: The Transnationalization of Pentecostalism on the West Coast of Africa," in Religion Crossing Boundaries: Transnational Religion and Social Dynamics in Africa and the New African Diaspora, eds. Afe Adogame and Jim Spickard (Netherlands and Boston: Brill, 2010); Levitt, 2004.

82. Noret, 2010; Levitt, 2004.

83. Noret, 2010; Levitt, 2004.

84. Manuel Castells, "Toward a Sociology of the Network Society," Contemporary Sociology 29 (2000): 693–699; Noret, 2010; Levitt and Jaworsky, 2007.

85. Peter Marina, Getting the Holy Ghost: Urban Ethnography in a Brooklyn Pentecostal Tongue-Speaking Church (Lanham, MD: Lexington Books, 2014).

CHAPTER 3

Charismatic Ethnography in the Charismatic Caribbean

Chasing religious leaders in the Caribbean involves a journey into a world far removed from the sandy beaches and coconut rum cocktails of tourist pleasure zones. It's the type of research that uses the traditional methodological approaches to learn about previously unfamiliar worlds that involve taking copious field notes and recording hours of conversations and church services, becoming fully immersed into the public and private worlds of Caribbean religious life. But this type of research into the lesser-known spaces of Caribbean religious life also requires moving beyond the conventional strategies of ethnography.[1]

This research uses an ethnographic approach that captures unique insight into Caribbean religious life focusing primarily on religious leaders and their mainstay activities, from presiding over their various church services to preaching at religious revivals to engaging in religious transnational activities crossing borders throughout the region. This ethnography involves extensive formal and informal interviews along with direct observation and participation with religious leaders in both their public and private lives, allowing for the collection and analysis of layered and engaging data. The results of this process include the production of hundreds of journal notes, stunning pictures, and videos of religious activities, demonic possessions and exorcisms, dozens of interviews, life-changing testimonials, and stories that provide unique insights into the lives of religious leaders crossing borders and impacting local regions throughout the Caribbean. The analysis of these data provides for both a historical and theoretical overview of the sociological work on religion

© The Author(s) 2016   63
P. Marina, *Chasing Religion in the Caribbean*,
DOI 10.1057/978-1-137-56100-8_3

in late modernity, global religious networking, the relationship between religion and culture, and the Weberian concept of charisma as central analytical frames. Further, this research also captures an important moment in the modern Caribbean world where the previously divided Christian churches attempt to join forces and unite to become a stronger force in shaping Caribbean life as they realize more power among the political and economic elite of the region. But this requires moving beyond the tenets of most qualitative research and into a methodological world that involves new and creative approaches that make it possible to venture into the deep Caribbean.

Chasing religion in the Caribbean involves eliminating fancy titles and formalities. The conversations with dozens of religious leaders move seamlessly from life experiences and religious perspectives to discussions and debates on a wide variety of issues, including controversial ones. While some skeptical outsiders might wonder if preachers of the poor pimp their flock, preachers wonder about the dangers of non-black academics writing about the world of black people, knowing how well that often works out for them. The boundaries between the researcher and the researched eventually dissolve to become a more egalitarian relationship among individuals who share a common interest. Perhaps most importantly, one of the main goals throughout this process is to capture the voice of religious leaders to explain their own subjective experiences and worldviews.

Topics of discussion involve a wide variety of issues, including hell and homosexuality, sin and salvation, religion and politics, sexuality and morality, and other highly controversial topics. Religious leaders relish the opportunity to interrogate the limited worldview of an academic while they found similar critique thought provoking. Literally preaching to the choir gets tedious at times, even for the most passionate preacher. Intellectually sparring with academics allows preachers to test their ideas beyond an all too agreeing congregation. Such open dialogue and brutal honesty helps form relationships of mutual respect and admiration. This in turn opens doors to new insights and experiences, challenges and debates, and opportunities to change one's thinking and transform the self. In full disclosure, sometimes the debates with religious leaders lead to heated discussions, yet we almost always found time to share a laugh together and appreciate the joys of life, like eating fresh mangos and agreeing that perhaps it is indeed God that put the best mangos in Antigua.

THE SOFT CARIBBEAN

Caribbean island hopping with religious leaders uncovers a world far removed from travel journals and blogs. Borrowing from a Rabansque view[2] of the soft city, venturing into the "soft Caribbean" captures social life revealing how people carve out their biographies and craft unique identities when confronting the challenges of everyday life. Although some scholars depict religion as the sigh behind Marx's alienation rooted in false consciousness, or the force keeping at bay Durkheim's anomie rooted in social transformation, or the hope behind the problems of rationality trapping humans in an iron cage of routinization, Charismatic Christians in the Caribbean seem to use it more as a source of empowerment. That is, the Charismatic movement in the Caribbean is a collective response to shared structural problems. Instead of being primarily shaped by religion and its doctrines and beliefs, Pentecostals keep the individual front and center, retaining their ability to shape the religion, just as much and if not more, than the religion shapes them. Theologians may start from the premise of God's existence; sociologists, on the other hand, examine religion as a human product. Humans have the agency to fashion religion in their own image, to witness their subjective imprint on the objective forms they create. And people understand their experiences through various forms of communication—and here in the English-speaking Caribbean with strong African roots and history of European colonization—storytelling serves as a primary vehicle where religious adherents make sense of their lives. Personal travel with religious leaders throughout the region moves beyond the concrete church and into the soft religious spaces where people tell stories about their joys and sufferings. And these stories reveal a remarkable agency and belonging to a religion that defies, in many ways, its intended structural positions.

In general, and for Charismatic Christianity as an institutional movement in the Caribbean, religion is not the sigh of the oppressed but rather how the oppressed find solutions to their sigh. Religion is not to keep anomie at bay but rather offers a way to plunge into the depths below it to transcend above it. Religion is the defiant stubborn force behind the "parent" bureaucratic institutions, while also envious of its position.

For the individual, Charismatic Christianity serves as a vehicle to reinvent the self and find alternative paths to dignity and strength. People transform their identities while at the same time transforming the meaning behind the movement. The Charismatic movement in the Caribbean is a constantly active verb that responds to the new and ongoing challenges of everyday life. It is a creative cultural response to collectively experienced problems. In the religiously influenced cultural world, people find a solution to their problems, real or perceived, in the human quest to transcend beyond the ordinary. And religion is all about the super-ordinary. It's about realizing life's greatest mysteries and confronting fears of the unknown, including the meaning of existence and the inevitable death that faces us all. It is the place where souls get saved or cast to hell, fortunes are gained or lost, and favor is granted or dissolved. In religious life, hope remains in the face of despair while identities shift and the past becomes reinterpreted. The present is recast in a new light through storytelling and testimonies, and belief is constantly renegotiated.

Entering the "soft Caribbean" of the religious world opens up new windows to explore human creativity and its limitations, its processes of assimilation and resistance, the extent of its agency and structural limitations, and its ability to retain charisma in a world that increasingly denies it. Charismatic Christianity in the Caribbean is one type of subcultural project that people create in a world steeped in inequalities of wealth found in highly unequal tourist-driven economies and uncertainties of identity found in the age of hyper-plurality and over-saturating information. In his view of the modern city, Jonathan Raban commented that living in cities is an art that requires artful analysis and insights.[3] Perhaps too is religious life, with its various styles and forms of worship, which requires a vocabulary of art and style to describe it. Like New Orleans jazz, it is best to improvise, relying on something that goes beyond the standardized training. The scientific study of religious life offers incredible insight and discoveries into human religious phenomenon, but relying strictly on science tenets and its dogmatic tools of investigation can trap research on religious life into its own iron cage.

HOLY GHOST SCIENCE AND THE ETHNOGRAPHIC STUDY OF RELIGION

Many Charismatic Christians believe that the Holy Ghost resides in them the moment they become born-again. They call this the in-dwelling. God, an external entity existing independently of humans, begins to dwell in the new born-again. Once this happens, God can use the body of the believer as a vessel to disseminate information. This is what happens when people speak in tongues. The Holy Ghost comes upon the speaker to communicate, often to deliver an important message. This is called "getting the Holy Ghost." Even the less humble preachers will readily claim that the performances of miracles and healings must be attributed to the Holy Ghost, not its human vessel.

Similarly, many social scientists have a peculiar belief system that I call "Holy Ghost Science." These academics seem to believe that science resides in them the moment they become doctors of philosophy. They call this person a "social scientist." Science, an external entity existing independently of humans, begins to dwell in the newly minted PhD. Once this happens, science can use the body of the social scientist as a vessel to collect data and disseminate information. This is what happens when social scientists speak at conferences and classrooms as well as publish in journals. Science comes upon the objective and value-neutral social scientist to communicate, often to deliver a message they deem important. This is called "getting the Scientific Holy Ghost." Even the less humble social scientists will readily claim that the careful analysis of numbers, statistics, and variables must be attributed to the travails of science, not its human vessel. Additionally, the way many social scientists speak and the words they use can sometimes sound like tongue speaking to the uninitiated.

Welcome to the world of Holy Ghost Science!

THE GENESIS OF CHASING RELIGION IN THE CARIBBEAN

The original contact made for this research began in the Afro-Caribbean Brooklyn neighborhood of Brownsville during a separate research project on tongue-speaking Pentecostals. From Afro-Caribbean Brooklyn to Antigua, the home base for this project, new contacts develop in Trinidad, St. Lucia, Barbados, Dominica, St. Kitts, St. Martin, Nevis, Haiti, Barbuda, and Montserrat. Bishop Bradford, Antiguan-born Brooklyn bishop, became the initial contact. He is also the person who charismatically networks in an attempt to unify the previously divided churches discussed earlier. Bishop Bradford serves as the *point d'entrée* who opens the doors to the Caribbean world. As is often the case in research, timing is essential.

Bishop Bradford works closely with Apostle Stephen Andrew (Apostle), the head pastor of the Antigua mega-church St. John's Pentecostal House of Restoration Church (SJPC), to achieve the dream of multi-church unity. Apostle agrees to provide a forum for him and to bring together religious leaders from various church denominations around the island. SJPC is so large one can easily locate it while flying over the small island.

It also houses a studio for the religiously inspired Abundant Life Radio, a popular Caribbean radio station. Apostle's SJPC might very well be the largest Pentecostal congregation in the Caribbean. Taking into account both his large congregation and radio following, Apostle has well-developed contacts with religious leaders throughout the Caribbean. He also hails from Trinidad, where many Charismatic Christian leaders get their formal training from PAWI, the Caribbean version of the US-based Assemblies of God. Not only is his church one of the largest Pentecostal churches in the Caribbean, Apostle presides over the largest congregation in PAWI. As a man of means and connections, establishing rapport with this well-connected religious authority proves key.

To appear before Apostle, one must first comply with the rules and regulations posted outside his office, detailing the proper way to present oneself before the preacher. Assured our appearance is up to snuff, Bradford and I met with Apostle to discuss the previous night's exorcism described in the introduction. This meeting provides an opportunity to make an impression on Apostle in the hopes of gaining access to his many Caribbean contacts. We discuss our ideas about God and men, and moving from topic to topic, we talk about a variety of issues from the politics of the death penalty to the role of the church in political and cultural affairs.

We find a mutual respect and we each enjoy the intellectual sparring. He wants to discuss his ideas to test intellectual waters beyond his "choir." He enjoys exchanging ideas with a non-believing "intellectual" from an American university, as it is similarly a delight to debate with a mega-church "rock star" preacher resembling the television evangelist I vaguely remember seeing on TV as a child. We are aware of our own respective positions—a perceived "liberal" intellectual and equally perceived fundamentalist "conservative" Christian Apostle—and find appreciation for one another, despite our conflicting views. Somehow, though different, we make a connection.

This connection is evident when Apostle becomes seemingly more relaxed, without Goffman's front stage performances, and willing to loosen the intense scowl of a religious leader serving as a father figure to his flock. Soon, Apostle began to make jokes around me, even teasing me in his thick Caribbean accent, "Peter, you crazy man, you crazy, you different, weird, but I like you." But respect always remained. And in the Charismatic Christian world, humility is a virtue that shows respect. A preacher in his church holds more power than a judge in a courtroom. Humility plays an important role in securing the confidence of religious leaders. After explaining this research project, the conversation proceeds as follows:

Marina: So is this cool with you? I'm not invasive. I don't do anything you tell me not to do. I'm under your authority. You tell me not to do something; I don't do it. You tell me it's okay; I do it. This is your place and I respect it.

Apostle: Very nice. If it is cool with Bishop Bradford, it is cool with me.

Marina: That's the story that I want to write, the struggles, the pains, the difficulties, and the successes and the challenges and the beauty and the joy and all of it.

Apostle: You'll get them all. What I can do for him (looking at both me and Bradford), if he wishes, I can probably take him to Trinidad for some days. I can let you meet other ministers in Trinidad. I have connections. I can get you to Trinidad.

Viola. Over the next few months and multiple trips to Antigua, Apostle helps establish contacts with church leaders, preachers, and congregation members on ten other islands. Secretaries provide the names and contact numbers of church leaders who are in turn given dates of my itinerary. The rest is up to chance and improvisation.

Sometimes the contact information is completely wrong. Sometimes these religious leaders forget about the arrival dates, some take great pains to accommodate the research, others initially act with indifference, while some are almost hostile, and still others skeptical about the purposes of the research. Some religious leaders do not believe that Apostle has the right to "sanction" a non-believer to write a book about born-again religious leaders. At times, religious leaders are hard to find; some are off island while others live in remote villages difficult to access. But one way or another, I find them. Sometimes it takes knocking on doors in faraway villages inquiring as to the whereabouts of preachers. Other times it involves long bus rides from one end of an island to another or propeller and jet-engine planes, private and public buses and boats, and moto bikes and maxi taxis. It didn't matter; the job is to get it done. As stated from the outset, this research literally chases religion in the Caribbean.

Gaining Entrée to the Private Lives of Religious Leaders and Pastors

Gaining entrée into a research setting involves an ongoing process throughout the entire research project. Each new site requires starting from scratch, meeting new religious leaders and their adherents. Although Apostle's office set up the initial contacts, a strange researcher is still viewed with suspicion. And every time a new contact is made, the process of winning confidence and some degree of trust begins anew. It's daunting at times, as a non-born again and non-black outsider without any ties to the English-speaking Caribbean, to constantly start over and over again and again from scratch. Of course, being associated with Apostle helps open more than a few doors.

Sometimes it is as easy as "Ya mon, no worries." At other times, it's nearly impossible. Contact numbers are sometimes wrong since PAWI preachers often move to new churches or travel to preach on other islands. Sometimes preachers don't want to be found, but they are found anyway, at least eventually. Sometimes bus travel across entire countries results in a preacher, who initially agrees to meet, telling me he will not speak to a non-born-again conducting research. Fortunately, in that instance, a chance encounter with a radio deejay led to an important contact with prominent and well-known preachers in the country. At least initially, most preachers and religious leaders reluctantly agree to meet, and usually do so only to accommodate Apostle's request. Others are skeptical about the intentions of the research. Some found it fascinating that an outsider wants to know about their world, let alone write about it. Others seem eager to show an academic from the USA their supernatural world of miracles. Sometimes the ethnographic doors opens, while other times they close. But every time the door shuts, another opens. When it comes to Charismatic church doors, the ethnographer must move beyond ethnographic charisma and venture into an ethnography of the soul.

REACHING THE ETHNOGRAPHIC *IT*: SOULFUL ETHNOGRAPHY IN THE STUDY OF RELIGION

The jazzman riffs "EE-yah!" and "EE-de-lee-yah!" to a transcending Kerouac in constant search of this abstract but certain thing called *it*.[4] Before him it was Dickenson[5] reaching that inevitable moment of *it* until the fly buzzes and Emerson's[6] search for *it* in the nature and soul of the universe. Sometimes *it* finds symbolic expression in places like Melville's whale,[7] Gilman's yellow wallpaper,[8] or Faith in Hawthorne's "Young Goodman Brown."[9] Sometimes *it* is in the production of the thing itself like "Jack the Dripper's" abstract expressionism where Pollock must be "*in* my painting, ... to let it come through."[10] But *it* is never the thing itself; it's not the finger but where the finger is pointing, not the symbol but the soulful meaning given to that symbol. Sometimes *it* is forced upon the tortured innocent soul like Sugar in Bambara's "The Lesson"[11] or Huck Finn's confrontation with hypocrisy in his adventures with Tom Sawyer where "a sound heart and a deformed conscience come into collision and conscience suffers defeat."[12] At other times, *it* is a desperate search that must continue, no matter what the end might bring like at the end of Hemingway's double-barreled shotgun.[13] Sometimes people never see *it* while at other times *it* slaps them in the face and they still can't recognize *it*. *It* remains an underlying theme that the great novelists, essayists, poets, beatniks, creatives, mads, artists, intellectuals, and those who push to move beyond and search for something more attempt to achieve.

And that is the challenge of ethnography—the search for *it*—our ethnographic call to arms, and our renewed promise as Mills once reminded us with the sociological imagination. We need an ethnographic imagination of the soul. It's the quest for something more that moves beyond the tenets of science. Soulful ethnography is the search for the ethnographic *it*.

It's not just in fantasy literature or eccentric artists where colorful characters come alive to search for this magical tragic beautiful *it* but also in the so-called ordinary characters of everyday life where people, in the carving out of their own biographies, get the Holy Ghost,[14] find the rush in Contreras's drug dealer robbery,[15] perfect Williams's con in the art of the hustle,[16] realize Daynes's hope and redemption in reggae music,[17] experience the self through the exploration of Grazian's nocturnal economy,[18] despair in the inhumane criminal injustice system of Brotherton's immigrant deportation policy,[19] or discover Wacquant's learning something about the soul through the "flesh, nerves, and senses" from the "sweet science of bruising."[20] Whether down and out in New Orleans[21] or chasing religion in the Caribbean, the characters discovered in the research process seem to have one common theme that links together this project we call the experience of humanity—the endless search for *it* and the wanting for something more. And that's how you connect with others and establish rapport.

If ethnography involves the use of the body as a research instrument to capture the carnal dimensions of life, it also requires the ethnographic soul to capture *it* that is central to the human experience. Soulful ethnography is about letting go in order to hang on, losing it to find it, questioning the self to understand the self, lying to find truth, deceiving for clarity, knowing sadness to realize joy, obliterating all common sense to find some grasp of reality. It's about freeing the academically trained self from scientific doctrine, to forget about being a research scholar, a professor, a sociologist, an academic, a category, and shedding one's very identity to get to the heart and soul of things. It's about getting lost to rediscover. It's about being outside oneself to get inside the ethnography—the only place to find oneself again. The soulful ethnographer becomes fully enraptured into the ethnography and gets inside "the it" within it. One realizes what it's all about only after becoming lost in it and forgetting that any research is actually taking place. Fear of messing up the research and blurring the picture or making changes or destroying it all vanishes. The ethnography becomes a reality sue generis but not in some reified way. It belongs to the characters and the researcher and for all those moving to the groove of the pounding ethnographic beat—but only if you can hear *it*. Unlike pretenses of objectivity and the positivistic doctrine of detachment, separation from the process and from the characters and their *it* would result in the work's utter destruction and could create a portrait that unrealistically depicts life without the soul. The more contact, the more inside the ethnographic soul, the better the portrait, the more muddy, the closer the harmony one has to the underlying *it* that lies dormant in the deepest of souls.

The religious world stubbornly denies the disenchanting, sterile aspects of ordinary life. In the study of the supernatural, in the study of religion, people search for it in the world of winged angels, horned devils, evil spirits, tarot cards, monsters and magic and mayhem and superheroes and unicorns and all that is utterly fantastic about the human imagination. The religious mind stubbornly retains its capacity for creativity, and its search for meaning in a world seemingly in short supply of it.

The ethnographic study of religion offers a fascinating and rewarding field of intellectual inquiry. It is divinely human. It claims to offer something as grand as salvation and as simultaneously simple and complex as unconditional love while encompassing all the blurriness and contradictions of social life. Soulful ethnography of religion reveals a world where people experience the extremes in life from speaking in tongues to getting demonically possessed and from dancing to the ecstatic joys of life to falling down to your knees to Huxley's *mysterium tremendum* and Otto's numinous experience.[22] It taps into the most intimate and personal aspects of lived experience ranging from heightened transcendental states of awareness to a deep love relationship with deities. Indeed, what joy surpasses a perceived profound love of a creator and what conjures more fears than the torment and dread of hell? How much more powerful can a human become who serves as a warrior of God, a destroyer of evil, an exorcist of demons, and a savior of the world? Here we find martyrs and villains and killers and victims. Religious experience is part of this search for *it* that brings out the extremes of pure selfishness and unwavering altruism to the brink of suicide and the forces that keep it at bay. The extremes extend wider than the biblical parting of the sea.

Yet there is joy in the mundane practices of everyday life, like the first sip of coffee in the morning, a smoke before bed, and a drink while witnessing the sunset. It can also be found hiding in the seemingly mundane practices of life where the sacred exists even in the profane. *It* lies quiet within the simple pleasures people derive from hearing their preacher's voice for the past 20 years, smelling church incense, and recalling past holiday services with the faint ring of Christmas bells in the far distance. It also brings the frustration of feeling that—no matter how much one asks—God never responds. Soulful ethnography looks into the subjective feelings others have wondering about what God might look like, imagining what heaven means, and inquiring about its location. Ethnography of the soul searches for *it* listening to conversations people have with their friends about their spiritual worldviews, personal feelings about belonging to God's kingdom, and skepticism of outsiders too blind to see the obvious reality of God.

Wait. Here arrives the inevitable question to the researcher of religious worlds. Are you a believer? In other words, do you know *it?* How can you write about *it* if you don't understand, or worse, not believe? You just got called out. What do you expect, when your research calls out others? Do you know *it?* "Do you believe," as the curious wide-eyed face stares at you waiting for reply. No rule or science or method or principle or purple-hearted pagan will get you out of this one.

It is not about God, belief, adherence to church membership, or conformity to group rules. It is about the very thing of the human condition. Do you know *it,* the beat and rhythm and "butt-scarred drums," and the "EE-de-lee-yah,"[23] the window before the fly buzzes,[24] the thing that links us all, the lust and desire, hurt of betrayal and ecstasy of love, and the rejection and inclusion to all and nothing that makes us a life always burning, burning. *It* is the thing we always knew but didn't know we knew. Do you have *it?*

Does immersion into the ethnographic odyssey take you away and whisk you into a world of endless possibility? Does the journey bring you to the brink of *it?* Let's take a glimpse into religious life in Trinidad.

As the deep hot Caribbean air weighs heavily on us all, the spirit of the crowd gives the humidity a sort of magic that seems to uplift everyone not above or through the density, but deeper within it. The crowd no longer forms a congregation; it unravels, blows up, and reforms too many times to call it any congregation. It is Durkheim's collective solidarity[25] mixed with a deeply, lonely, highly individualized and isolating anomie that somehow does not frighten. The woman next to me wails in some sort of despair that cracks through the barriers of pains beyond pains, which allows her to rejoice. She found her *it* and collapses in ecstasy with not a movement more. A jumping man falls from his feet and desperately clamors, crawling hands and knees to some seemingly invisible object, perhaps his *it*. Everyone clamors, reaching beyond with not just the body and the performance of rituals and gestures, and prostrating and collapsing, and the shouts of strange nonsensical words. They move beyond Goffman's facework[26] and Hochschild's emotional labor.[27] They move with the soul. They engage in soul work.

And from that you can never return, or at least return and be the same again—like poor Young Goodman Brown.[28] It's a bridge-burn, a transformative moment where you walk through a threshold that cannot be undone. You cannot unsee it. The individuals consumed in this collective nomic isolation engage in the wildest of acts, gyrating their bodies, rolling their eyes up and into their sockets, jumping up and down with fists clenched in their air and the man up front does not lead but rather orchestrates the melodic, thumping conduit into a passageway that is easy to suspect leads to some sort of *it* at the end of this crazy road. And I am no longer me, nor do I care about sociology or academia or my name or any sort of manufactured identity. I feel that feeling of that proverbial window that leads to I don't know what but something more and maybe *it*.

Yes, I convert but not into a born-again Christian or Vodou practitioner, but into a soulful ethnographer and do so each and every time when conducting ethnographic research.

The manifest function of the question "Are you a believer?" is less important than the latent, "Do you have *it*?" No one really cares of "yes" or "no," religiously "unmusical"[29] religious research can produce great ethnographic art while believers make a mess of things who believe without having *it*. What people really want to know is not if you believe in their God but if you have *it*. Well, do you have *it*? And if you don't, the result may become an ethnographic mess.

Similarly, when doing fieldwork on religion, "the field" always attempts to convert us. Attempts to convert us have more meaning if we relate it to the concept of *it*, and bringing us to the point where seeing *it*, their *it*, becomes a possibility. The researched want you to understand, want to bring you to their *it*. Convert. Yes, convert.

Not in some religious way or to a religious group, unless so inclined. Convert into something else; lose yourself and your social place on the earth. Like Pollock, get inside the painting and lose yourself in it, which is where you will find the subject matter in question.

Be a passionate lover and a misanthropic mule, a staunch believer and cynical skeptic, hopeful romantic and hopeless nihilist, selfish and selfless, and genuinely honest in a way that reveals all the deceit. Throw down your reservations and pretenses and move into new ethnographic realms of possibility.

That is the point of attempts to convert, to bring the researcher to *it*, the best way possible that others have to bring the researcher to *it* within the limits of the world under investigation. It's a treacherous journey; some never leave when they come close to *it*. Some go native while others take it so far they receive the scorn of the academic community. *It* involves risk and uncertainty, much like in the real lives of the people we study. *It* involves feeling the tragic anomie of others and unlocks the anomie that exists buried within us all. *It* involves surrendering, much like the religious do to their deities for self-empowerment. *It* harnesses into the deepest subjective experiences of inequality and the intense joys and sufferings that derive from such experiences. *It* is about reveling in your own vulnerabilities that spill out all over the place like the music that spills out of church doors on Sunday afternoons.

Do you have *it* and will you convert into something else, something more? Will you rise above the ethnographic ordinary?

Do you have ethnographic soul?

CONCLUSION

Whether it's the remote rural villages of Dominica and Montserrat or the big urban metropolis of Trinidad and Port au Prince, or the capital cities of St. John's and Bridgetown, each research experience brings unique challenges requiring different strategies. In the end, ethnographic charisma along with its complementary methodological improvisation opens doors to enter deep into the worlds of Caribbean religious life. Now enter into the life of religious leaders deep in the Caribbean islands.

NOTES

1. See Appendix for further elaboration on the methodological underpinnings of this book.
2. Jonathan Raban, *Soft City* (New York: E.P. Dutton, 1974). Jonathan Raban describes the soft city the following way: "Living in cities is an art, and we need the vocabulary of art, of style, to describe the peculiar

relationship between man and material that exists in the continual creative play of urban living. The city as we imagine it, then, soft city of illusion, myth, aspiration, and nightmare, is as real, maybe more real, than the hard city one can locate on maps in statistics, in monographs on urban sociology and demography and architecture."

3. *Ibid.*
4. Jack Kerouac, *On the Road* (New York: Viking, 1997).
5. Emily Dickinson, *The Poems of Emily Dickinson, Reading Edition*, ed. R.W. Franklin (Cambridge, MA: Belknap Press, 1999).
6. Ralph Waldo Emerson, *Emerson on Transcendentalism*, ed. Edward L. Ericson (New York: Ungar, 1986).
7. Herman Melville, *Moby Dick*, ed. Tony Tanner (Oxford: Oxford University Press, 1998).
8. Charlotte Perkins Gilman and Lynne Sharon Schwartz, *The Yellow Wallpaper and Other Writings* (New York, NY: Bantam Books, 1989).
9. Nathaniel Hawthorne, *Young Goodman Brown* (Charlottesville, VA: University of Virginia Library, 1996).
10. Pepe Karmel and Kirk Varnedoe, *Jackson Pollock: Interviews, Articles, and Reviews* (New York: Museum of Modern Art, 1999).
11. Linda Janet Holmes, *Savoring the Salt: The Legacy of Toni Cade Bambara* (Philadelphia: Temple University Press, 2007). "The Lesson" is a story about a well-intentioned schoolteacher sending her poor black students from Harlem to Manhattan's expensive FAO Schwartz toy store. The students are exposed to the world outside of their oppressed community, and in the process of this contradiction find tragic enlightenment bringing them to the window if what can be argues as *it*—ushering a moment of crisis in the underlying reality of the social world.
12. Victor Doyno, *Writing Huck Finn: Mark Twain's Creative Process* (Philadelphia: University of Pennsylvania Press, 1991).
13. James R. Mellow, *Hemingway: A Life without Consequences* (Boston: Houghton Mifflin, 1992).
14. Peter Marina, *Getting the Holy Ghost: Urban Ethnography in a Brooklyn Pentecostal Tongue-speaking Church* (Lexington, KY: Lexington Books, 2013).
15. Randol Contreras, *The Stickup Kids Race, Drugs, Violence, and the American Dream* (Berkeley, CA: University of California Press, 2013).
16. Terry Williams and Trevor B. Milton, *The Con Men: Hustling in New York City* (New York, NY: Columbia University Press, 2015).
17. Sarah Daynes, *Time and Memory in Reggae Music the Politics of Hope* (Manchester, UK: Manchester University Press, 2010).
18. David Grazian, *On the Make the Hustle of Urban Nightlife* (Chicago: University of Chicago Press, 2008).

19. David C. Brotherton and Luis Barrios, *Banished to the Homeland Dominican Deportees and Their Stories of Exile* (New York: Columbia University Press, 2011).

20. Loi Wacquant, *Body & Soul: Notebooks of an Apprentice Boxer* (Oxford: Oxford University Press, 2004).

21. (Upcoming book) Peter Marina, *Down and Out in New Orleans: Notes from the Urban Underbelly* (New York: Columbia University Press, n.d.).

22. Rudolph Otto and John W. Harvey, *The Idea of the Holy* (2nd ed., Oxford: Oxford University Press, 1958); Aldous Huxley, *The Doors of Perception and Heaven and Hell* (New York: Harper Perennial, 2009). Rudolph Otto's work titled *The Idea of the Holy* discusses the numinous experience to describe the awe of God's power when one becomes aware of the divine presence. Similarly, Huxley's *The Doors of Perception and Heaven and Hell* states, "The literature of religious experience abounds in references to the pains and terrors overwhelming those who have come, too suddenly, face to face with some manifestation of the *mysterium tremendum*. In theological language, this fear is due to the incompatibility between man's egotism and the divine purity, between man's self-aggravated separateness and the infinity of God."

23. Kerouac, 1997.

24. Emily Dickinson, "I Heard a Fly Buzz—When I Died," in Dickinson, 1999.

25. Emil Durkheim, W.D. Halls, and Lewis Coser, *The Division of Labor in Society* (New York: Palgrave Macmillan, 1984).

26. Erving Goffman, *The Presentation of Self in Everyday Life* (Garden City, NY: Doubleday, 1959).

27. Arlie Russell Hochschild, "Emotion Work, Feeling Rules, and Social Structure," *American Journal of Sociology* 85 (1979): 551–575.

28. Hawthorne, 1996.

29. William H. Swatos and Peter Kivisto, "Max Weber as 'Christian Sociologist,'" *Journal for the Scientific Study of Religion* 30 (1991): 347–362. Weber said in a letter to Ferdinand Toennies on February 9, 1909, "It is true that I am absolutely unmusical religiously and have no need or ability to erect any psychic edifices of a religious character within me. But a thorough self-examination has told me that I am neither antireligious *nor irreligious*."

CHAPTER 4

Antigua

Ethnographic Notes: Juxtaposing Religious Scenes

The end of the second hour of the church service approaches as the congregation gasps in exhaustion from the physical exertion of highly energized praise and worship. This mega-million dollar church, located in the Upper Gambles neighborhood just outside of Antigua's capital in downtown St. John's, attracts an audience that expects a religious show for their spiritual souls. The congregation yearns and burns for something more as they clamor for spiritual nourishment from a mega-star preacher man on fire with the Holy Ghost mojo. They simply call this man who embodies pure charisma "Apostle." Apostle, wearing a brilliant burgundy tunic fit for elite African royalty, talks about wrapping up the sermon, bringing it to completion after a long emotional journey filled with tears of sorrow and joy, but nobody believes him. He probably doesn't believe himself. The service includes almost an hour of religiously inspired Caribbean music from a well-trained choir and worship and praise team, tithes, announcements, numerous testimonies, a one to two hour preaching sermon, communion, and often altar calls that involve what is best described as rapid exorcisms. The preaching concludes as an assistant offers communion where congregation members eat bread.

Suddenly, Apostle moves from solemn communion to prosperity theology. He goes into a "double" rant promising this new year is about double everything—double salary, double income, double contracts, and double anointing. He prophesizes every member of the congregation will receive money to pay off their loans; mad money for everyone. He says, "Everybody say double seven times," to which they comply. It is all about prosperity and hope. The crowd receives this information with great excitement as they

© The Author(s) 2016
P. Marina, *Chasing Religion in the Caribbean*,
DOI 10.1057/978-1-137-56100-8_4

jump, cheer, and applaud. A husband and wife with children on their laps look at each other with relief that their burdens will finally come to an end. A member of the congregation holds her sick child who needs a new heart and must find a way to travel to Barbados to get that new heart, or die. Apostle prays for healing, asks God for a new heart, and says, "It is done."

Immediately after the communion and message of "double" everything, as people return to their seats, a man holding a microphone standing stiffly in front of the church offers a chilling testimony.

He reports on the three spirits invading Antigua this carnival season. The reports follow from intelligence gathered from the other Caribbean Islands warning the people of Antigua of this impending attack. The "Puka" spirit from Jamaica penetrates the body and takes it airborne. The "Spirit of Sue" from Japan to America to Antigua creates the illusion of mental illness. Medication proves useless as doctors, he claims, will medicate the inflicted without avail, leading the unfortunate victim into the "crazy house." The man reports that this demon will make the possessed "Speak like you are going crazy" and "Start running like you are crazy." The "Shakira Spirit" is an old male wizard spirit that forces heterosexuals into homosexuality, forcing young straight men into gay and bisexual behaviors. The audience gasps in horror with sounds of "Ohhhh" and "Hallelujah, amen, Jesus!" with each new introduction of evil spirits to this Carnival culture.

To Pentecostals, the carnival season celebrates sin and debauchery that invites evil spirits into the island leaving its inhabitants vulnerable to demonic possession. The culture of carnival for the religiously unmusical serves as a release from the mundane world of work and routine. Thousands take to the streets parading for hours and reveling for days while drinking and dancing in the streets. To Charismatic Christians, the cultural of carnival celebration masks the real carnival of evil where demonic forces prey upon the weak souls who have strayed away from God.

Spirit possession reveals how religious and scientific knowledge not only coexist but also flourish in a post-modern world that blends pre-modern miracles with modern rationality. Pentecostals in the English-speaking Caribbean simultaneously believe in the power of western medicine while also believing in the supernatural world of miracles. Pentecostals live in a reality where physical and spiritual forces threaten to inflict harm and disease. Demons possess the body and take on the appearance of a physical or mental disease. They have the ability to create illusions that mimic the symptoms of diseases like cancer or bipolar, or as many Pentecostals believe, the "disease" of homosexuality. Though Pentecostals engage in prayer rituals for people with physical and mental diseases, the purpose is to empower the administrator of medicine or the inflicted to remain strong while undergoing scientific treatment. The main purpose of prayer ritual is to cure spiritual diseases, especially ones that appear to be physical or mental to the untrained eye. Pentecostals believe that those with the gift of discernment can tell when a disease is spiritual even if it looks to be simply physical or mental. It is, of course, useless to apply western medicine to spiritual diseases, even the ones that closely resemble physical and mental symptoms. Rather, spiritual diseases require a preacher while physical and mental diseases require western medical treatment. And spiritual diseases run rampant in Antigua during carnival season.

Hundreds of congregation members in this two-story church respond to these frightful warnings with intense individualized prayers.

"Antigua must be saved."

If communion reflects routine rituals characteristic of large bureaucratic institutions, what follows shatters any perception that large and institutionally affiliated churches have lost its charismatic flare, at least here in the Americas south of the United States.

...

Meanwhile up the road and down the Caribbean block in a small little church in downtown St. John's right next to the central market a man with cornrows gently speaks to an audience. Pastor Matthew Noyce offers biblically inspired practical advice to his twenty-member congregation. There's no yelling, demonic possessions, warnings of evil spirits, garments of royalty, nor loud sound system that blasts religious music throughout the church. Matthew prefers simplicity but he is far from simple. He defies institutionalization through his blue-collar charisma, or the grassroots oriented charisma that stems from his hard work pastoring to the local community, that spreads his Pentecostal message far beyond the walls of his small church, which sits on the second floor above a small Caribbean food wholesale and retail grocery and across the street from an active and boisterous neighborhood basketball court. Matthew built the church from scratch, piecemeal, slowly putting in plumbing, air conditioners, folding chairs, musical instruments,[1] lighting, a small stereo and sound system, projector, and all the other essentials for running a church.

Matthew stands behind a lectern wearing a short-sleeve black button down shirt and slacks discussing a biblical passage from Exodus about a character named Joshua fighting for God. The service started about a half an hour late; Matthew served as a guest preacher at Bethany Moravian Church in the small township of Piggotts in St George's Parish earlier this morning. To make matters worse, his video man failed to show up with no prior. But Matthew quickly recovered and his reliable friend took care of the job allowing the service to commence. He preaches in a casual, almost informal tone as he speaks to his audience in a personal and intimate manner. The music compliments the more informal setting atypical of many Caribbean

Pentecostal Churches. The church musical ensemble consists of three band members on keyboard, drums, and guitar along with his wife singing gospel songs such as "I'm Trading my Sorrows." After the music, Matthew engages his audience, sometimes asking questions while calmly preaching. He talks his preach, no frills here, but it's far from boring, at least to this attentive congregation who hang on to his every word.

Matthew's sermons often include jokes and frequent references to popular culture, but always return to practical wisdom that audience members know well. In a tiny house in the nearly deserted island of Barbuda, the owner of a small but powerful radio station called Abundant Life Radio offered to broadcast Matthew on its Caribbean air waves. His message reached local, and shortly after, inspired international audiences throughout the Caribbean delighted with Matthew's unconventional approach to preaching. But Matthew refuses to take credit. Instead he takes on a radically egalitarian approach to his church proclaiming, "In God's kingdom, there is only one star, and his name is Jesus. In His kingdom, there are many servants. Anything, everything we do for God is an act of service. There are no superstars in His kingdom."

Like seemingly all Pentecostal pastors, Matthew promises to keep his talk short, but continues to tell his captive audience what he finds to be an important message from Exodus 17 Verse 9 regarding Joshua's fight with Amalek. He looks at his congregation with concern and compassion explaining, "We live moment to moment in this gift that God has given us called life." Sometimes, Matthew tells us, we get ambushed. But we must still fight. He says, "Anybody who doesn't fight in this life has given up. But you are a soldier in this fight called life." Matthew talks about fighting the good fight, something he knows quite well from his days prior to becoming a self-made pastor without any formal training or institutional belonging. We all have a story, one that involves a fight against injustice, or a struggle to overcome obstacles no matter how large or small, or a battle with inner demons that threaten to consume us. Matthew says, "In order to have a great testimony you have to have a great test." The congregation responds with testimonies and stories about tackling mountains and defying odds. Others can no longer restrain their bursting feelings as they collapse on to the church floor.

...

Meanwhile back in Upper Gambles, hundreds of congregation members struggle with the demons of carnival season. Church pews begin to empty as believers crowd in front of the huge stage where a large musical ensemble performs to the ebb and flow of emotional energy spreading throughout the impressive church.

Apostle changes his wardrobe from the elaborate maroon garments to a cape-like black trench coat symbolizing a transition from preacher to healer. He's ready to get to work. About a hundred people pack together around the stage area standing and jumping, wildly swinging and twirling, shouting and screaming, crying and praying, tongue-speaking and wailing, and shaking their bodies with hands frantically grasping towards the heavens as if desperately preventing the pull of invisible forces into the subterranean world.

Many of the people need an extra dose of prayer to overcome trying times; others suspect demons have penetrated their bodies to control their minds toward an evil agenda. Still others find themselves backsliding and unsaved knowing it's a sure path to hell, while some struggle to keep anomie at bay with the many fears that plague us all, if we only stop to think about it.

It's carnival time, it's carnival time and we got demons in our mind.

Apostle pierces his eyes in, through, above, beyond, within, and inside the congregation members and lets out a primordial shriek that echoes like the thunder of God striking vengeance upon the wicked.

He calls out audience members using not their names or any known identities but rather using his spiritual abilities to call out their inflictions.

First he calls to someone "caught" in an unequally yoked relationship; a young woman approaches the altar crying. Screams of "hallelujah" follow with further screams of "Jeeeeesus" repeated many times along with people nearly falling all over themselves in spiritual rapture.

In a surreal dizzying moment one feels the sudden stream pulling away from reality to a new altered state that goes beyond, between, and within multiple realities. With each new infliction announced, the music thunders as speeding strobe lights flash brilliant colors while the church frequently shifts its illumination from bright to dark with laser shows periodically adding color to the pumping, fluctuating, flickering lights. Through the light shows, flag twirlers with huge waving flags dance and run back and forth like background performer "Hip-hop Honeys" going buck wild in rap videos. Meanwhile, the music thumps and occasionally the sounds of sparking fireworks crack as congregation members wail and speak in tongues.

In the jam packed space, one woman dangerously shakes her body with hands clamped on each side of her head that violently rocks back and forth while she shouts at the top of her lungs. Numerous church leaders attend to her. Everyone breaks from the confines of social control like Emerson's "nature without check with original energy." It's a full-blown spiritual mosh pit.

People engage in both individual and collective acts of screaming and praying, prophesizing and praising, worshiping and wrestling with sinister demons. They're jumping and moving in every direction. It's layers upon layers of activity; fragments upon fragments, never seeming to coalesce into a whole. Here people create a reality that cannot deny their existence. Perhaps through religion they subvert their own alienation and flip the script of false consciousness.

The next announcement calls for someone experiencing sexual violence, rape. A woman approaches the altar.

Another is about someone engaged who is making a big mistake and should not get married; a woman approaches the altar.

The next speaks of someone's daughter who is getting abused; a mother approaches the altar.

Another announcement calls for a particular person receiving threats about going to church and submitting to God. Funds will be withheld if they continue to attend church and live a Christian life; a man approaches.

Apostle sings along with the band about something called the "overflow" as people can no longer wait for release from this frenzied state. Now Apostle no longer sings but rather gives another primal scream at the heavens before proceeding in soldier-like march to approach his waiting audience like a prowling lion towards its waiting lamb.

...

Back in Matthew's small but growing church, Matthew stands in front of the lectern with a look of genuine concern asking his congregation members if anyone wants to approach the altar, "Does anyone want a little extra prayer? Is anyone not living the Christian life that they should be living?" If you are having trouble talking to God, if you are in need of a supernatural intervention" He stops to look at his audience standing in complete silence with their averting eyes looking towards the ground. Matthew pauses, contemplates his audience with a forehead wrinkled with concern, and says, "Just talk to God. Say, "God, open up my eyes. I'm thirty, thirty-five, forty, and now my life isn't the way I want it to be. I've been fighting so much in the natural, but now, the truth is, God, I'm losing the battle. I need your help now." ... Even in the audience, if you need help even where you are, begin to talk to God. You need a supernatural intervention. We need the power of God to set us free.

He talks more about the troubles that torture us all, and explains that, at the end of the day, we need to "enter the spiritual world" to be healed and blessed to continue our fight. Matthew prays out loud and then tells people to open up and speak to God. Everyone responds to his request. They start talking to God out loud—collectively but individually. Matthew continues to speak over them, speaking of the power of God's love and mercy, urging his congregation to speak. He says, "The spirit is willing but the flesh is weak."

Sensing that "unclean" spirits currently disrupt the lives of his congregation members, many of which he knows well, Matthew uses his pastoral abilities to channel God's power to heal those now approaching the altar. Matthew continues:

We break every generational curse over the lives of young people. We rebuke every unclean spirit, in Jesus's name. We break every curse over our life, over our children. We speak life and break up every wicked invite of the devil, in the name of Jesus. You were nailed, my God, on wood, on the cross. You became a curse, my God, so we will not be cursed. You became a blessing, by your strikes, almighty God, we are here."

Most of his congregation now stands together praying either silently or out loud in the space between the folding chairs and altar. Matthew places a gentle hand on their heads to pray over those most in need of it. But he wants them to talk along with him and speak directly to God. He calmly says, "There is life and death in the power of the tongue. We tear down this morning, my God, every curse spoken over your people. We declare that no weapon is formed against your people, my God, they shall prosper."

Matthew talks something about "generational curses," "yolks of bondage," and "Egyptian spirits" believed to impact a people steeped in a long history of African religious practices, slavery, colonization and forced Christianization, and the distinct religious practices that result from this history. As the pastor requests his audience to speak to God, Matthew speaks directly to evil stating, "Any unclean spirit this morning, we command you to loose God's people, and to let them go. I command every unclean spirit to be removed this morning and to leave God's people, in the name of Jesus. The blood compels you to leave now, in the name of Jesus. Up and out, every unclean spirit. Every unclean spirit, I tell you to leave now, in the name of Jesus. Up and out." He now speaks directly to God, "Your word declares, my God, that we shall be set free. My God, we warfare this morning in the spirit, not in the natural. My God, we are going at the roots this morning, generational cursing, long-standing sins."

As Matthew talks to God and demons, he lays hands on his congregation members assuring that God loves them, that God forgives those who forgive others who have trespassed against them, and that they will find freedom in the love of God. He watches over his flock as they pray, and after a few minutes, asks them to take their seats for the conclusion of the service.

...

Meanwhile, the roof almost blows off the top of St. John's Pentecostal House of Restoration Church. As Bishop approaches his congregation like a war-torn soldier does to a final battle, fire seems to spread to each of the church members as some begin heaving like a dying man struggling for his last breath, while others perform a wide variety of spiritually influenced behaviors that include crying, twirling, prostrating, screaming, shivering, convulsing, tongue speaking, collapsing to the floor, violent shaking, quiet prayer, loud wild prayer, rapid prayer, jumping, solemn deep worship, and shouts joyous praise. It's a radical motley of embodied spiritually fueled performances.

Bishop must have invisible electric fire bolts shooting from his hands. As the band supplies the tunes, the congregation sings:

It's raining, it's pouring, the spirit is flowing
I feel the anointing for healing and miracles
It's raining and pouring over me
It's raining, it's pouring, the spirit is flowing

Apostle sings into the microphone holding it with one hand while laying his other hand on the heads of the spiritually intoxicated. About a hundred people stand waiting for their turn at the spiritual juice bar. Each head he touches produces peculiar and unique responses. Some people immediately collapse to the ground like a ton of bricks, while the knees of others seem to buckle succumbing to the pressure of gravity suddenly working against them. Still others gently fall backwards as if losing consciousness and fainting to the ground, while some folks fall sideways, forward, or wildly stumble in every direction before hitting the ground. Sometimes Apostle palms their face like a basketball as it struggles with his grasp forming circles and circles until the spiritual charge slays them to the ground. People begin to collapse all over the place, running into others, grabbing onto walls, steps, holding on to the carpet as if the Earth is trying to cast them off its axis. One woman pukes in a bucket vomiting out a demon that once polluted her soul.

Bodies lay sprawled all over the floor like Armageddon just struck the unsuspecting world. Still dozens of the hundred once standing bodies remain upright even if prostrate, heaving and screaming out to the heavens. The gospel song now becomes a melodic chant:

Healing Water flow over my soul
Healing water overflow, overflow
Overflow, overflow, overflow, overflow, overflow
Overflow, overflow, overflow, overflow, overflow

Apostle filled with Holy Ghost fire springs into action laying hands on people in rapid succession as they immediately drop. Now free of the microphone, he lays hands on people as they speak in tongues, pray out loud, and struggle with tormenting demons. It's a series of many exorcisms happening one after another with each head the hand touches. It's an unstructured assembly line of exorcisms. Sometimes Apostle touches a head, and as the body begins to collapse he already tends to the next head that drops immediately after. At other times, he uses both his hands simultaneously to drop two heads at a time. He now runs around the church tapping heads one by one as the bodies attached to those heads crumble to the ground. It's the Fordism of exorcism or perhaps the mcdonaldization of exorcism,[2] not for its lack of quality but for the assembly line efficiency of the procedure. We've reached a state of rapid exorcisms knocking out bodies in rapid succession. These speed exorcisms are like speed dating but with God's soldiers casting out demons. No matter how big or small, the bodies attached to the head go down, down.

Only a few bodies remain standing surrounded by a mass of people lying seemingly lifeless all over the church floor. Apostle grabs the microphone, screams into it, shouts "overflow, overflow," and touches another head dropping at first wobbly and then hard to the carpet. Like a creature in its last moments of resistance, Apostle screams raw and mighty while placing his hands on the last remnants of standing humans until bodies lay about the floor, a spiritual warfare battlefield where everyone dies. Apostle then drops to his knees, bellows out one last time, before prostrating with two hands on the floor while his wife covers him with a red cape.

INTRODUCTION TO ANTIGUA

Within the reef-lined beaches of Waladli, the "Carib" name for Antigua,[3] the scene above juxtaposes two radically different Pentecostal Churches with dia-metrically opposing pastors—Apostle Andrews and Pastor Matthew Noyce. Both men are extraordinary but for different reasons: Apostle leads one of the largest Pentecostal churches in the entire Caribbean while Pastor Noyce heads one of the smallest. They both defy institutionalization in their own right, the former from within an institution while the latter free from its shackles. Using months of observations and hundreds of hours interviewing religious leaders and pastors, including Apostle and Noyce, as well as using ethnographic scenes of beach baptisms, Sunday church services, exorcisms, and go-alongs in the everyday life of religious leaders, the sections below navigate the religious worlds of Apostle's large PAWI church and Pastor Noyce's small Pentecostal churches in Antigua to reveal how various types of charisma impacts religion in the island and beyond to its Caribbean neighbors.

A brief religious demographic portrait of Antigua reveals a country that identifies strongly with Christianity. A whopping 93 % of Antigua's 2014-estimated population of 91,295 people claims Christianity as their religious identification.[4] According to the 2011 census, the Anglican Church is the largest religious group, accounting for 17.6 % of the population, while Seventh-day Adventists (12.4 %), Pentecostals (12.2 %), and Moravians (8.3 %) make up a combined almost 40 % of the population. Roman Catholics remain a minority of the Christian population at 8.2 %

while Methodists sit at 5.6 %. Those with unspecified or no religious beliefs account for 12 % of the population. Baptists, Church of God, and Wesleyan Holiness members each have less than 5 % of the population. Another 12.2 % of the population belongs to other religions while Rastafarians, Muslims, Hindus, and Bahá'i members constitute less than 2 % of the population. While these hard numbers reveal a country composed of a definite religious identity, the soft Caribbean island of Antigua showcases a world where religious life deeply penetrates into the culture of the people.

RELIGION AND CULTURE IN ANTIGUA

The tranquil island of Antigua sits amidst the calm Caribbean waters and the wild Atlantic Ocean deep in the Leeward Islands. Although its shape from above looks like a bug that squashed on your car's windshield, the soft built environment of Antigua's sancroscapes reflect a rich and layered culture steeped in religion. Outdoor restaurants place huge billboards of biblical passages such as 53rd Psalms right next to their simple menus serving vegetable roti and the Caribbean version of bread pudding. Large and small churches from a variety of Christian denominations flood the nine-by-twelve-mile interior of the island's jagged coastline. Schools with names like "Divine Academy of Excellence" proudly display their Christian symbols on the façade of its buildings. A boy near a table filled with mangos sits on a public community bench with words proclaiming "For God so loved the world, that He gave His only begotten son, that whosoever believeth in Him should not perish but have everlasting life." Cars pass city streets with Christian inspired bumper stickers, claiming the power and importance of Jesus and His ability to offer salvation while worship and praise songs blare out its windows. Religiously inspired music from Soca (soul calypso) to gospel plays as workers sing gentle lyrics such as "Here I am to worship, You are altogether worthy" in public libraries and retail stores while also spilling out of public school buildings and even the airport outside St. John's.

Religion and culture deeply intertwine and penetrate into the social world of Antigua. Social life is interpreted and judged from a strictly born-again Christian lens. Locals explain that selling alcohol past midnight on the Christian holy day of lent is illegal and punishable with jail time. Although it's generally not enforced, homosexuality also remains illegal. Many Christians on the island express the importance of keeping homosexuality illegal as an important symbolic expression of their culture. Even fairly typical everyday behaviors such as drinking alcohol and smoking marijuana are understood through a Christian lens. Many religiously influenced Antiguans interpret these acts as backsliding or turning away from God. Few "respectable" men, and especially women, frequent any of the local drinking establishments on the island. In fact, most of the bars serve tourists in the quays and resorts. The few bars that cater to locals outside the tourist areas often involve drug use and prostitution. Any who patronize these bars are at best seen as demonically possessed victims, and at worst, evildoers rejecting God and salvation. In short, respectable men and women do not go to bars or drink, especially in public. In this overwhelmingly Christian population, many Antiguans see the world as a dichotomy between good and evil. In such a world where the unruly forces of Obeah are believed to still threaten the island, religious leaders become important people of power and respect in the dual-island nation-state. The stories of Apostle and Pastor Matthew below focus on how religious leaders and pastors impact religious life in Antigua and spread their influence beyond its borders throughout the Caribbean juxtaposing the worlds of large-institutional and small-unaffiliated Caribbean Pentecostal churches.

THE LARGE INSTITUTIONAL AND SMALL NON-INSTITUTIONAL CHURCHES OF THE CARIBBEAN

In the Caribbean world of Pentecostalism where Charismatic and institutional power struggle in a postmodern theater that combines secular attitudes toward the supernatural and religious perspectives toward the secular world, a common theme emerges that reflects a similar tension— free will and determination. In both sociology and Pentecostal theology, at least here in the English-speaking Caribbean, the concepts of free will and agency relate to charisma—not so much in the Weberian sense to impart the perception of superhuman abilities—but rather in the ability to impact the world beyond the confines of limiting structural conditions. Although not all people with agency have charisma, those with charisma possess human agency. This is best revealed looking at the remarkable stories of Pentecostal leaders in the Caribbean and their ability, originally starting with limited resources, to make a big impact on regional affairs.

Many Pentecostal preachers in the Caribbean, often from conditions of poverty, overcome seemingly insurmountable odds to become influential religious leaders within and beyond their borders. Although institutionalization might be the death nail of charisma in Pentecostal churches in the USA north of the Caribbean, charisma can still thrive within institutions between the two large American continents. And though charisma remains big in small places free from excessive institutionalization, like in small storefront churches in the inner city of the USA, it can easily die in small places in the Caribbean world.[5]

The stories of Apostle and Mathew Noyce demonstrate how human agency among Pentecostal preachers leads to the rise of Charismatic figures that become influential religious leaders within their respective churches. Pastor Matthew and Apostle offer two comparative approaches to understanding how religious groups like Pentecostals use various types of networking strategies to impact their home communities while spreading to other countries throughout the English-speaking Caribbean. The sections below describe two radically different Pentecostal pastors and their religious influences before developing a typology to explain how religious leaders within Pentecostalism establish networks to impact their respective countries and the Caribbean world beyond its borders.

Apostle Stephen Andrews and the Large Pentecostal Church of PAWI

Apostle describes his formative years as one of humble beginnings. He was reared in the Trinidadian borough of Arima, located about 30 kilometers outside Port of Spain and just east of Piarco International Airport. Although his family came from near impoverished conditions, none of the children knew it. In fact, he holds fond memories of his childhood, growing up under pleasant conditions. Unlike some Pentecostal pastors, Apostle remembers remaining "obedient" throughout his childhood and young adult life, respecting authority, conforming to rules and expectations, and easily avoiding trouble. Although Apostle hails from Trinidad and Tobago, he has become fully immersed in the social fabric of Antiguan life, even referring to himself as Trini-Antiguan. It makes sense that Antigua serves as another home, Apostle heads St. John's Pentecostal Church, PAWI's largest church in the island, and perhaps the Caribbean. He's an outsider turned insider as many of the religiously inspired people of Antigua have fully embraced him as a legitimate religious leader—a force of God with the ability to influence political and economic life on the island. It's easy to realize that perhaps PAWI needs Apostle more than Apostle needs them, though no one admits it.

Apostle spreads his religious influence beyond Antigua traveling to other Caribbean islands as well as various countries in Africa and North and South America. Besides personal travel, his voice extends within and beyond these political borders using various media sources to spread his influence throughout the region and beyond. He uses a second radio station for Barbuda's Abundant Life Radio right in his own Antiguan church to broadcast a live weekly radio show. He preaches on the internet using live video and audio streaming of his sermons and broadcasts of another weekly radio program called "Hope for the Nation" discussing the social problems within the Caribbean region. Recently, he created yet a new radio program on Sunday afternoon on Red Hot Radio. Apostle also owns a credit union, nursery and daycare, pre- and primary schools, and makes gospel albums with some of the island's religiously inspired musicians.

Already the presiding bishop of Antigua and Barbuda, Apostle recently received a promotion within PAWI to become the presiding bishop over the dual-island nation-state of St. Kitts and Nevis. Although Apostle continues to grow within the institutional structures of PAWI, it's his charisma that allows him to increase his power and influence in Antigua and beyond. Let's take a closer look at how charisma operates within the confines of an institution.

Apostle's Networking Strategies

Apostle holds an official title within the PAWI bureaucratic structure, but it's his charisma that moves him up the ranks. Ordinary pastors rely on official procedures to seek promotion within an organization; Apostle relies primarily on charisma for upward mobility. Just as Napoleon took the crown from the hands of Pope Pius VII in the coronation ceremony indicating Charismatic supremacy over the institutionalized church, Apostle titles himself as "Apostle"—no such title exists within PAWI. He's officially a "Bishop" but the institution dares not prevent him from claiming such a title. PAWI offers Apostle access to powerful resource-rich networks, but Apostle relies on his own highly personal networks of friends in high places—from his personal connections to former Prime Minister Baldwin Spencer to influential but religiously unaffiliated religious leaders from the Caribbean—to establish connections.

He might be an official part of the institution, but he most often works outside of it. Apostle's credit union, nursery, daycare, schools, and gospel albums remain independent from PAWI. He still uses resources from PAWI's rich networks, but unlike most other pastors, does not rely on them. Rather, Apostle navigates freely between the formal institution and various informal religious and secular networks—from leaders in Antigua's music industry to other religious organizations outside PAWI. Although Apostle forms networks outside the institution, he creates a private inner circle of trusted friends from within PAWI—like "The Rev" and Trinidad's Bishop Andrews John (see Chapter 5)—that offer each other support and protection from those bureaucratic leaders strident about enforcing rules and laws. Even for powerful Charismatic religious leaders, inclusion within PAWI provides useful benefits. Having formal ties to the institution increases one's informal ties. Institutional legitimacy gives religious leaders "legitimate" access to leaders of political and economic institutions who rely on rank and status to enter the private circles of the country's elite. Further, though Apostle does not need to establish legitimacy with his 1000-members-plus church, titles such as "bishop" don't hurt. And though not in need of formal theological training and credentials, they remain plastered all over his office walls reminding everyone that this is a man of distinction. In short, people like Apostle might rely on personal charisma to head a church, while also using the institution for further legitimacy of title within the church. Access to PAWI also silences critics who might attempt to label those lacking credentials as fakers. Access to a credentialed legal institution better insulates powerful and wealthy religious leaders from suspicion of corruption or wrongdoing. The institution serves as a form of protection against perceptions of corruption. Just as Apostle relies primarily on charisma for upward mobility in the institution rather than its official rules and regulations, he refuses to allow the institution to stifle his influence and potential for growth. He uses his Charismatic qualities to defy institutional policies and limitations of its rules to build and establish churches and find external resources to grow.

Apostle crosses political borders to spread his influence throughout the Caribbean and beyond participating in PAWI general, national, and district conferences. PAWI also sends Apostle overseas to engage in missionary work, support struggling pastors, guest preach in struggling churches, oversee new churches, and other institutional business. While traveling abroad using PAWI resources, Apostle develops his own connections and informal friendships with political, religious, and economic leaders in the Caribbean, including the elite CARICOM, to spread his growing influence throughout the region. Further, his travels abroad using personal favors as a type of what I call "religious barter system" to travel across borders taking turns hosting other institutionally affiliated and non-affiliated churches with preachers abroad. Networking preachers informally make connections to take turns funding each other for opportunities to travel and guest preach. Sometimes Pentecostal pastors use favors in exchange for travel funding.

This charisma from within an institution juxtaposes Pastor Matthew's charisma that exists without institutional belonging. Prior to developing a typology for understanding Pentecostal networking strategies, the next section reveals the blue-collar charisma of Pastor Matthew and his biography of becoming a preacher.

Pastor Matthew Noyce and the Small Pentecostal Church

Pastor Matthew Noyce defies institutionalization and the pompous attitudes of some of the more conservative Pentecostal religious leaders basking in their positions of wealth, power, and authority confined within fancy church ivory towers. Although Pastor would probably deny it, his hair braided in cornrows—a highly unconventional style for a Pentecostal pastor and informally unaccepted within large Pentecostal institutions—symbolically resists institutionalization and subverts its arbitrary rules. He's a prototypical self-made man from humble beginnings. Pastor Matthew does not have any formal religious training, no theological background, no institutional belonging, and until relatively recently, no pulpit to preach on: He was, in fact, a preacher without a pulpit. He never attended church for much of his life nor did he think much about God or religion. Matthew became a Pentecostal pastor using what I call "blue-collar charisma" that has pushed his religious influence beyond the walls of his small church. First, let's take a glimpse into Matthew's biography and his path to becoming a pastor. The details of Matthew's life reported below derive from spending months of time with Matthew at his shop in the craft market, eating at his go-to lunch spot Nash's Place, running errands all over St. John's, and spending hours at his church during, before, and after church services.

THE ROAD TO BECOMING A PENTECOSTAL PASTOR
IN THE CARIBBEAN

Although Apostle serves as an "unusual" Charismatic religious leader with institutional power, Pastor Matthew offers a highly unique story of how, metaphorically speaking, small fish impact big waters. It's worth detailing Matthew's biography before developing a typology on Pentecostal religious networks and its influence in the English-speaking Caribbean.

As a teenager, Matthew began working for himself eventually developing a reputable fashion design business and even winning occasional awards for his clothing line. Like many young men, young Matthew spent most of his time fancying women. Ironically, it was a woman who provided the first steps to his path of becoming a born-again Christian and eventually a Pentecostal pastor. This young and pretty woman in his neighborhood expressed an interest in talking to Matthew.

> I remember this girl kept seeing me, meeting me, telling me, 'I want to see you.' So I knew that when a girl said she wanted to see me, I knew exactly what she wanted to see me for. And this girl was really pretty. And she lived only four to five blocks away from me. For some strange reason, I just could not make the time to go see her.

Eventually Matthew runs into this girl's brother at a Reggae concert who urges him to go visit his sister. Matthew accepts the offer with full expectations of engaging in a romantic relationship. What he finds instead is a woman engaged to be married who says God speaks to her. Matthew reports the events that happened on his first visit to her house:

> She says, "God says for me to speak to you." And I was like, "Really? And what does God want to say to me?" And she says, "God wants to help you. He says He loves you and he wants to help you." And I'm taken back. I'm a bit skeptical, like whatever. She says to me, "The gentleman that drives the church bus lives four homes down the road on my same block, he drives the church bus."

That Saturday night he goes out dancing at the Rabbit Night Club until the early morning hours. Although Matthew arrives home at around five in the morning he wakes up just in time for church. Matthew recalls:

> I woke up about eight-thirty and amazingly, I said, "Hey, that girl invited me to go to church." So I looked through the window and the bus that the guy drives is gone. And looking back on it, Peter, I don't know why, I'm in my boxer shorts and my vest, I put on my slippers, and I walk down to this guy's house. With the bus gone, I begin to tap on the door. And the guy comes out fixing his tie, I said, "Good morning, I want to come to church today, sir." He says, "Someone has just taken the bus. They'll be back in half

an hour. If you're ready by then, I'll drop you." And that church morning, it was eerie. It was a strange environment to me, people dancing … y'know what I mean? And I remember the guy preaching, and it was just as if he was speaking to me personally. I felt very uncomfortable. And I remember leaving church saying I would never come back here again.

But Matthew returns that same day to attend the Sunday night service. Although he wants to heed the altar call, he claims that something prevented him from getting saved that night. Unable to wait until the following week, Matthew attends a Wednesday night service with the sole intention of getting saved and surrendering his life to God. Like many Pentecostal stories of conversion, Matthew begins to disassociate himself from prior secular affiliations, especially all the women.

I remember going that Wednesday night, reaching home I began to write e-mails to tell girls, "Hey, I'm a Christian now, I don't know what it means, don't ask me any questions, I really don't know anything about it but I just know I'm not happy and I want to try this thing out." And I broke up all my relationships and just began to read the Bible and listen to sermons.

Matthew began attending church at Bible Believers Fellowship in the village of Clare Hall just outside of St. John's. One day Matthew received a Christian poem that made an impression on him, one that inspired him to read it out loud at a service. The poem stirred the emotions of people in the congregation, encouraging some of them to go receive the altar call. Matthew describes how "this one girl, she was sobbing, crying, the poem got a hold of her. It led her to the Lord. All she kept saying was 'That poem. That poem. That poem.' That's what the girl said at the altar. 'That poem.'" This encourages Matthew to continue reading poems to the congregation, eventually allowing Matthew to become more comfortable with public speaking.

Soon after joining the congregation, the head pastor offers Matthew a leadership position in the church to take over the Bible study program. Eventually Matthew begins to minister during some of the church services. As it turns out, much to his surprise, he was quite good at it. Matthew explains, "I remember the first time he gave me a chance to minister, it was a Friday night, and it was met with great success. A lot of people came and shook my hand. They said, 'Wow, wow, wow.' Then I began to do it a little more often."

After some time, Matthew encounters some negative experiences with other Christians, like irresponsible roommates, that disillusioned him to the Christian world. Matthew says:

> I said to myself, "Hey! I am done with this Christian business, I have no interest in Christians." I remember saying, "God, I love you, it's your people I have a problem with." Right? And I'm gonna stop going to church. But I'm going to be faithful, and I'm going to continue serving you, reading my Bible, but I'm just not going to Church. And then I stopped going to Church for almost two years. Went back to the club, girls, everything [makes noise to imply everything going fast].

After "backsliding" for about two years, Matthew encounters a woman while looking for an apartment to rent:

> I remember going down the road, meeting a lady, and I said, "Excuse me, miss, I heard you have an apartment for rent." She said, "Yeah, I do." As I walk in, she says, "You're running from God, son. And you're never going to be happy until you go back to God." True story. Shocked me like [imitates shock]! And I don't know if somebody told her, I really can't say if it was supernatural, but I know I had never spoken to this lady before. I said—tears running down—"Do you think God wants me back?" And she said she backslid for years and God took her back and she been saved now for years. [Makes noises to imply an explosion, then begins to pretend to cry.] I remember she prayed with me right there on her kitchen table.

Meanwhile, Matthew's former pastor called and sometimes sent letters throughout his backsliding days going to clubs, drinking, and dating women. Soon after encountering this woman while looking for an apartment, Matthew receives a letter from his pastor that stirs powerful emotions:

> On the side of the card is a cartoon driving the car and the tire bouncing off. There are three tires on the car, and I open it and it says, 'Things just aren't the same without you.' [Makes noises of frustration] Ahhhh! Tears, man, mashup mashup. And I remember calling him and saying, 'Well you know, I am weak with my life. He calls on my friend Orrin from church, and Orrin's a big dude. My pastor calls Orrin, calls some other young men that have been influential in my life, and then I put down the phone. Maybe half an hour all these guys are there. All these guys pull up, 'Yo! Glad to have you back!'

With the support of his pastor, Matthew becomes immersed in Christian life attending church and running the Bible study classes. He even began leading a Bible study class in a shop that he rented for his tailoring business.

> I remember praying for a young guy at night at my store, and a demon manifested. The guy was rolling, screaming, crawling on the ground, and the manager down there heard it. Now he wanted the whole complex locked down by seven o'clock. So eventually I had to move it from the craft market to my home in Potters (Village). I was there for a few years doing Bible Study on a Monday night at my home, and then I would preach occasionally at my church on a Friday night, and occasionally on a Sunday morning only for a special service.

Matthew explains how the pastor became influential in his life, acting as father figure and encouraging him to continue holding Bible study classes and grow within the church. Matthew Noyce learned from his pastor how to acquiesce to authority while learning to become a leader in his own right. Unfortunately, the untimely death of his pastor would change the direction of the church. Matthew recalls, "So I did everything with the consent of my pastor, I did nothing without it. Then eventually he died, and the regime changed." Matthew's hopes of becoming a church leader in the church quickly diminished with the passing of his leader. The death of his pastor plunged Matthew into the depths of religious anomie:

> I remember the pastor would say, 'Hey, if you weren't here on Friday night, you missed out! Wow!' He said that to the whole church. They would say to me, 'It's young men like Brother Matthew who serve as the future of this church!' So I had everything plotted out, eventually I'd be a pastor here. That's the only church I've ever been exposed to my entire life. I know nothing else but that church. You know? And then pastor died. It's interesting, the church, [sadly] that church. I remember, if I could look at my life in its entirety, that segment was the most challenging, both from the pressures at church, not being sure what was goin' on at church, to now losing friendships that I had built over ten years, and just [makes sound to indicate the friendships being cut off]. You know? No sure direction for the future. Just everything that you deem stable, all of a sudden it's gone. I remember that being the most challenging time in my entire life. Not knowing up from down. I remember that messed me up. Messed up.

As various religious leaders have related to me, the preacher who took over Bible Believers Fellowship turned against the former pastor now deceased.

This divided the church as many members of the congregation began to jump ship. Over time, Matthew became discouraged with the new pastor and left the church as well. This would change the direction of Matthew's life in profound ways.

Although Matthew no longer had access to a congregation or Bible study classes, he still receives messages from God to deliver to an audience. The irony of being a preacher without a pulpit brought with it a sense of humor. Matthew recalls, "I'm getting all these messages, little ideas for a sermon, and I'm putting them down on paper, and I'm thinking to myself, 'God, you really have a sense of humor. You're giving me all these sermons, all these nice ideas, and I have no outlet to preach them to.'" But ideas for an outlet would soon surface.

One day while watching television, Matthew hears a story about a Jamaican native and Muslim convert deported back to his country from Pakistan. The man received a gag order from the Jamaican government, preventing him from preaching unpopular religious ideas publicly. Instead, the man used the internet to blog religious messages using his home computer. Soon, this internet preacher found a large following. Matthew explains his moment of enlightenment, "While watching' that, I hear the voice of God saying to me, 'That's what I want you to do. Just record.'" Viola! Matthew begins the process of becoming an online preacher. He says, "I didn't know anything about recording, I knew nothing about audio. But Brother Orrin was always into music and editing. So I remember the very first time myself, Orrin and maybe five of us in Brother Orrin's home, with a little mic, and I preached my first audio message, my first sermon online—it's available online. It's called God's Preservatives."

As Matthew begins recording sermons into a microphone and storing them online, he comes into contact with the owner of a Christian radio station in the neighboring island of Barbuda, Antigua's sister island. Matthew makes a CD of sermons without any plans of distribution until God speaks to him with an idea. Matthew relates the events:

> So I have this CD, I have this sermon and I don't know what to do with it. I begin to ask God, 'What now? What next?' And God said to me, 'Send the CD.' It's incredible; God said to me, 'Send the CD to the gentleman in Barbuda.' I don't know his name, I don't listen to Christian radio, I know nothing about Christian radio—I play CDs in my car, I don't listen to radio.

This gentleman called Evangelist Clifton François is the creator and owner of Barbuda's Abundant Life Radio that broadcasts throughout the Caribbean. "I'm goinig to play this on the radio." And I'm like, [gasps]. And he says, "This thing really impacted me, and I am willing to give you a program every week on the radio station. But you have to promise to give me regular content. If you can give me regular content, I'll give you a spot." Eventually, Matthew's approach to delivering practical messages in a unique preaching style inspires a small but growing audience. This following leads to him becoming one of the most well-known religious voices in Antigua and the Caribbean and lands Matthew a prime time spot on the air. He says, "Every Thursday I would record, and upload it, and send the link to him in Barbuda. And then he said God spoke to him and told him there's a program that comes on every Sunday morning from eight to eight-thirty, and from eight-thirty to nine. He said to me, that God told him to put my program there. He moves these other two programs and gives me both spots."

Matthew reminisces about this moment while we eat at his favorite lunch spot, Nash's Place in downtown St. John's close to the market. He grows visibly excited as he recalls:

> Prime time. And he did it, and I remember the first one we did was called Potter's Clay. I was just walking over by the Woods (neighborhood) and this guy says, 'Hey! Yo! What a message! Potter's Clay—WOW!' And I [said], 'Ya, mon!' And he was like, 'Pshh! Boy, yo mon! Had me thinkin'! Yo!' Y'know? And then the guy in Barbuda began to get all this feedback.

As this continues for three years, Matthew becomes one of the most prominent radio voices in the English-speaking Caribbean. Meanwhile, as Matthew develops his own business as a shirt designer renting a vending space in the craft market, he preaches into a microphone and computer when business closes for the day. Matthew explains, "(Pointing to his computer and microphone) You see my pulpit? I built my pulpit. I had that down there (the craft market). My pulpit, my little mic plugged into my computer, and sometimes there was just (his friend) Kat and me. Alone. I was preaching my heart out. He's there sleeping, and I'm preaching, [yells like a Holy Man]." Preaching his heart out in the lonely vending space with his trusted friend Kat pays religious dividends as Matthew begins to receive increased attention from a now large audience of listeners. The amount of attention from so many different people from a variety of Christian denominations was a welcome surprise. Matthew relates, "All this feedback starts to come in from different denominations, and old people and young people, even this week I got encouragement from my Facebook. People just kept calling in and saying, 'I was depressed and you encouraged me. All this good stuff starts to pour in.'"

Though good stuff pours in, his wife grows concerned about their lack of church attendance, especially with a newborn son and young daughter in tow. As they began tentatively looking for a church, Matthew's friends offered advice that would only confirm ideas hovering somewhere in the back of his mind. He explains:

> A friend calls me saying, 'Why don't you start a church, Matthew?' And I laughed and laughed. I was like, 'Boy, you got to be kidding me!' Another friend, a Baptist pastor in St. Croix, says to me 'Why you don't just start a church?' I'm like, Boy! You guys crazy; you guys crack me up. I can honestly say that nowhere in my heart did I ever think about starting a church. I saw myself preaching, but I never ever thought I'd be preaching in my church. Ever.

At first, Matthew refuses to entertain this possibility. This begins to change when his friends continue to encourage him and his wife grows increasingly weary of missing out on the Sunday church scene. Now Matthew searches within himself to figure out the next steps. He explains, "So I'm getting pressure from home on going to church. I begin to seek God, asking, 'God, what do you want me to do?' So one day I'm passing through this neighborhood and this gentleman by the (basketball) courts, by the corner right down here, calls out to me." Although Matthew vaguely knew this man as the owner of the wholesale and retail Caribbean food store, this man knew Matthew well from his radio sermons. The man calls Matthew to his car shouting, "Good preaching! Good preaching! I heard you on the radio." It suddenly dawns on Matthew that this store has a vacant upstairs. Matthew recalls, "All of a sudden, I hear God saying, 'Go and ask the gentleman to show you the upstairs.' And I remember thinking to myself, no way am I doing this. I said 'God, I'm not going to do it.' Didn't think I'm qualified. I don't want this responsibility." He never gets around to asking the man to show him the upstairs space. Instead, the man approaches him with the idea stating that God told him to show Matthew the space for him to rent as a church. Matthew explains:

I remember, Brother Anthony can testify to this, I am passing one day and
he says to me, 'Brother Matthew, Brother Matthew, come here, come here!'
He says, 'I want to be obedient to God, God has been telling me to show
you upstairs. Can I show you upstairs?' I Didn't ask him. And I'm like,
whoa! So I go upstairs.

Matthew begins the blue-collar way starting from scratch without any
access to institutional resources. As he "chupes" his teeth, that teeth-
sucking sound Caribbean dwellers frequently make to express disapproval
or annoyance, Matthew recalls that starting a church offered mountainous
challenges with seemingly impossible odds. The first problem was finding the money, "I remember being really financially tight. Cash tight. My
finances dwindled down; business gets really slow in certain seasons. I can't
even buy groceries for my family. And then God says, 'Church.' I'm like,
[chupes his teeth], church? Really! Who's going to pay for this, Lord?"
Matthew needed to build his church starting with the basics of getting a
lectern, chairs, carpeting, sound system, some modest decorations, and
even electricity to run the lights and running water for the bathroom. He
works fast using all of his informal connections to get all the basic material
needed to at least hold a church service, barely. Matthew says, "I remember this vividly: it's a Friday afternoon, heading towards the first Sunday
in January, 2012, I tell my wife, we spent the whole December getting the
plumbing and the fixtures put in, 'We are gonna have church this Sunday.'
First Sunday in January 2012. We didn't know who was gonna come,
we have no chairs, we have no power in the building." Matthew found
a way when it seemed impossible. He even struggled with the Antigua
Public Utilities electricity company before running into another woman
who knew him from his radio sermons. She says to Matthew disappointed
after further delays with the electric company, "Noyce! Noyce! Come
here, come here! I'm hearing good things about you on the radio, what
you doing here?" Unexpectedly, this woman used her connections with
Antigua Public Utilities to expedite the electricity instillation in the new
church. While at the office, he also received a call from a friend, stating
that he sold Mathew's motorcycle to a medical student at the American
University of Antigua. This allows Matthew to buy 50 black chairs for his
first Sunday service in the first Sunday of the New Year. Matthew reports,
"We had sound, chairs, no instruments, no a cappella just clap our hand
sounds. We had speakers, chairs, and electricity that Sunday. And we had
about six people."

That church continues to grow as does his presence preaching all over the island—from Antigua's "Red Gate" or "Her Majesty's Prison" on Coronation Road to churches of various denominations throughout the island—as his radio show reaches even farther, extending his voice throughout the English-speaking Caribbean region. This growth does not happen on accident: It's the result of creative networking strategies without the luxuries of resource-rich institutional networks.

Pastor Matthew's Networking Strategies

Pastor Matthew remains completely free of any institution. He lacks any formal theological training or any official credentials that legitimate his position as a church pastor. In fact, he titles himself pastor; after all, he heads a church that he built from the ground up. As the story above explained, Matthew used his blue-collar charisma to make connections to locate church equipment, gather musicians, find audio and video technicians, and other specialists to help build the church. He also relies on his own schools to build, nail by nail, a running church from the proverbial sweat of his own brow.

Though he could travel to Trinidad for formal training, title, and position within PAWI, thus gaining access to its many powerful resources, Matthew prefers relying on his own personal informal networks. Lacking institutional resources, Matthew develops his own creative networks of support to transmit his sermons on the internet and radio, run the audio and visual equipment in his church, perform as the praise and worship team of his church, serve as church maintenance performing the duties of electrician and plumber, and assist with operating his various forms of social media. Matthew relies on his friendships and business connections to make things happen. He owns a small print shop in the central market. His employees also assist in his church business. In fact, many of his customers also attend his church.

Lacking high office in a religious hierarchy of ivory towers, Matthew prefers to remain on the ground floor, using highly personal approaches to minister to his neighborhood and becoming heavily involved in community life. People confide in him regarding personal matters both religious and secular. They look to their pastor as not only a man of God but also a personal friend to be counted on in the darkest of days. He also plays basketball with youths from the neighborhood and built a weight lifting space in his church building for people from the neighborhood to exercise. All this serves as another aspect of his ways of bonding with the community. But his religious influence extends beyond his neighborhood and local community. Matthew's access to Abundant Life Radio made him a minor religious celebrity in Antigua with his voice extending well beyond the island. His popularity on social media also has a large following as he develops creative religiously inspired slogans like "Sin is like a net: Easy to get into hard to get out" and "Safe sex: Get Married and be Faithful" (with a wedding ring inside a condom wrapper) to inspire his audience. This has gained him recognition throughout Antigua, prompting religious leaders and pastors of churches both large and small to invite him to guest preach. What is more, since Matthew lacks any official credentials or theological training, he offers little threat to other pastors who sometimes become paranoid that another more Charismatic pastor will steal their members away. And though Matthew is Charismatic, he's atypical of many Charismatic pastors like Apostle that uses over-the-top methods to provide thrilling church performances. Instead, he develops innovative preaching styles that offer an alternative approach to theatrical Pentecostal Church performances. He uses the Bible to offer practical advice with real-world examples that help people with their everyday life. He seldom yells or raises his voice. Rather, he speaks gently and informally into the microphone in a calm soothing manner. His slight lisp actually makes his voice sound distinct from others and only adds to his charisma.

Lack of institutional belonging offers some advantages that other pastors find difficult to enjoy. Matthew regularly guest preaches at churches of various Christian denominations—from Moravian to Seventh-day Adventists to Methodists—that help to spread his influence beyond the ears of Pentecostal followers. As a result, Matthew uses both institutions and independent Charismatic church pastors to establish connections and create networks. Although he networks informally with religious pastors of institutions, Matthew does not deal with the institution itself.

The advantages of lacking institutional affiliations allows Matthew to not only preach in unconventional ways but also appear in ways highly unusual for a "proper" Pentecostal preacher with braided cornrows and attire typical of most other working and middle-class Antiguans. Lacking institutional belonging requires Pentecostal pastors to become—what I call "Religious Charismatic Mavericks"—who develop creative strategies to form their own networks that provide the same resources as institutions. Just as the excluded members are denied access to institutional resources and support must develop their own alternative forms of organization, independent pastors must use their creativity to develop their own connections to acquire resources for themselves that institutions would otherwise offer. Although Matthew travels far less than his PAWI colleagues, he successfully spreads his influence across borders using his vast social media and radio networks.

CHARISMA AND RELIGIOUS NETWORKING IN THE CARIBBEAN

The networking strategies of Pastor Matthew and Apostle offer comparative approaches to understand how Pentecostal pastors use various networking strategies to impact their home communities while spreading their influence throughout the English-speaking Caribbean. Extending the scholarship presented in Chap. 2 on transnationalization "from above and below" as well as "extended and negotiated" transnational religious organization, this section develops a typology to understand how Pentecostal leaders create networks to impact their local communities and spread throughout the English-speaking Caribbean. The types of transnational religious networking in the Caribbean include (1) Institutional-Charismatic Networking (ICN), (2) Institutional-Formal Networking (IFN), (3) Charismatic-Institutional Networking (CIN), and (4) Charismatic-Informal Networking (CFN). These typologies below serve as ideal types that explain the various forms of transnational networks Pentecostal pastors and leaders develop to impact their local communities and spread throughout the Caribbean.

(1) **Institutional-Charismatic Networking:** Pentecostal pastors and religious leaders with ICN strategies hold official positions within the bureaucracy of the institution. Though part of official institution, they often work outside of it. These pastors and religious leaders use resources both internal and external to the institution. They navigate freely between the formal institution and various other informal religious networks. But they are not limited to making connections with religious institutions; rather they establish networks with both secular and religious organizations. In fact, they use their positions within high institutional places to enter the private inner circles of powerful people who hold high political and economic positions. ICN involves establishing formal networks inside the institution as well as networks outside of it. Formal ties within the institution increase the informal ties outside of it. Not only do these

pastors and religious leaders join the private circles of the elite outside their organizations, but they also form their own private inner circles within their institution. They rely on personal charisma to head a church and use their institutional belonging to achieve further legitimacy within the church. Their institutional belonging adds official credentials to the Charismatic power. ICN pastors and religious leaders use the institution as a form of protection against perceptions of corruption, but refuse to accept the limitations of its bureaucratic rules and regulations. They use their Charismatic qualities to defy institutional policies and the limitations of its rules to build and establish churches and resources and grow while also relying primarily on charisma for upward mobility in the institution, rather than its official rules and regulations. ICN pastors and religious leaders use personal favors and a "barter" system approach to travel across borders taking turns hosting other institutionally affiliated and non-affiliated preachers abroad.

(2) **Institutional-Formal Networking:** Pentecostal pastors and religious leaders who rely on IFN occupy official positions within the power structure of the institution. They rely strictly on their institution to develop connections. These leaders turn inward into the institution, closed off to others external to the institution. They received formal training within the institution and find validation through its bureaucratic system of rewards and promotions. In order to get these promotions, they go through official channels conforming to the institution's formal rules, regulations, and policies for promotion. Their vision does not extend beyond the institution, for they live and breathe the institution. The institution made them. IFN pastors and religious leaders find their legitimacy to head a church through the titles their institutions bestow upon them. Their authority derives strictly from the institution, for without it they are rendered impotent. They stand in front of congregations as pastors simply because the institution allows them to do so. These men and women are institutionalized bureaucratic cogs in a machine.

IFN pastors and religious leaders develop friendships primarily with others of similar rank and status within the organization, often skeptical of superiors and inferiors, and especially outsiders. They engage in institution-to-institution networking with other powerful religious organizations to travel throughout the region. The institution provides their primary means of travel on official functions to establish new churches, conduct missionary work, and attend general, national, and district conferences, among other things. Without the institution, these powerful IFN pastors and religious leaders would plunder into the world of the ordinary.

(3) **Charismatic-Institutional Networking:** CIN involves pastors and religious leaders who serve in complementary roles or as quasi-members of large and powerful institutions. They use a special skill, expertise, or Charismatic ability to network with institutions, though they remain loosely affiliated with them. They have charisma within the institution in a Weberian sense, as other pastors and religious leaders perceive their supernatural qualities as gifts that bring power. These gifts such as discernment, healing, wisdom, and counsel serve as potential cures to some of the problems and struggles that sometimes occur within a church. Pastors and bishops might call upon these men with special gifts to cure an illness within the church, a Pentecostal version of a medicine man. As a result, CIN pastors and religious leaders often serve as guest preachers on their home island as well as the Caribbean beyond. They travel across Caribbean borders using invitations from religious institutions abroad to fix problems and reinvigorate churches in danger of losing their mojo. Perhaps this is another reason why the large Pentecostal Church in the Caribbean somehow retains its charisma while large Pentecostal Churches in the north fair quite differently. CIN pastors and religious leaders use their Charismatic qualities to network directly with institutions and frequently use numerous institutions to make connections, informal friendships, and official networks. These men and women navigate freely through official channels, using "legitimate" organizations within various religious denominations to make their impact. While some rely on their pure Charismatic qualities to network with large institutions, others rely more on their official credentials and quasi-membership to acquire religious capital and status within various organizations. They serve almost as honorary members, occupying roles such as councilors and advisors of the institution in matters ranging from finance to marketing to spiritual matters and political affairs. Though lacking official full-fledged membership in an institution, their loose religious affiliations and networking strategies with various institutions allow these pastors and religious leaders the ability to influence their home countries and the Caribbean region beyond.

(4) **Charismatic-Informal Networking:** CFN pastors and religious leaders remain free of any large and bureaucratically organized institution. They're not trying to join the social clubs of the religious elite in high places or get invitations to play in their posh gold clubs. Rather, they rely completely on informal networks of support from the community.

They make friends with people from high and low places from multiple walks of life; religious leaders to plumbers and electricians to radio broadcasters to musicians to even Rastafarians. Their networks consist of friendships and business connections as well as hundreds of people on social media who remain in constant communication. These pastors and religious leaders use highly personal approaches to minister becoming heavily involved in the everyday life of the community. They often rely on their blue-collar charisma to build churches and establish networks one nail at a time getting their hands dirty in their do-it-yourself approach. Although they remain free from institutions, they will use both institutions and other independent Charismatic leaders to establish connections and create networks, but with no strings attached. They informally network with large institutions, establishing connections with its Charismatic leaders, not the institution itself. Lacking the funds of elite institutional dwellers, they use social media and radio to spread influence across the Caribbean. While institutionally free, they use their independence to an advantage, often developing unconventional methods to deliver their Pentecostal messages. And because they operate without the luxuries of an institution, they must be innovative in their approach to make their impact in the community and beyond. CFN pastors and religious leaders must become—what I call "Pentecostal Mavericks"—using their Charismatic abilities to develop innovative approaches to preach, establish creative networks of support, and spread their influence. As a result, they keep the Pentecostal movement unpredictable and creative as they stay away from the norms of most Pentecostal preachers, especially in the large institutionally affiliated church. Their innovative preaching styles offer an alternative approach to Pentecostalism that keeps the old and wise movement yet somehow making appear new and definitely refreshing. Although they spread religious messages across political borders mainly using social media and radio, they sometimes receive invitations from other religious leaders abroad to host or guest preach in church services of various denominations both large and small.

CONCLUSION: RELIGIOUS NETWORKING IN THE CARIBBEAN

These typologies serve as ideal types to compare the transnational religious networking strategies in the English-speaking Caribbean. Apostle most closely resembles the ICN strategy while Pastor Matthew employs a CFN approach. Of course, pastors and religious leaders may begin their careers using one approach and develop other approaches depending on multiple factors, ranging from their level of structural inclusion and exclusion to their own personal choices. Some pastors and religious leaders are denied access to institutions of power and ideology while others refuse to join such organizations. Pastors and religious leaders have access to different opportunity structures and uneven access to the dominant institutions.

The pastors and religious leaders of Antigua and Barbuda, Trinidad and Tobago, St. Lucia, Barbados, Dominica, St. Kitts and Nevis, and Montserrat use these networking strategies in various forms. Some strictly use one form over the other, like how Evangelist Peter Augustine Pastor Cameron Robins of Dominica (see Chapter 6) relies strictly on IFN strategies to make an impact in his community and beyond. Others like Bishop Andrews John of Trinidad (see Chapter 5) closely resemble Apostle in his ICN approach. Still others like traveling preacher Larry Scott of St. Lucia (see Chapter 6) clearly develop a CIN approach to spread Pentecostalism throughout the Caribbean. While Pentecostal leaders like Bishop Bartholomew and Reverend Kenneth Francis of St. Kitts and Nevis use a mix of ICN and IFN approaches, others adhere specifically to one strategy, like how Pastor Tony Allen of Montserrat relies strictly on his IFN approach (see Chapter 7). The networking strategies that Pentecostal pastors and religious leaders develop variously impact their home communities and the places they settle abroad. These different strategies also impact the strength and vitality of the Pentecostal movement as it spreads throughout the English-speaking Caribbean. As will be seen in the countries of Trinidad and Tobago, St. Lucia, Barbados, Dominica, St. Kitts and Nevis, and Montserrat, the Pentecostal movement in the Caribbean retains its charisma and powerful impact on the religious, political, and cultural life of the Caribbean where pastors and leaders use charisma in their approaches to regionally networking throughout the island. As the Pentecostal movement flourishes in the Caribbean impacting the social, political, cultural, and economic life with the ICN strategies of The Rev (see below) and Apostle as well as the CFN approach of Pastor Matthew, how do other English-speaking Caribbean counties fair? Let's look next to Trinidad. First, journal notes from the Caribbean capture a glimpse into the clashing perspectives of a PAWI Pentecostal leader and a secular sociologist that takes unexpected turns in a journey of enlightenment and self-discovery.

Journal Notes: Island Hopping to Antigua, St. Martin, and Barbuda

Reverend Henri "The Rev" Nigel serves as the head pastor of Barbuda Pentecostal Church and World Missions Executive Director of PAWI. Our travels together throughout the Caribbean islands of Antigua, Barbuda, and St. Martin involve hours of discussion on topics such as PAWI's role in the Caribbean, Pentecostal institutionalization, charismatic religious leaders and the "special men" of PAWI, the decentralization of PAWI from Trinidad to other small Caribbean countries, Caribbean religious networking, and the future of Pentecostalism in the region. But it's the end of our journey where a fascinating and descriptive story unfolds that involves a casual conversation that turned intense, leading to clashing sociological and religious ideas on free will, agency, and charisma among the crashing waves at the exact point where the peaceful Caribbean Sea meets the turbulent Atlantic Ocean.

Barbuda's 175 square kilometers of largely flat land in the middle of the northeastern Caribbean Leeward Islands feels like a desert island outside of its small village capital of Codrington. We pull out of the driveway of The Rev's house located right next to his church near the island's tiny airport to travel through the country's on its only main road, which is nothing more than a semi-paved street. We travel to the northern parts of the island to see deserted and remote beaches with pink-tinted sand from the island's coral reefs and later drive to the western Atlantic side of the island only to see miles of remote islands, the wild ocean, caves filled with stalagmites and stalactites, and breathtaking cliffs overlooking the joining of the Caribbean and Atlantic waters. Throughout the journey, we casually discuss matters concerning theology, philosophy, the existence of God, morality, reality versus truth, religious beliefs and practices, and so on until we reach the intense topic of free will and determination.

After hours of driving, we leave the SUV to walk on coral limestone towards the spectacular crashing Atlantic coast bracing ourselves against the hard blowing wind while discussing the weight of historical forces and all the factors, decisions, chance events, and inter-contingencies that must have happened in order for a New Orleans-born son of Cuban immigrant parents to come into contact with a Pentecostal leader with African roots from the remote island of Barbuda. We marvel at the remarkable events throughout hundreds and thousands of years of history necessary to make this moment for us—two men from completely different walks of life with completely different orientations to reality—happen that involves discussing our disparate perspectives from the world perspectives of western social science and Afro-Caribbean religious practices. But conflict sometimes produces highly surprising results.

Marina: It's a wonder how situations beyond our control shape our lives in ways beyond our imaginations. We believe in the fallacy of free will, but so many external factors that shape us that undermine such notions.

Rev: Free will exists, it's your God given ability to make decisions ever day that impacts your life.

Marina: Yes, but we don't choose the circumstances surrounding those decisions. Even the language we are using right now, we did not really choose it.

Rev: You choose to speak or not to speak; you can always decide to speak another language. You can also speak in tongues.

Marina: Yes again, but your speaking English is the direct result of an ancestral past ripped out of Africa and placed in a world of English-speaking colonizing slave owners forcing the language on your people. That's beyond your control.

Rev: It was people making decisions based on their free will that led to this moment of me making decisions based on free will.

Marina: But your free will is limited to the set of circumstances to other people's decisions that produced the world you live in.

Rev: And it's free will that remains, then as now.

As we walk, we carefully navigate between the gaps that can easily lead to one falling through holes that lead to the treacherous seas. The hard blowing wind and the sounds of waves crashing on coral reefs pervade the warm tropical Caribbean air. We begin to realize that perhaps we agree; it's the usual problem of semantics that stem from seemingly radically different perspectives from the conflicting point of views of a secular academic and Pentecostal theologian.

Marina: Ah, the theological concept of free will reminds me of the sociological concept of agency. Agency involves a person making alternative decisions that go against the external pressures that powerfully shape and influence our lives.

Rev: That sounds like free will.

Marina: It is, but limited free will. Nothing happens in a vacuum.

We take turns offering scenarios demonstrating our respective points of free will and human agency finally getting to the issues of gang formation and why a young person might join a gang. While Rev argues that kids use their free will to join a gang when they could have made the decision to join a church, I explain the structural conditions that can lead to gang formation.

Marina: Young people form gangs when they find themselves excluded from institutions that offer resources and support. When they are excluded from jobs that offer respect, political decisions that impact their lives, education that empowers them, and other support networks, they have to create their own institutions. Gangs are creative cultural solutions to the collective structural problems young people face that provide them with institutional resources otherwise denied. Gangs would probably not exist if everyone had institutional access to resources, support, and power.

Rev: But kids are still freely making the decision to join the gang, they could form schools or alternative organizations that offer support, or work within the system to change their conditions.

Marina: Sometimes gangs become exactly that; they have the potential to become something unexpected, like turning political and denouncing violence. The point is, we all have the ability to make decisions, but most of us find ourselves in highly unequal positions that impact our life chances tremendously. What about Apostle Stephen Andrews? He was poor and now he's one of the most successful and wealthiest pastors in the Caribbean. How did that happen?

As we near the coast, the crashing waves begin to echo off the canyons in the distance as the wind kicks up. The heightened sense of the energy and power of the Caribbean Sea meeting the volatile Atlantic mirrors the escalating debate. Rev raises his left eyebrow while he responds to my question about Apostle.

Rev: Andrews is unusual, a rarity. He's not like most men.

Marina: He was expected to be poor, to stay a poor man in Trinidad but he became more. He became something unexpected.

Rev: Again, Andrews is extra-ordinary.

Marina: What do you mean? What makes him extra-ordinary?

Rev: He made his way to the top without anything, self-made man. He still does things that are extra-ordinary. Like even in PAWI, he can do much more than other church leaders. PAWI allows him to do more; he has less limits.

Marina: He has agency, he operated within the limited conditions of poverty and made unexpected decision that put him in power. Now he operates within the limiting conditions of an institution and still does more than what is expected. That's agency.

Rev: That's free will

Marina: Rev, your free will is my agency's brother.

Rev: Free will and agency.

Marina: Free will and agency.

Rev: It's ...

Rev and Marina (simultaneously): Charisma.

We look at each other while taking our final steps towards a cliff at the edge of the island where it looks like the world ends. We realize the power of free will and agency, and how the theological and sociological concepts reveal the ability of humans to overcome odds both big and small. The Pentecostal concept of free will and the sociological concept of agency impacts both secular and religious worlds. It's the resiliency of a young woman defying patriarchal domination or how teachers inspire students despite stifling standardized educational curriculums or how an inner city youth picks up a trombone instead of following his big brother's dangerous path to the grave. It's also how religious leaders from small places make big impacts in places around the world.

A powerful realization dawns on both of us. Perhaps it is our agency that allows us to think beyond the limited confines of science and religion where two seemingly contradictory and conflicting views coalesced into this transcendental realization of the sheer power of human will and the endless possibility of its potential. Perhaps we found, if only for a moment, it. As we nod in unspoken agreement, we suddenly gasp, almost losing our breath, as our eyes cast over a 125-foot cliff to capture the divine view of the violent Atlantic meeting the tranquil Caribbean waters that somehow gently combine two radically different and opposed waters into a single unified body.

NOTES

1. I personally shipped Matthew his church keyboard while in the USA.
2. George Ritzer, *The McDonaldization of Society: An Investigation Into the Changing Character of Contemporary Social Life* (Thousand Oaks, CA: Pine Forge Press, 1996). George Ritzer's clever book *The McDonaldization of Society* inspired my use of the phrase the mcdonaldization of exorcism.
3. This is according to my interview with Antigua's well-known archaeologist Reginald Murphy at Nelson's Dockyard near my apartment "Jackie's Place" in English Harbour.
4. This section derives its data from the following sources: (1) The Pew Forum on Religious and Public Life, *The Global Religious Landscape: A Report on the Size and Distribution of the World's Major Religious Groups as of 2010* (Washington, DC: Pew Research Center, 2012); (2) United States Department of State, *2014 Report on International Religious Freedom—Antigua and Barbuda* (Washington, DC: USDS, 2015); (3) The Center for the Study of Global Christianity, *World Christian Database* (South Hamilton, MA: Center for the Study of Global Christianity, Gordon-Conwell Theological Seminary).
5. Peter Marina, *Getting the Holy Ghost: Urban Ethnography in a Brooklyn Pentecostal Tongue-Speaking Church* (Lantham, MA: Lexington Books, 2014). In my book, I argue that against the sociological scholarship that charisma is in decline in the USA, showing how charisma remains strong in the small inner city institutionally unaffiliated churches.

CHAPTER 5

Trinidad

Fieldnotes: Ethnographic Observations of a Trinidad Exorcism

Something peculiar stirs in the dense tropical air on an island so close to South America it nearly kisses Venezuela. It's a regular weekly mid-day revival held at a theater on Park and St. Vincent Streets in the heart of downtown Port of Spain. About sixty people attend the event hoping for an afternoon spiritual jolt like lovers do an afternoon delight. Others tend to perhaps more urgent matters.

The crowd reflects the diversity of the island with believers from African, Indian, and mixed Afro-Indian descents. Here on Rainbow Island, culinary delights such as callaloo reflect the great diversity and multiculturalism found in the people, culture, and religious beliefs of Trinidad.[1] This is a society historically built on racial and ethnic mixing best revealed in its cultural and religious productions where Hindu Indo-Trinidadian religious practices coalesce with Afro-Caribbean Pentecostalism equipped to handle the supernatural wonders from a variety of cultures. To religious leaders like the locally popular mega-preacher Bishop Andrew John (Bishop), this variety of supernatural entities serve as simply different spirits to contend with in a much larger battle between good and evil.

Apostle, the mega-preacher from Trinidad, traveled from his home base of Antigua to help his friend christen the opening of his fourth new church. For now, Apostle merely observes his friend Bishop lead a spiritual hour of afternoon revival. Bishop, a large and towering man who only a few months ago endured triple bypass surgery after suffering a heart attack, speaks in a prophetic tone offering spiritual guidance to an approving crowd nodding their heads while shouting "Amen, Amen." Most of the people in the audience wear business attire typical of middle-class office workers. It's

© The Author(s) 2016
P. Marina, *Chasing Religion in the Caribbean*,
DOI 10.1057/978-1-137-56100-8_5

lunchtime, and instead of eating a big plate of callaloo, they're feeding their souls instead.

Bishop casts his gaze upon the crowd as if scouring deep into their exposed consciousness, like a father suspecting a child of transgression. Bishop senses defiance amidst the flock. Like a stone-faced child repressing emotions to hide inner guilt and remorse, a short and plump Indo-Trinidadian woman gives up the ghost exposing the existence of a dormant sordid entity within the body. Except this entity is no ghost and this woman is certainly no child. It's a demon and the demon makes frightening noises.

She wails strange dramatic contralto noises from the depths of her vocal folds while falling towards the ground in dramatic fashion. This rotund woman shows off surprising athleticism while lying on her back, jolting her torso up and down as if the floor shoots electrical shocks from beneath her. The crowd forms a semi-circle around her convulsing body. While the audience members show concern, Bishop exudes a cool, almost blasé ho-hum attitude of indifference, as if this is a typical, mundane, and everyday occurrence.

But his words express the grave dangers that lie hidden deep within the depths of these waters surrounding the island. If God indeed never died here in the Caribbean, perhaps it's because Satan thrives here too. Bishop explains how Satan and his entourage continue to attack the region, hell bent on destroying the Caribbean and its colorful people. And the demon inside this woman serves as yet another battle in a long and historical war between God and his fallen angel.

Bishop knows evil but evil does not frighten when God's got your back. This spiritual war requires tapping deep into God's arsenal; it requires Holy Ghost power. Throughout the Christian English-speaking Caribbean world, it is believed that bishops serve as the generals of God's spiritual warriors. These men fight demons and cast them to hell. They free the innocent of spiritual bindings, hexes, and unholy curses. In this case, it is believed, demonic Hindu spirits possess this woman and determine her will—full control.

Moving from deep and low vocal ranges to higher pitches, the sounds conjure images of Hindu chants from centuries past. The echo bounces all over the walls. It starts with a low gurgling that gradually coalesces to a low-pitched animalistic growl amplified with the reverberation from the sound-scape of the theater. It's the opposite of Otto's Mysterious Tremendum. It's the sounds of fear that derive from a sinister entity trying desperately to swallow and consume a soul. It's Durkheim's anomie; the fight to wrestle control from a demon attempting to destroy your connection to the world. The congregation witnesses this woman experiencing the type of nomic rupture that plunges an individual into the depths of despair and terror.

As this eerie sound continues, one wonders if this woman's breath will soon be ripped from her lungs. The dark theater seems to turn even darker. This is not anyone's idea of a Caribbean vacation.

The crowd perceives this woman to be in a state of demonic bondage; they watch while hoping for her release from it. Like the Holy Ghost is believed to move through spiritual realms during times of intense prayer, the wind carries the soft melodic chants of worshippers in this spiritual war against pure evil, manifested.

There is no music, no contrived props or manufactured modifiers to affect the emotional mood of the place. This is a theater, but the stage is not preset nor the performances ready-made. Rather, the scene relies on pure energy; sheer will the only motivation. It's the raw energy of the praying crowd and the demonically possessed woman and the warrior preacher that produce this supernatural moment. It's charisma par excellence. These spiritual battles happen at unpredictable times and places. Unlike the more institutionalized and structured Charismatic churches that exist just north of the Caribbean, the charisma that remains in these churches remain better equipped to handle spontaneous spiritual outbursts and perceived demonic attacks. More audience members gravitate towards the front of the theater where the demon menaces. The whispering wind carries the soft spoken words of congregants acting as God's angels, making sounds of sweet Jesus while the women emits low pitched gurgling noises. The woman stands to her feet and suddenly shrills as her body gyrates like a shuttle about to blast off to the heavens.

Bishop places his hands on the woman's head, confronts the demon personally and directly showing aggression and confidence. He draws the woman's face towards his own, nose touching nose, speaking directly to the demon. Like a general, Bishop commands:

"In Jesus's name, get out of her!

Out of her! In the name of Jesus, out of her right now!

Loose her (shouting). Out of her! Out of her! (Shouting louder with veins popping out of his neck)

Yes! Spill out of her! Yes! Out of her! Out. Out. Out [repeats].

Just now, I want you to see the power of God."

As the women falls to the floor, he directs some of the spectators to lift this woman from the ground commanding, "Pick her up." Supportive members of the audience swiftly lift the woman to her feet. Bishop mocks the demon, speaking to it with condescension. He calmly requests:

"Talk to me. What's your name? What Is Your Name? (Slowly and deliberately)

Talk to me. What's your name? (Slightly faster and more matter-of-fact)

What Is Your Name? (Rapidly and with force) What's your name?"

Like the Hollywood depiction of a demon struck with holy water, the woman responds to each question with shrills and shrieks, eeeeeeh, urrrrrrrrrr, ahhhhhhhhhhh.

The possessed woman, in a screeching tone, wails out in an inordinately distressing emotional outburst that causes a tangible sense of panic in the theater. Less calm but still cool, Bishop asks, "What's your name? I command you to speak!" The woman roars like an animal in horrid pain, like a lamb getting its limbs torn. Bishop screams, "Out! Out!"

The sounds range from high-pitched tones to throaty low-pitched growls surprising for a woman of such small stature. At times she simply groans and growls, winding up, stopping, winding up again to stop and suddenly bursting out frantically. The moans and shrieks move the crowd to quietly repeat, "Jesus, Jesus."

Bishop whispers directly into the woman's ear, saying in a matter-of-fact tone, "You have no power here. You know, you have no power here." He moves in closer to repeat the same phrase making a personal and private statement for only the demon to hear. He grabs her throat while commanding the woman, rather, the demon possessing the woman, to look at him.

"I command that you go completely free."

He wraps his left arm around the woman's shoulder pressing her head on his wide and broad chest, and with his right hand holds a microphone to speak for the entire audience to hear. Bishop says, "This is a little bit different today (noticing my filming of this event), it's just more proof people in the media recognize how wicked the devil is and how he manifests."

As he says this, the woman bellows out a visceral shriek while slowly descending towards the ground as if floating. Bishop directs two women near the scene to push her back up towards his waiting hands. The high intensity, ferocious sound emits such terror that members of the audience gasp.

The wind carries the words, "The Lord rebukes you" and "The blood of Jesus is against you" that become further amplified in the theater.

Despite the frantic moment and the almost tangible panic and fear, Bishop continues with urgency, still remaining composed, and a bit arrogant and condescending of the demon. Satan is no match for this. His attitude is as blasé as Simmel's indifferent urban dweller.[2] He's developed the demonic blasé attitude.

The crowd remains intense as some audience members begin chanting in the background to support this spiritual battle to release this victim from its demon.

Bishop grabs the woman's upper neck and jaw ordering her to look at him again. While his enormous hand completely covers her jowl, the woman hisses while spreading both arms to either side flailing them like a broken baby bird attempting to take its first flight.

Bishop orders the congregation members assisting him with the woman to continue restraining the woman and keeping her vertical. He says,

"Hold her up. Let's hold her up.

{While talking to the theater audience} Watch me. Watch me. Watch me. Watch me now."

The possessed woman yelps and screams.

Bishop states, "Now watch it go now" and suddenly takes his right hand holding the jowl and plunges it directly into the woman's torso screaming, "Loose her."

The woman falls screaming to the ground screaming like a slain animal from a bloody dagger. Audience members standing directly behind the woman ease her to the ground. As they turn her over, Bishop orders, "Right now, in Jesus's name."

She immediately begins coughing and spitting up a white foamy substance signifying the departure of the demon. Once done, Bishop requests the audience members to help her up. He says, "Right now. Pick her up. Amen, amen. C'mon lift your hands up. Give God thanks. Thank God. C'mon. Give God thanks."

The audience members applaud perceiving this moment as another victory against Satan and his unrelenting evil. Bishop tells the woman now standing to lift her arms in the air to celebrate her newly found liberation. She waves her hands in the air though maintains a facial expression still in distress.

As Bishop repeats, "Give God thanks. Hallelujah. C'mon let's give God praise. Hallelujah. Hallelujah. Hallelujah," the woman bounces up and down with a relieved but still strained facial expression and hands sporadically waving.

Exorcisms in the religious world of the English-speaking Caribbean occur as often as rain, and seem just as natural. At least, to the people who live in the religious world of Caribbean life, this is the normal taken for granted reality of everyday life. Culture and religion remain intertwined here in the Caribbean where supernatural forces still shape the knowledge systems of these historical islands.

This is the everyday world of PAWI's Bishop Andrew John. Welcome to charismatic religious life in the highly institutionalized Pentecostal church in Trinidad.

INTRODUCTION TO TRINIDAD

This explosive exorcism scene during an afternoon prayer hour highlights how a highly institutionalized PAWI church maintains charisma despite the modernizing forces of rationality. It also shows how religion and cultures blend into the everyday life of these Port of Spain urban dwellers. Here, in this "New York" of the Caribbean, Port of Spain keeps a cosmopolitan attitude coupled with a religious state of mind. Trinidad serves as the heart of Charismatic Christian institutionalization where the central power structure of PAWI resides. An analysis of the tenuous balance between charisma and institutionalization within the Charismatic movement in Trinidad follows using ethnographic observations and interviews with PAWI religious leaders. This analysis reveals how religious leaders of the most powerful and bureaucratically organized Pentecostal Church skillfully, even if sometimes precariously, navigate their Charismatic authority within an authoritative bureaucratic institution while also balancing Charismatic and modern routinizing forces in their both church services and religious networking across the Caribbean. The ethnographic findings reveal how Charismatic religion impacts the social, economic, and political Caribbean world, right in the heart of Trinidad. Finally, religious leaders, including million-dollar mega-churches, respond to the critical view that perhaps they serve as "poverty pimps" opening new churches and collecting money from largely poor and dispossessed classes.

ARRIVING TO TRINIDAD

The plane from Antigua hops to St. Lucia, Barbados, and St. Vincent and the Grenadines all the way down to the twin island Republic of Trinidad and Tobago, the last of the Windward Islands. The capital Port of Spain bursts with colors of every kind where the visualscapes coalesce with the soundscapes of the bustling city a stone's throw away from Venezuela. On Charlotte Street between Park Street and Independence Square just east of Woodford Square, political subversives shout speeches of civil discontent. This is not your typical laid-back Caribbean city; it's rough and edgy, fast and cosmopolitan, diverse and bursting, and oozing with life and culture. Trinidad refuses to pamper tourists or cater to their needs; rather, the locals treat their few tourists with indifference. The country still benefits from the oil and gas industry leaving it less dependent on the shackles of a tourist-intensive economy. This bustling city does not keep religious practice behind private doors. Rather, locals practice their religious beliefs in public places, like the exorcism in the beginning of this chapter, which was performed in a wide-open downtown theater in broad daylight.

Trinidad geographically sits south of all major islands in the Caribbean and the first major island on the continental shelf of South America. Port of Spain serves as the economic and cultural heart of the country. Although the diversity does not rival the great American metropolis of New York, Port of Spain is one of the most diverse cities in the English-speaking

Caribbean. Perhaps the popular local dish callaloo, Trinidad's version of New Orleans style gumbo, best symbolizes the multiculturalism of this highly unique culture. As of the 2012 Trinidad and Tobago Census, the dual-island nation-state has a population of about 1.3 million composed of people self-described as being of African Afro-Trinidadian (39.5 %), East Indian Indo-Trinidadian (29.5 %), mixed descent (23 %), and other (8 %). Many of these groups overlap heavily due to racial and ethnic mixing. For example, "Dougla" is a common term used to describe a person of African and East Indian descent but may self-identify as either group. Walking through Port of Spain one can hear the many sounds of Trinidad's diverse population including English, Caribbean Hindustani (a Hindi dialect), French, Spanish, and Chinese. Although Catholicism was once the dominant religion in Trinidad, Protestantism now dominates the religious practices in the country with approximately 12 % Pentecostal and other Evangelicals, 7 % Baptists, 6 % Anglicans, 4 % Seventh-Day Adventists, 2.5 % Presbyterian/Congregationalists, other 1 % various other Protestant groups. Due to the large Indo-Trinidadian population, Hindu (18.2 %) is the dominant non-Christian religion in the country, while the country also is 5 % Muslim.

As in much of the English-speaking Caribbean, religion and culture intertwine in a myriad of ways. Trinidad's many churches, composed of various religious groups and faiths, hold services almost every day of the week. The worship and praise music from these services spill onto city streets giving a religious flare to the urban beat of the city's soundscapes. Religious symbols permeate the hard built urban environment of Port of Spain while cars blast religious sermons and music for all to hear. Trinidad's many festivals—from the Christian celebrations of the Santa Rosa Festival, Christmas, and Easter to the Hindu celebrations of Diwali and Phagwa—reflect the religious diversity of the country. Although the racial and ethnic experiment of equality and multiculturalism in Trinidad has many of the same problems found in the USA, the diversity adds to the vibrant religious culture of the region. While religion might influence belongingness and interconnectedness of a country's diverse inhabitants, Trinidadians of both Indian and African descent develop a sense of identity from their racial, ethnic, and religious belonging while interethnic and racial mixing influence their unique form of multicultural politics.[3]

Trinidad serves as the headquarters of the PAWI—the central power structure of the Pentecostal movement in the Caribbean and epicenter of Charismatic Christian institutionalization. PAWI offers a prime example of how religious charisma transforms to a highly bureaucratic and hierarchical institution similar to the Catholic Church, though most PAWI leaders refuse to admit it. Pentecostalism spreads in unique ways to each Caribbean country, and the way it spreads impacts its influence in the regions it permeates. Pentecostalism in Trinidad serves as a unique example of how charisma remains within a now mature and wise religious movement that has reached the maturity of institutionalization. Trinidad serves as a launching point beyond Antigua and Barbuda to better understand how Charismatic religion moves across borders in the Caribbean world.

GO-ALONG ETHNOGRAPHY WITH APOSTLE ANDREWS AND BISHOP JOHN

Apostle Andrews (Apostle) and Bishop John (Bishop) met years ago while formally training to become religious leaders at PAWI's "The West Indian School of Theology" located in Maracas Valley, St. Joseph, just 13 kilometers west-southwest of Port of Spain. Now they're God's rock stars, oozing confidence everywhere they go, as others seem to defer to these men who look even larger than they stand. The ethnographer becomes but a shadow following the Big Two—"Apostle" and "Bishop"—as they conduct their everyday activities. The daily lives of these two men involve such "routines" as participating in radio interviews, performing exorcisms on the demonically possessed, leading healing rituals and spiritual revivals, as well as their regular church services that often involve tongue-speaking, spiritual warfare, and religious empowerment. Confident of their "divine" mission, these men readily open up their public and private lives, including their thoughts and feelings prior to and after these "mundane" everyday events.

The plane lands at 12:30 in the afternoon at Piarco International Airport just 15 miles east of Port of Spain. Apostle strolls out of the airport in Hollywood style business attire, and like a celebrity, waits for his chauffeur to take him to the Hilton just northeast of Queen's Park Savannah where one of the world's largest roundabouts circles the huge park. He takes in a large breath, absorbing the moment of his return home, in the same region as his current residence in Antigua but still seemingly worlds apart. He looks left and right with a huge genuine grin on his face, though his eyes remain hidden behind dark shades. Born in the Trinidadian borough of Arima, Apostle left his country as an ordinary man living in or near poverty conditions. Now he returns home as one of the richest and most successful Pentecostal preachers in the West Indies and beyond. Apostle holds power and prestige with the Pentecostal movement in the Caribbean. This puts him in a position of power over his friend and colleague Bishop, who has just opened his fourth PAWI-affiliated church in the island of Trinidad under the auspices of Covenant House of Praise, though this new church sits outside of his jurisdiction in the suburb of Barataria. Formal PAWI rules prohibit pastors from opening new churches outside their jurisdiction, but Bishop is no ordinary man.

Bishop Andrew John and his Fourth New Church

At the age of 57, Bishop's list of credentials resembles a religious version of a distinguished professor from Oxford. He has a Bachelor's and Master's Degree in Theology from Florida's Jacksonville Theological Seminary and is a graduate of the West Indies School of Theology with a Theology degree. Bishop received an Honorary Doctorate from St. Thomas Christian College. He serves as the president of Caribbean Ministers International and sits as a member of the International College of Bishops.

Bishop became a born-again Christian 40 years ago and has served as a pastor for over 35 years. Now he is the Senior Pastor of the Covenant House of Praise with five locations in Trinidad. Ordained as a minister with the PAWI, he has held various titles within its ranks that include serving as a member of the PAWI's General Executive, Men's Ministries General Director, bishop of the North West District, the Men's Director and Youth Director, member of the Board of Directors of the West Indies School of Theology, and Missions Promoter of the organization. But his positions of status go beyond PAWI.

He holds power as an Executive Member of the Evangelical Council of Churches of Trinidad and Tobago and the Full Gospel Association of Trinidad and Tobago. He also helps promote national conferences featuring big name international speakers from around the world. Outside of his institutional affiliations, Bishop works in the community offering preschool, nursery, and adult education through his Covenant Foundation Learning Center. His church also owns real estate property throughout Trinidad. Bishop the "Apostle of Prayer" reaches large audiences throughout Trinidad and the broader Caribbean hosting the morning show "City Prayer" on 98.1 FM that broadcasts live from the Globe Cinema in Port of Spain through Family Focus Broadcasting, where Bishop sits as an Advisor to the Board of Directors. Aside from his many community events, from revival meetings to church services, he reaches audiences beyond his community through the use of radio and social media helping to grow his ministry throughout the Caribbean. But the path to becoming one of the most successful religious leaders in Trinidad involved humble beginnings.

Bishop's mother was too young to raise him. Instead, his Salvation Army street preacher great aunt Martha Clark took over the job while also raising her other children in the streets of Trinidad. It did not take long for the young Bishop to become accustomed to the world of street preachers as, he says, "We played around her skirt." This early childhood experience provided the context for which Bishop developed the drive to become a religious leader. The world of street preachers became part of his everyday experiences, part of his cultural milieu that led to his ascent to some of the highest ranks within the Pentecostal West Indies power structure. But his success was nearly derailed less than a year ago when he suffered a heart attack that required triple bypass surgery.

Bishop ignored early warnings of his heart condition when he refused to complete treatment after suffering from what his doctors later reported as a minor heart attack on Christmas Eve. Although he eventually checked into the hospital that night at the urging of his son, he never followed through to seek treatment for his condition. On a trip two years later, while guest preaching at local churches in Florida and attended a T.D. Jakes conference in Orlando, he went shopping with his 25-member church crew from Trinidad where, as he describes it, "I literally shopped until I dropped." Tests from the Florida hospital found that not only did he suffer from heart disease but also an aneurism that required immediate surgery. Bishop now opens his fourth new church only three months removed from triple bypass surgery. He performs his functions as a religious leader without any noticeable evidence that he suffered a heart attack and endured a serious surgery. Even his preaching remains on fire with the thunder of a Charismatic Christian pastor.

Charismatic Christian religious leaders often bring guests to preach at their services during special events, especially to christen the establishment of a new church. Bishop hands over the church reigns to his trusted confidant Apostle to guest preach for four straight days.

Bishop's fourth new church in the Port of Spain suburb of Barataria sits inside a plain and simple building on a busy avenue. But like many Pentecostal churches, the unimpressive façade outside the building hides the impressive energy inside its walls. After a warm greeting complete with a "bear hug" common among long-established friends, Apostle and Bishop enter the church filled to capacity. Wearing a plain black t-shirt, gray sports jacket with a white handkerchief sticking out of the pocket, and khaki pants, Bishop walks to the lectern with a macho swagger and imposing confidence. He introduces Apostle as the guest preacher for the next four nights. But for most of the congregation, the introduction was mere formality. Most members of this congregation already know the Apostle from frequent visits to the church for important occasions such as this. Apostle and Bishop often travel back and forth between Antigua and Trinidad using informal networks of support to foster the growth of their churches. This reveals how Charismatic leaders within sterile bureaucratic organization retain charisma within an institution despite its tendency to extinguish the fire.

CHARISMATIC INFORMAL NETWORKS WITHIN THE IRON CAGE OF RATIONALITY

Religious leaders in large institutionalized churches such as PAWI often rely on their formal networks of support to wield power and authority as well as accomplish their respective missions. When institutions mature to resemble Weber's iron cage of (ir)rationality, Charismatic religious leaders emerge to "re-charismaticize" the cold and dry institutions from its web of rules, dogmas, and procedures. These Charismatic leaders begin to create and rely on their informal networks of support over their institutional connections.

Although Bishop and Apostle have access to institutional resources and power within the ranks of PAWI—that offers everything from church guidance and counseling to financial assistance to guest preachers for special events—they create their own Charismatic informal networks of support to empower their churches and spread their influence throughout the Caribbean. Ironically, it's the high degree of formal institutionalization in the Charismatic Christian Church in the Caribbean that allows charisma to informally flourish within its hierarchical ranks. When institutionalization produces rigid bureaucracy, it sparks charisma and reinvigorates the institution from the long slumber of modernity.

Religious pastors holding high positions emerge as potentially Charismatic when they become skeptical of other administratively motivated religious leaders more focused on the bureaucratic rules, policies, and regulations of the organization. These now Charismatic pastors begin to challenge the rule enforcing bureaucrats eager to enforce discipline. Charisma in all its forms necessarily resists institutionalization and subverts its domination. Pastors lose trust of other religious leaders within an institution obsessed with formal rules, regulations, and procedures. This becomes evident with the trust relationships that emerge among religious leaders, especially when inviting others within the private spaces of their home congregations.

Allowing outsiders from the high ranks of PAWI into their churches subject pastors to institutional scrutiny from rule and policy obsessed bureaucratic religious leaders. Informal networks of support protect preachers from hosting unfamiliar religious leaders, often people they distrust or find suspicious. Friends and other trusted connections, on the other hand, form what I call "informal charismatic trust networks" that become increasingly important for an institution where rules and regulations dominate religious policy and the message of the movement. As a result, pastors create their own networks to provide for themselves access to resources both inside and out of their institutions. Sometimes religious leaders within PAWI will turn to other trusted religious leaders for support from within the organization, just like Apostle and Bishop. At other times, these same religious leaders develop informal networks from outside the organization, and beyond the control of it. Charismatic religious leaders often establish these outside informal networks with other religious leaders, radio and television stations, political leaders, and successful businessmen. Whether inside or outside of their formal institutions, pastors develop their own sense of charisma establishing these informal networks of support through making friendships and agreements with people in places of power.

Further, Charismatic men such as Bishop and Apostle cannot operate within the limitations of bureaucratic control and institutional domination. They certainly did not rise from poverty to become millionaire preachers through conforming to any system. The pressure within the cold iron cage of rationality explodes into a Charismatic mess that gives rise to "informal charismatic trust networks" that empower Charismatic leaders to spread their influence throughout the Caribbean.

Charismatic Preaching in Trinidad: Insights into Apostle's First Night Guest Preaching

Apostle, announced as the "powerful man of Almighty God," offers a testimonial about a missionary trip to Barbados that involves a discussion about Satan's activities in the Caribbean. In this story, Apostle reports that a man approached him after that meeting in Barbados stating that he was a Satanist. The Apostle explains:

> I came across a very interesting man who openly said to me, "I am a Satanist." As he looked me in the eyes, he said, "I hate you." I replied, "Well, I love you because my love is stronger than evil." He said something that I will never forget. He says, "We know who you are. We heard about you messing with our work in Antigua."

This story lays the groundwork for another story that involves a nearly tragic event that connects to this demonic warning. The story shows how Caribbean Pentecostals, and their leaders, rely on testimonies to show how supernatural forces work to forecast future events, and serve as warnings to overcome potential tragedies. It is these types of stories that penetrate deeply into the culture of the Caribbean. This particular event happened three months after the warning on a missionary trip to Trinidad. In this story, Andrews explains how Satan actively attempts to sabotage God's will through intervening in the lives of religious leaders. In this case, Satan causes a car accident to keep him from fulfilling God's divine plan. He says:

> It was late. I was preaching on a missionary trip with a group of believers from Antigua. I drove south to pick my wife up and my two kids along with two other members. I was just about two minutes away from Barataria when the car crashed. Everybody in the car fell asleep, including myself. When the car hit the wall, I could recall my wife calling that name, Jesus! And that awoke me, but it was too late. The vehicle turned over and hit the road and at the end of the day it was written off. The wheels were spinning while the engine was running. I could hear the cry of one of my children. We were upside down and my hand somehow dragged in the road and split open and blood started pouring out. Eventually one of our members, he was in the vehicle, stuck in the middle of the road, and then came to my rescue to help get me out of the vehicle. According to my wife, she said I was fine. But broken glass (was in my arm), and (I) ended up in the hospital.

Apostle recalls the excruciating pain in his arm and the events leading to the surgery needed to repair it. As the nurse gave him an anesthetic, he realizes his mortality and experiences a transcendental state of awareness where his spirit elevates out his body and into the supernatural realm. He meets a man who asks, "Son, what are you doing here?" Without waiting for a reply to this rhetorical question, the man informs Apostle, "Satan tried to take you out. Go back to Antigua and finish my work." Staring at the congregation with watering eyes, the Apostle says with trembling words, "And in that moment, I jumped up with tears in my eyes."

This story resonates with church congregation members who believe that the supernatural world shapes the physical world of everyday life. The message is clear; Satan's forces operate in our daily life and threaten to destroy us. The latent function of the story serves to convey the message that he is indeed a man on a direct mission from God. Stories such as this serve as a way for preachers to establish their importance and legitimacy to preach in front of the congregation in a more humble way rather than listing off credentials. Practically, it also opens the way for a transition to shift the mood from an intense emotional atmosphere to one of determination and rejoice.

Suddenly, the Apostle shouts with force how the power of Jesus elevates the soul and all who seek out the divine. But he warns, transitioning once again to an intense moment of fear, about the dangers of the "contaminated soul" using a biblical character named "Haran" to substantiate his message about how contaminated souls get stuck in places while those who follow God refuse to get stuck in either physical or mental places. Rather, like Abram on the way to Canaan, they move on to perform God's will. Moving between personal anecdotes to empowering messages for the congregation, Apostle claims that his work in Antigua is a prophetic destination while the congregation members have a divinely inspired road. Apostle says, "You are going somewhere-ah. You will not stop-ah. You shall go on-ah. God will deliver-aah." Aahuh. Aahuh. Aahuh. Andrews slowly begins the incantation, "My love is stronger than evil! I am going somewhere" as the crowd repeats it in a slow, melodic chant. As the congregation chants, the Apostle states, "Beware of the contamination of your soul because one day, it will hinder your momentum."

The sweat pours from his forehead as his suit becomes drenched with the perspiration from such fervent physical exertion. He shouts at one moment and falls to his knees at another. His stories suddenly yet somehow smoothly move from personal stories to prophetic messages. At times he cries with tears streaming down his face while, almost immediately, he regains complete composure turning determined and resilient. In fact, resiliency becomes the message. In the face of adversity, one must move forward and beyond.

The preaching now refocuses on the power of positive thinking and the dangers of negativity. Negative thinking, he says, characterizes the contaminated soul. Negative thinking makes people stuck and prevents those who harbor such thoughts from fulfilling their destiny that is part of God's plan. Apostle begs the congregation to think in positive ways to complete God's ordained destination for the believer. The message, like Stuart "I'm good enough" Little, is to think positive.

Pulling it back for a moment, Apostle looks around the congregation in silence giving the audience time to reflect. His silence emits the feeling similar to the calm before a hurricane. In a low whisper, he begins to repeat the phrase, "The danger of a contaminated soul" that becomes a full-blown chant that paves the way for another story about avoiding the negativity of a contaminated soul:

> I was told to go to the bank and I listened to that voice for one minute and went to the bank and the bank turned me down. He turned to me saying, "You're not gonna get this money." And I turned to him, in the midst of the disappointment, and said, "Sir, I will build that building (referring to his new million-dollar church in Antigua) debt free, and you will hear of it."

This message shows how material forces, including institutions such as banks, attempt to hold down the fire, the Charismatic will of God. His message relates that institutions must now disempower the people, must not hold them down in their mission to achieve their will, a divine will. The belief is that demonic forces enter into human vessels who sit in high places of power, like money-lending banks, and attempt to hold people down. Many Pentecostals believe that these demonic forces influence people to obstruct God's will. And Satan does not choose these demons at random. Rather, he assigns them to attack specific targets, people with power. In this context, the believer must do whatever it takes to prevent Satan and his forces from impeding one's destiny to carry out God's will, including resisting and subverting the institution. Resisting institutional power becomes a moral imperative to achieve a higher purpose, a noble endeavor for a born-again believer believed to be a soldier in God's army. Andrews explains, at first in a matter-of-fact tone, "You see, there are those that are assigned to hinder you from getting to the place that you're supposed to get to." Apostle continues the pattern of moving between danger and resiliency. The bank, symbolic of an institutional obstacle to prevent God's will of building a new church in Antigua, obstructs divine design. The believer, refusing to show the character of the contaminated soul, must show resiliency. The message is that born-again Christians must use their agency[4] to become their own Charismatic leaders to subvert illegitimate forms of power, sometimes in the form of institutions and their leaders, to achieve the will of God. Resiliency and charisma in the face of overwhelming outside forces becomes the new message.

Apostle paces the room like a lion pondering his prey. He walks then runs as he screams, "Sometimes you have to walk over some people. You've got to run over them. You've got to shove over them. They're not going to stop you. You have to run through them because God ordained you." Although Pentecostals espouse values of peace, that does not translate to turning the other cheek. Satan must be defeated, never allowed to win. Charisma must defy control, for it's charisma that has the power to run over and shove institutional domination.

The screaming turns to joy as the congregation responds with unchecked excitement while jumping to their feet. Apostle shouts like an announcer to the heavy weight fight, "Give him some classic praise. Hallelujah! Hallelujah! Hallelujah! Hallelujah! Hallelujah! Hallelujah!" Wild and raw and free, the apostle paces back and forth on the dais where an elaborate glass lectern stands of a fleur-de-lis carpet. He urges the congregation to consider that it is not always Satan that serves as the enemy, but the negativity that results from his influence. Show resolve, he pleas, and unwavering belief in God that He casts away all doubts about His ability.

Apostle redirects attention to the establishment of Bishop's fourth new church in Trinidad, one that violates PAWI's institutional policy. Apostle proclaims, "If your bishop was a doubter, he would still be holding on to one church that he's PAWI officially allowed [by PAWI]. He understands that's what God wants for him. Very few people understand that." Now fixing his gaze upon the congregation, he points to them stating with certainty, "But if you hear from God, forget about your credits. If you know what you love, forget about what they're saying. If you know that it's God, you keep on going." This message shows Pentecostal leaders believe that God's law carries more legitimate weight that the rules and regulations of man's law embodied in institutions. Bishop might be violating the formal rules of PAWI but his primary mandate requires listening to God. Charisma trumps the institution. The congregation must become Charismatic too.

Like a Pentecostal version of New Orleans's Rebirth Brass Band "Do whatcha wanna," Apostle advises the congregation to adhere to the Charismatic defiance of institutionalization, "I say do what you gotta do, and learn to overcome evil. Learn to love those that hurt me and do good to them." He claims that listening to God allowed Bishop to open up his fourth church, against institutionalization. He returns to the message getting stuck, indicating that man's law embedded in the modern institution stifles us and prevents God's will from realization. Now fully animated and building steam, he loudly proclaims, "We have a purpose, a destiny to fulfill the will of God." The Charismatic Apostle emphatically screams, "I'm going somewhere. Are you going somewhere tonight? There is a destination. And you cannot avoid it; do not let anything hinder your onward momentum. There is a destination." Charisma allows for movement beyond the ordinary. Perhaps channeling Weber himself, the preacher argues for the congregation to listen to God directly and defy any obstacles that prevent the actualization of God's will. It's all about resilience and agency to achieve great things. He says, "I became pregnant with visions and dreams of what I wanted to do for God. I knew that it just wasn't what he wanted for me. I knew he wanted something bigger and more majestic. I knew that I couldn't stop when people wanted me to stop."

Apostle presses the congregation to overcome seemingly insurmountable obstacles to fulfill God's will. The enemies are those who attempt to prevent that will from realization. Sometimes Satan permeates people and institutions, as well as religious leaders within them. Regardless of the enemy, one must disappoint their enemies to achieve higher, more divine purposes.

> I rose up one day and God said to me, "Stephen, disappoint your enemies." I said, "What do you mean by that?" He said, "Disappoint them by exceeding expectations. They expect you to give up. Don't ever give up. They expect you to die. Don't ever die. They expect you to stop. Don't ever stop. They expect you to throw your hands up and say, 'I've had enough.' Don't ever do that.'" God said, "Disappoint them by living, by continuing, by preaching, by praying, and I ask that you disappoint your enemies." Because God told me these things, I'm living the way I'm living.

Charisma, that's the message. The Charismatic figure talks directly to God and overcomes human obstacles that try to prevent divine will. Apostle uses his informal Charismatic religious networking as evidence:

> The Lord spoke to me one day and says, "Stephen, I want you to partnership with Abundant Life Radio. It is a twenty-four hour gospel radio station in Barbuda. There is [previously] none in Antigua. So, people came to me and said, "Well, pastor, you can start your own radio station." I said,

"Yes I can. But if I do, I will compete with one that already exists." And that would create competition and division among the body of Christ. If I do, I will divide the listeners. I said, "Noooooooo!" And I put everything together in our church needed for radio. I called the CEO of Abundant Life Radio. I said, "We're going to have an appointment. Instead of starting my own, I'll pay for and carry Abundant Life Radio. We have better equipment in the [church] facility, but that doesn't make me the boss. God is tired of the competition."

Apostle explains how the congregation must look at how nothing, including man's laws, has stopped Bishop from building his fourth church, despite all the obstacles. He encourages the congregation members to heed this example within their own lives. Apostle chants "You are my strength; strength like a lion" as the congregation begins to dance in a highly emotional state repeating, "You are my strength; strength like a lion."

Strength like the lion reaches to me.
You are my strength; strength like a lion.
Strength like a lion.
Strength like a lion.
Charisma is the strength of the lion with the power to free the jungle from its institutional colonization.

Networking in Trinidad: Religious Leaders of PAWI

The above event of Apostle's first night of guest preaching for Bishop's new church best exemplifies how Charismatic networking operates in the everyday practices of religious leaders. Later that evening after the first church service, Apostle and Bishop discuss the importance of spreading the Charismatic Christian message to the Caribbean while at a restaurant in the Port of Spain neighborhood of Woodbrook. Andrews describes this mission as "carrying the burden to deliverance" to fulfill God's plans. This networking continues on the radio waves of the Caribbean.

We meet the next day at 8 a.m. for an interview with I.S.A.A.C 98.1 FM Christian Radio Family Focus Broadcasting Network. Religiously inspired radio stations in the Caribbean network together with other stations to multiply their broadcasts to other islands. For example, the radio station Family Focus links up with the popular Abundant Life Radio to broadcast religious messages throughout the Caribbean. Networking through radio serves as an essential way to broadcast the Charismatic Christian message and spread its influence, both for the well-established Institutionalized Pentecostal Church as well as for the small independent church.

Bishop owns and operates a large three-story building that hosts a radio station located deep in the heart of Port of Spain that he paid over a million dollars for in cash. The radio station is heard throughout the Caribbean and beyond through its Web site. It certainly reaches Antigua and Barbuda. After hearing about my research on the radio, an interested caller from Antigua explains how the Pentecostal movement spread to the Caribbean from Montserrat eventually forming the PAWI. She goes on to explain how Charismatic religious leaders link and connect through PAWI in Trinidad. The Apostle and Bishop agree with the caller explaining how their informal friendship began from their formal training to become leaders at PAWI's West Indies School of Theology for ministerial training. It is through this organization that many pastors, both large and small, form connections and empower themselves and their ministries. As described above, Bishop and Apostle sit in high places of power within the vertically arranged institutional structure of PAWI where authority is unevenly distributed. Bishop and Apostle are Charismatic figures of authority within an institutional authoritative system. Within authoritative institutions like PAWI, two types of figures emerge—What I call the "Bureaucrasaurus" and "Charismaticrats."

MEET THE BUREAUCRASAURUS AND CHARISMATICRATS

The Bureaucrasaurus, Instituticus Modernicus, has a tiny head, long neck, rotund belly, short arms, and no doubt, small tail. Its miniscule head holds just enough information to process the procedures of the bureaucratic machine, stamping all the forms and ensuring the following of rules and regulations according to its bylaws. The wee brain inside the skull produces simplistic factual knowledge systems of mechanistic codes and procedures merely for the functioning of the system void of emotions and creativity. The elongated neck serves as a vertical space to hold gradational levels of hierarchy where each level controls the level below and is controlled by the level above to make for a more efficient centralized decision-making process. The fat round belly serves as a mega-warehouse filing system for storing stamped forms, meeting minutes, outcomes of disciplinary hearings, organizational procedures, official letters, doctrines, dogmas, and procedures to keep for the smooth functioning of its mundane operations. The short arms indicate the now long faded hope of desperately reaching out for something more but never to any avail. The pitiful tail exposes its real inner shame and humiliation that only the enforcement of rules and authority redeems, even if only imagined.[5]

The Bureaucrasaurus serves as obstructive bureaucrats more concerned with gaining personal control, power, and influence within an organization rather than pursuing its actual goals. They use formal rules, procedures, and guidelines to rise in organizational rank, often at the expense of others within it. In the case of organizations like PAWI, the Bureaucrasaurus becomes myopic, one-dimensional creatures hell bent on following and enforcing rules rather than the Charismatic message of Pentecostalism that ignited the great worldwide movement. We cannot know for sure if these men and women attempt to achieve personal gain through kicking other people in the teeth, or if they simply are an exaggerated version of Robert Merton's[6] ritualist succumbing to the defeat of personal failure while using rules to hold others down—a Charismatic-blocker.

Charismaticrats, on the other hand, refer to Charismatic religious leaders who retain their charisma despite involvement within an authoritative institution with a hierarchical and bureaucratic power structure. These Charismatic leaders derive their authority more through their ability to impart the perception of their superhuman abilities to others (direct access to God) rather than through their institutional belonging. They negotiate with the institution offering a mutually beneficial relationship that empowers both the institution and the leader. For the institution, Charismatic leaders make the institution seem more Charismatic and increases membership of the overall organization while also acquiring religious leaders of economic and political influence. For the Charismaticrats, institutional belonging enhances their Charismatic perceptions through participation into a power structure that their own charisma empowers for the institution. They find what I call "lagniappe legitimacy"[7] that offers extra authority to their already established but informal Charismatic authority which increases their "official" legitimacy to members of their congregation. They also receive an added prestige of position within a "respected" official organization—like a professor finds when appointed to a posh Ivy League university.

They take on leadership roles but refuse to apply harsh or strict rules to themselves or others. Rather, they do not attempt to hold others down and expect the same treatment—and when others try to hold them down, sometimes they have to "walk over," "run over," and "shove" people in their way. Just like the Pentecostal movement in small churches throughout the USA and Caribbean, they successfully balance the forces of charisma and bureaucratic rule. They take on the radical philosophy of "Do what you want" so long it's using personal charisma to fulfill God's mission. While the institution provides mutual benefits, Charismaticrats allow for minor control and oversight of their churches. But when they have a mission to accomplish, their charisma and Charismatic networking takes precedence over the institution though not its original mission. What is more, these men climb into the high ranks institutional authority using their personal Charismatic qualities and, in so doing, achieve large congregational followings and political and economic influence. Just like the "Too big to fail" American corporations, they become "Too big to control" religious leaders within the great religious institutions of their time. And that exactly describes Apostle and Bishop, "Too big to control" Charismaticrats. Ironically, Charismaticrats help balance charisma and the rationalizing forces of modernity threatening to succumb the great Pentecostal movement into an institutional iron cage.

WHY DOES CHARISMA CHOOSE TO REMAIN IN CHECK?

As Bishop opened his new church, Apostle received a large promotion within the ranks of PAWI and now leads 16 churches in Antigua, Barbuda, and St. Kitts. Both men have some of the largest churches in their respective countries with large national and international followings. The path to success within PAWI and their own largely independent churches grew simultaneously with their friendship. As mentioned above, although they first met at the West Indies School of Theology, it was a more natural and informal setting that led to their networking.

Bishop fondly recalls first meeting Apostle, "When I was going through the leadership of the organization, you see a kindred spirit, you get closer to them because they share the same vision, the personal vision that you share. You are able to make connections and establish relationships out of those contacts." While Bishop trained to become a "missions" leader in the organization, Apostle was training to be a mission's promoter, or what he calls an itinerant speaker traveling throughout the Caribbean guest appearing in various churches. Meeting people in PAWI's official theological school as well as the apprentice-type training traveling throughout the Caribbean guest preaching where—despite the formal institutional organization of PAWI and its bureaucracy—Charismatic Christian leaders established these Charismatic forms of networking that lead to their success both in and out of PAWI. Apostle recalls, "So you went through [the institution], and you meet guys and develop relationships. You see each other grow. Because we were not what we are today, we all grew together. This is where we made relationships to help each other grow." In fact, Apostle served as an itinerant speaker for four years prior to becoming a full-time pastor allowing him to develop vast networks with dozens of preachers and religious leaders throughout the Caribbean and beyond, including with many preachers from the Caribbean now preaching in the USA. These men of charisma now hold wealth, power, and influence. This begs the question of why Charismatic religious leaders with wealth and power remain under the control and influence of large and sometimes stifling bureaucratic structures. Perhaps finding success as religious leaders served as their original motivation to join PAWI, but what now keeps these now powerful religious leaders within it?

In the Caribbean world plagued with political and economic corruption, Charismatic religious leaders in the Caribbean need to protect themselves from perceptions of corruption. The perception of corruption will destroy the charisma of most religious leaders. Institutional belonging offers protection from such scandals that can destroy reputations. Bishop and Apostle call it accountability. Bishop says, "You don't want to be like a runaway horse. So you need somebody [pastors] who wants to be accountable to their congregation so that they provide a sense of safety." Bishop continues:

> You can easily become so independent that you become dangerous to your own self. You want to be in that place where you have coverage in terms of your accountability financially, morally, and spiritually. You want accountability of your social relationship with your congregation, you want to have fellas who can become like your reagents that will be there with you and give you a good complement to what you are doing.

The benefits of institutional belonging, both Apostle and Bishop stress, never threaten their highly independent churches in just about all regards, including in the churches' financing and governance.

Aside from accountability, successful pastors find other personal and practical reasons for remaining in the highly institutionalized PAWI. For Bishop, it provides the opportunity to make genuine friendships with other leaders to avoid what he calls the loneliness of the religious leaders.

Those on top, he holds, have few people to serve as private confidants. Leaders with high status in a community and organization have fewer friendships and less people to confide in about personal matters. Simply put, life is lonely at the top. As Bishop puts it, "The ministry, as much as you have thousands of people around you, can be a very lonely place for a leader. This is because you are influencing hundreds of people from all walks of life. When you are an established church in a nation or a community, who do you go to share your personal struggles?" It's difficult to confide with other people lower on the socio-religious hierarchy, they look up to their leaders. As a result, developing friendships with other religious leaders who share power within a central organization offers the opportunity relate to a confidant who wields similar power and shares common concerns. Of course, religious leaders must be careful with whom they share their concerns with, so as not to make one vulnerable to others seeking power and prestige in the organization. Access to the formal institution allows the opportunity to form genuine relationships and develop Charismatic networks; it takes personal charisma to realize those opportunities.

Bishop explains the need to make oneself vulnerable to others in order to establish a genuine relationship where leaders can fully express their concerns and fears. He admits, "You need someone who you can relate to, who can see you and your humanity. [Someone] you can feel comfortable with letting down your hair. You need that kind of camaraderie where you can relate to people at that personal level who also share a lot of common things with you." This form of mutual camaraderie offers both a sense of comfort and the opportunity to continue traveling around the Caribbean to network and preach to others from around the region. It also creates a sense of home while traveling to neighboring countries. As Apostle warmly expresses to his friend, "I can go there any time [Bishop's church]. His home is like my home; my home is like his home. The relationship is a personal friendship that we have developed."

PAWI membership involves other informal benefits that keep Charismatic religious leaders in the organization. Influential religious leaders, much like highly valued professors in a university, rely on knowledge beyond the theoretical ideas found in textbooks. Rather, they use their personal experiences beyond their formal theological training to incorporate experience "in the field" that involves conducting ministerial works in the real world of everyday life. For example, Bishop explains that bringing Apostle to guest preach for the initiation of his fourth new church offers his congregation new experiences from his own personal connections to "high men of God." Apostle states, "This is not theoretical experience; rather, he is so experienced that he has walked the walk. You don't want somebody who just speaks from a textbook. You want to speak from experience." As a result, bringing in a Charismatic religious figure with "rock star"—as many people consider Apostle—attributes increases the status of other Charismatic religious leaders through their personal connections. It also helps that Apostle's radio voice with Abundant Life Radio transmits to thousands of listeners throughout the Caribbean, further increasing the legitimization of another pastor and giving added pertinence to his mission. With a well-known religious leader guest preaching, a pastor opening a new church gives his new project a sense of increased legitimacy and importance, as well as offers the chance to increase attendance in the precarious early days of the church's growth. Bishop confidently expresses, "Like Friday night, I guarantee you Saturday night, we will not have an empty seat in the congregation. ... By Friday night, God willing, we're going to have problems in the car parking lot."

In short, Charismatic religious leaders and their authoritative institutions serve as a mutually beneficial relationship. While Charismaticrats help retain charisma in an institution, Bureaucrasaurus's attempt to reinforce the institutions rules and policies over institutionalizes the movement into a rigid bureaucracy which, in turn, creates the need for Charismatic religious leaders to continue creating "informal charismatic trust networks." Although Institutional charisma opens the door, personal charisma allows one to walk through it.

Religious Leaders and Politics in the Caribbean

At the posh Hilton Hotel in Port of Spain overlooking the Gulf of Paria, servers scurry about waiting on patrons, bussing tables, and keeping pace to fill up the breakfast buffet for a hungry Thursday morning crowd. Apostle and Bishop seem relaxed after a radio interview about my research and their upcoming trip to Jerusalem. Perhaps this is why they spoke openly and candidly for hours discussing the Charismatic movement in the Caribbean and its impact on politics throughout the region. As Bishop puts it, politics in Trinidad needs to move "from police and thief to police and priest." Apostle and Bishop believe that if the secularized state produced a Trinidadian society composed of "police and thief," the new direction of the country should be one where the church plays a vital role in the country's affairs transforming it to the influences of "police and priest."

But this involves a new and emerging role of religion and politics in Trinidad forming the trio "The big three"—Government, Police/Military, and Church—to impact the political and economic future of the region.

Bishop claims to have the ear of the political elite in Trinidad, especially when an Afro-Trinidadian, the ethnic Indo-Trinidadian and the first female Prime Minister of Trinidad and Tobago, Kamla Persad-Bissessar. Although she is born of Hindu parents, the Prime Minister claims to be both Hindu and Baptist. Perhaps because she is a Prime Minister with a Hindu background in a majority Christian country, she does not seek religious council with any known religious group in Trinidad, claiming instead to seek guidance in her "personal faith" in God.[8] But even while an ethnic Indo-Trinidadian with a Hindu background holds political power, Bishop says he enjoys the ear of the political opposition who often seek his council on public and private matters. Of course, he claims, such council must be kept behind closed doors due to the tenuous political relationship between Indo- and Afro-Trinidadians, especially as it relates to political and religious issues. Despite the ethnic and racial tensions that exist between Indo-and Afro-Trinidadians, it's visually evident that many people of Indian descent attend Apostle's church. He argues that this is a positive sign for the health of a nation when two "races" attend the same church admitting that, "very rarely do we find so many African pastors having so many Indians in his ministries, like how I have."

Both Apostle and Bishop prefer born-again Christians to rule the country. They agree that, "The bible shows [that] when the righteous rule, the nation is at peace." When asked if the nation was at peace when the opposition (People's National Movement) was in power, Apostle rationalizes that the nation fell short of achieving peace because of former Prime Minister Patrick Manning's backsliding, a term known to many Charismatic Christians that refers to a born-again believer who has turned away from God. This is one reason why many Christian leaders in the English-speaking Caribbean, such as Apostle and Bishop, believe that the church must play a larger role in the politics and economics of a country.

Commenting on a recent conference in Trinidad that involved a discussion on the church's role in the country's affairs, Bishop states, "For the first time, the church has really stuck in to be the balance of the socio-economic strength of the country as well as the political and conscious voice. So long ago it used to be police and thief, now, for the transformation of Trinidad & Tobago, its gotta be police and priests." He argues that the church is now becoming part of the "Big Three" that involves the church's emerging role along with the government and military to lead the country. The military, he explains, cannot operate unfettered without any checks and balances. The only other institution that can balance the behavior of the police and assist in their efforts to make the streets safe, what he refers to as improving the moral conduct of society, is the church. He argues, "The church must work with the police and military; they are the two worlds that bring the moral conduct of the country into sharp focus." While the church works with the police to regulate both police behavior and the behavior of potentially violent members of the community, the church must also work closely with the government, regardless of who holds power. Bishop suggests that the church's role in public affairs should no longer be kept behind closed doors. Just like the Charismatic movement pushed religion from the private to the public, Bishop argues that, "The church must rise to be a very visible partner with the police and government."

Just as many other leaders of the Charismatic movement in the Caribbean argue, Apostle and Bishop believe that without the role of the church in public affairs, it is impossible to trust the government (Prime Minister and cabinet) and military (including police). As Bishop puts it, "The government cannot function as a failed state and the military cannot function if they are not trusted. And the institution to hold those two projects together is the church." According to both Bishop and Apostle, the government, military, and church—or "The Big Three"—must work simultaneously together to lead the Caribbean region into the future. Almost as if stating on a microphone to world leaders, Bishop proclaims, "So the church cannot do it alone. The police cannot do it alone. The government cannot do it alone. All three of us realize we need one another." Perhaps the economic and political elite of the Caribbean heard this message as a dramatic turning point recently occurred in the Caribbean. The first steps of increased visibility began in the first months of 2014.

THE BIG THREE: CARICOM THE NEW ROLE
OF RELIGION IN THE CARIBBEAN

The CARICOM held its first Regional Inter-Faith Conference to invite the input of FBOs into the CARICOM Change Process on Monday, February 17, 2014 at the Jolly Harbour Resort in Antigua and Barbuda. This meeting happened due to a request from Antigua and Barbuda's Prime Minister Baldwin Spencer for religious faiths to become involved in the CARICOM change process. At this meeting, CARICOM officially asked religious leaders in the Caribbean to join the ranks of power in the political and economic affairs of the region. Perhaps Bishop's claim that religion is now one of the "big three" is more than simply unwarranted bravado.

The CARICOM is an organization established in 1973 that is composed of 15 mainly English-Speaking nations including Antigua and Barbuda, Bahamas, Barbados, Belize, Dominica, Grenada, Guyana, Haiti, Jamaica, Montserrat, St. Kitts and Nevis, St. Lucia, St. Vincent and the Grenadines, Suriname, and Trinidad and Tobago. According to its website, CARICOM seeks to promote economic integration and cooperation among its members, ensure the equitable sharing of benefits of integration, and coordinate foreign policy. CARICOM coordinates economic policies and development planning, devises and institutes special projects for LDCs within its jurisdiction, operates as a regional single market for many of its members, and handles regional trade disputes. Although dominantly made up of the English-speaking Caribbean countries, French-Speaking Suriname and Creole-speaking Haiti joined, respectively, in 1995 and 2002.

The first CARICOM Inter-Faith Service and Conference called for religious organizations to work closely with political and economic leaders to shape responses to the many challenges that face the region, especially the social and political issues of the Caribbean community. According to the Jamaican Observer, this conference involved religious leaders of "all faiths practiced in the community" as well as leaders of national and regional umbrella FBOs. The leaders of CARICOM invited religious leaders to emerge as a stronger force shaping the political and economic affairs of the English-speaking Caribbean creating a regional consultative process for religious groups to shape the decision-making process in the Caribbean. If the call in areas north of the Caribbean is to separate church and state, the opposite phenomenon is happening in the Caribbean where political and economic leaders of the region call for religious leaders to make a larger impact in the Caribbean. As Bishop proclaims, the "Prime Minister and her cabinet have the power to run the country. The police have the power to keep the country protected and safe. The church is the voice of the conscience. ... We need men who hail from God to speak to the nation."

The only problem, of course, is what happens to well-meaning religious leaders when they join the rank and file of the political and economic elite. Once in power, these leaders often become part of the Black Urban Regime Coalition[9] that supports the global elite including investors from the tourist industry at the expense of the people. Powerful grassroots organizations and social movements, like the Charismatic Christian movement, that once defended the people of the Caribbean community become vulnerable to being co-opted into the hands of the political and economic elite using the thin veil of neo-liberal economic policies to policy makers, nonprofit organizations, non-governmental organizations, the elite of the tourist regime, and real estate investment teams. As the political and economic elite of the Caribbean, including CARICOM, continues supporting big investors and tourist vultures, often at the expense of their supporters, the people of the Caribbean are put in harm's way of an avalanche of problems threatening to crush their region.[10]

MR. BIGS: THE POLITICAL, ECONOMIC, AND RELIGIOUS ELITE

The church's new role in shaping the Caribbean region increases today but still remains in its infancy stage. As religious leaders attempt to unite the Christian churches to become a larger voice shaping regional affairs, it also remains unclear how religious leaders will play a larger role and exactly how it will provide leadership as well as toward what issues. Many Charismatic religious leaders in the Caribbean seem obsessed with the usual suspect issues: street crime and violence, homosexuality, and gay marriage.

Ending our conversation at the Hilton, we discuss the problems of violence in Trinidad, a relevant topic in the recent spike in violent crime in Port of Spain. I challenge these religious leaders on their uncritical stance that ignores the social conditions that produce social problems while condemning the most vulnerable populations for the issues that plague their society, often the same people that attend their churches. The conversation is reported at length below:

> Marina: One of my biggest criticisms of the charismatic movement is that it's not critical enough. It keeps on attacking, saying, 'Oh, well they're just criminals, they're just gangsters.' Well, what produces the gangs? Gangs, in my view, are one of many creative responses to collectively experienced structural problems. So if you live in poverty, and you're marginalized, and you live in the ghetto, and you look at the police who come into your community and lock your brothers and sisters up as terrorists, then you're going to form organizations to protect you from the inequality and violence. So under that logic, it makes sense that people form gangs. They're trying to protect themselves from the structural inequalities and oppressions they collectively face. If you end the structural inequalities, then you end the

need for the creation of gangs. So why not look at the real source of the problem and help create an economic system that fosters greater equality and a political system that supports it? Instead, you want to join the ranks of the very systems that create the problems you want to solve.

English-speaking Caribbean Pentecostal leaders seem quite aware of the problems associated with church growth and its increasing institutionalization. These issues take on a central interest to religious leaders in Trinidad, and as it turns out, to leaders throughout the entire English-speaking Caribbean world. At the CARICOM Inter-Faith Service and Conference, Bishop spoke about how the problems of Trinidad changed from the easily identifiable racial and ethnic segregation and colonialism to a new but less visible enemy from within a new capitalist economy that has moved Trinidad from a shared economy for the nationals to a new one owned and controlled by a new economic elite. Bishop says, "Capitalism is now being reborn, and the nationals have become wealthy. And prejudism [sic], which dealt with colonialism, has been out of Mr. Bigs—all the big fellas: big religious leaders, big business-wise, and big political." The conversation continues below:

Marina: That's called post-colonialism. It's a new form of colonialism.

Bishop: Right. It's a new form of colonialism, so the church has to now be ready with the government and the police to now break up the revolution that's taking place among the poor people. Because they are now looking, as you [Peter] said, to perform their own defenses to fight against these forces.

Apostle: As you were saying (looking at me), and you were right in many ways, that our main problem deals with the institution of government right down to the church. A lot of compromises are being made, and these compromises prevent bringing about any radical changes.

Both Apostle and Bishop agree that the region needs more radical change, while also holding to the idea that these changes must be done from within the system. The problem with making changes in the system, they admit, is how church growth eventually leads to the same type of bureaucratic structure as their governmental systems. Once the church becomes institutionalized in this way, and vies for power, it joins the hierarchy of the political and economic elite. Once that happens, as Bishop admits, religious leaders make compromises and, eventually acquiesce to power or join in their endeavors. These men understand the problems associated with working outside the legitimate institutions of power. Bishop explains,

"To really bring about radical change, one has to understand martyrdom. When we look at history, from Martin Luther right down to Malcolm X, these people have to pay a price with their lives. If we interfere with the problems, the problems will interfere with us, too." Everyone nods in agreement on what happens if you go against "the man."

> Marina: Well where's our next Mahatma Ghandi, Martin Luther King and
>
> Malcolm X? Where? Who is it?
>
> Apostle: We don't know. They're in the making. They may be listening.
>
> Marina: Might be you?
>
> Apostle: Never know, might be you!
>
> [Everyone laughs]

Religious leaders like Apostle and Bishop know the problems associated with power and institutionalization within the "Big Three." They are well aware that when the church grows too big and becomes legitimated into the power structures of society, it joins those very existing power structures. They also know that growing too large and powerful makes the church vulnerable to becoming static, and worse, far removed from the people. They openly admit this fear, especially since these men serve as big players in the Charismatic movement of the Caribbean. They embody the very meaning of the big fish. Power and high position, they argue, must not necessarily side with power elite when joining its ranks. Apostle and Bishop express that they must become the elite and powerful to challenge power—particularly the government and economic elite—without joining them. They want to be part of the "Big Three" to fight the existing power structures while also admitting that the allure of power grants access to privilege that, once achieved, often becomes the very thing they are fighting against.

As we discussed the problem of placing blame on individual pathology while ignoring the structural conditions that produce the pathologies such as crime, poverty, homelessness, and environmental destruction, they agreed explaining, "We [The Pentecostal movement in the Caribbean] are not scratching where it itches." This focus to bring a large-scale change to the Charismatic churches in the Caribbean, to "scratch where it itches," they claim, now takes precedence in their mission to impart change. They urge the importance of "addressing the real hurts," and those hurts, they state, stem from the government and capitalism. They claim to want to become the powerful not to join power, but to change power.

Apostle and Bishop stress the necessity to remember their humble beginnings, engage in community activism, creating democracy in the church, outsmarting the elite by joining them to change them, creating grassroots organizations, and using social media to create personal and intimate connections with a large body of followers throughout the Caribbean to change the tide of power. In short, these religious leaders believe that a new Charismatic leader must also have the ability to defy the modern forces of rationality to resist institutional control and siding with the power elite. As Apostle puts it, "To end the structural inequality, we have to get men like Bishop John and others who possess a different mindset. So that when they get into the position to implement these changes, they can then implement these changes from within the system despite the system." Perhaps the rise of the Charismaticrats over the Bureaucrasaurus within the Charismatic Christian Movement will serve as a starting point for fomenting political and economic change in the region and keep the fire alive that sparked the original Pentecostal Movement in the Caribbean. At least in Trinidad, the Pentecostal movement in Trinidad continues its Charismatic fire that places its leaders, like Bishop and Apostle, on the same tables as the political and economic elite of CARICOM.

POVERTY PIMPS

Many outsiders to the Pentecostal Movement might view wealthy religious leaders with million-dollar buildings that house radio stations and multimillion dollar mega-churches as poverty pimps, pimping the poor for their own wealth. Religious leaders like Bishop and Apostle seem aware of this perception of many members of the mainstream secular world. To this view Bishop responds, "Let me say this, take a closer look into my life. Inspect my life and look at what I do for the people." They explain how many of the small everyday activities often go unnoticed, nor do they ever catch media attention, like waking up at three in the morning to a phone call from a congregant in crisis, or giving money to a congregant about to have furniture repossessed, or staying for two hours after church service to administer guidance to a member. Much of this resembles the life of university professors who become increasingly evaluated with quantitative numbers and pseudo-scientific formulas that measure "productivity." As many university professors offer countless unrecognized hours to help students with papers, grasping ideas, studying for exams, writing comments on papers, advising students, preparing for talks, and engaging on rich ethnographic work, the pastor finds the same plight. At least the go-alongs conducted with these pastors reveal a world where these religious leaders dedicate themselves to serving others, while also reaping the benefits of success. Outsiders must decide for themselves if religious leaders pimp the poor, but whatever the perception, it takes close inspection into the lives of religious leaders in the world where these religious lives transpire in the deep Caribbean.

NOTES

1. Trinidad is one of the islands of the dual-island nation-state of Trinidad and Tobago.
2. Georg Simmel, *The Metropolis and Mental Life. The Sociology of Georg Simmel* (New York: Free Press, 1976). Simmel argues that the urban dweller develops internal self-defensive mechanisms due to the overstimulation inhabitants of the metropolis receive in everyday life. One characteristic that develops from this internal defense system is an attitude of indifference, or what he calls the blasé attitude.
3. Aisha Khan, *Callaloo Nation: Metaphors of Race and Religious Identity among South Asians in Trinidad* (Charlotte, NC: Duke University Press, 2004).
4. This message sounds strikingly similar to the sociological concept of agency, perhaps the most beautiful concept in the English language. Agency refers to the ability of people to resist the outside structural forces that impinge upon human will. The concept holds that human beings are not determined but rather have the potential to use their limited free will when making decisions. Though free will is theologically possibility, it's a sociological impossibility. Humans remain limited within the historical period in which they live, their locations within highly unequal structural conditions, and their cultural milieus that respond to their collectively experienced structural problems. Human agency refers this to the ability of humans to make their own decisions in alternative ways to the structural pressures imposed upon them. A common theme in Pentecostal discourse is one of humans displaying a great propensity for agency, or the ability to respond to overwhelming external pressures in unexpected ways. For Pentecostals, the believer must not only deal with the external pressures of institutional forces pushing them toward certain expected responses, but also demonic forces challenging them at every turn. Although human

agency is often credited to God, it is the individual who defies all odds by surrendering their will to God. In this sense, power is found through submission.

5. This section borrows from Jock Young's "datasaur" in The Criminological Imagination (2011) critiquing positivism in mainstream criminology.

6. Sociologist Robert Merton develops a typology of five normative responses to the contradictions of cultural goals and institutional means of society. Merton's ritualists give up on their chances of achieving the cultural goals of society accepting their fate into mediocrity while also upholding the very institutions that keep them in check. Ritualists continue to subscribe to the institutional rules and policies, but reject the cultural goals of society accepting their fate into obscurity.

7. Lagniappe is a New Orleans Cajun Creole term that translates to "A little something extra." The term "lagniappe legitimacy" refers to "a little something extra" legitimacy a Charismatic religious leader receives in a formal institution.

8. See:http://www.nationnews.com/nationnews/news/50075/meet-pm-kamla#sthash.n7wa7qtP.dpuf

9. See: Adolph Reed, "The Black Urban Regime: Structural Origins and Constraints," Comparative Urban and Community Research: An Annual Review 1 (published simultaneously as Power, Community, and the City), ed. Michael Peter Smith (New Brunswick, NJ: Transaction Books, 1988).

10. Polly Pattullo, Last Resorts: The Cost of Tourism in the Caribbean (London and New York: Latin America Bureau Monthly Review Press, 2005).

CHAPTER 6

St. Lucia, Barbados, and Dominica

The Pentecostal movement exemplifies some of the great tensions of late modernity, especially between charisma and the process of institutionalization. In a fully institutionalized world, bureaucratic organization, hierarchical structure, imposed order, and scientific predictability become the order of the day and permeate every aspect of modern life. In this fully institutionalized world, reality becomes demystified, cold, calculable, and sterile, with little room for the supernatural world in all its complexities. It is Weber's iron cage of bureaucratic rationality. Weber's classic notion of charisma, on the other hand, refers to a world of innovation, spontaneity, and enchantment that permeates multiple spheres of social life, from religion to politics.[1] Charismatic leaders and movements have the ability to challenge traditional authority and a fully rationalistic world where routine, regulation, and efficiency dominate the world, even if irrational. These tensions play out in our late modern society, perhaps best exemplified in our great social and religious movements like Pentecostalism.

Scholarship on Pentecostalism and its relationship with modernity has focused on the problems for religion when it becomes institutionalized arguing that the Pentecostal movement increasingly resembles an institutional order like the Catholic Church.[2, 3] In Weber's almost Orwellian description of rationality permeating every aspect of social life, the fire of the original Pentecostal hardens into a cold and sterile institution.[4, 5] Religious movements lose their autonomy and become part of the larger society, incorporating its values and sharing its problems, developing

© The Author(s) 2016
P. Marina, *Chasing Religion in the Caribbean*,
DOI 10.1057/978-1-137-56100-8_6

"uncritical acceptance" of conservative views on national and international politics.[6] Religious movements become alienating when rituals organize and stabilize worship into an objective and systematic form. They lose autonomy and undergo a process of routinization where Weber's predictable, calculable, controllable, and efficient iron cage comes to life. Powerful ideas turn to systematic sets of principles or rules where the spirit (religious experience) is substituted for the letter (doctrine) and religious participants become religious followers.[7]

The institutionalization of Pentecostalism would be a great threat to culture as a verb, to the resistant potential of the Pentecostal movement and its ability to be a force for social change. It would be, in the end, the death of the most important and interesting aspect of the movement. Margaret Poloma argued that Pentecostalism was losing its Charismatic influences that sparked the movement as it became increasingly institutionalized. In this process of institutionalization, the Charismatic movement and its leaders join the rank and file of existing power structures and lose their potential to offer alternative solutions to modern problems, including inequality and marginality.[8] She later argued that Pentecostalism itself needs revitalization with her study of the Toronto Blessing where worship can be understood not only in relationship to religious vitality but also as a form of institutional resistance.[9] At least in the Western world, even the most astute scholars of Pentecostalism hold that it is almost impossible to prevent the movement from institutionalizing, even when periodic revivals happen. This rationalization threatens the vitality of the movement to remain a force in shaping the world today and may even lead to its eventual decline into obscurity, even in the great Caribbean islands, unless some experience of revitalization occurs.[10] However, the problem with theories forecasting the inevitability of institutionalization is that they tend to be deterministic and do not allow for observing ways in which institutionalization may be resisted or even moderated through ongoing practices of charisma.[11]

The Charismatic qualities of Pentecostalism in the Caribbean illustrate how religious leaders attempt to retain the movement's vitality as they negotiate charisma, church growth, and institutionalization. Religious leaders and pastors of the Charismatic movement in St. Lucia, Barbados, and Dominica provide insight into understanding how the Charismatic church responds and navigates through new experiences as they continue to grow and spread throughout the Caribbean. This chapter discusses issues, themes, and networking strategies within the

Charismatic movement in the English-speaking Caribbean as well as other ethnographic insights into each country focusing on questions related to institutionalization, including (1) how the Charismatic church handles church growth and power, (2) how the Charismatic church deals with both external adversity and internal conflicts, and (3) how the Charismatic church simultaneously undergoes the processes of centralization and decentralization. These themes relate to how the church struggles to maintain charisma as it continues to experience the process of institutionalization.

St. Lucia

Mountainous St. Lucia in the eastern Caribbean Sea sits exactly 14 degrees north of the equator just northwest of Barbados and directly south of French-speaking Martinique. As each Caribbean country displays a unique and vibrant culture, St. Lucia blends traditional Afro-Caribbean religion with a strong respect and fear of Obeah along with a mixture of traditional conservative and Rastafarian influences. The influences of its French Catholic colonialism persist today as Catholics compose 62 % of a population who speak English and what St. Lucians refer to as "Patwah," or a type of Antillean Creole that combines St. Lucian Creole French with Carib and African languages. According to the Pew Research Center, Christians compose 91 % of the population while the unaffiliated (6 %) and other religious groups, like Rastafarians, make up the rest of the country's religious demographic. While Catholics dominate the religious portrait of St. Lucia, Protestants make up almost 30 % of the total Christian population which includes Seventh-Day Adventist (10.4 %), Pentecostal (8.9 %), and others including Baptists, Evangelicals, and Jehovah's Witnesses.

The politeness of its people blends with a "rough and tumble" urbanism where the men display machismo attitudes and women, at least publicly, play second fiddle. While the economy depends largely on two industries—offshore banking and tourism—a cocktail of African, East Indian, French, and English influences shape the culture. Research in St. Lucia offers access into the life of traveling Pentecostal preacher Larry Scott who uses CIN strategies to influence his home island and the Caribbean beyond. He establishes religious networks using both Charismatic and institutional approaches. Traveling preachers like Larry Scott demonstrate how global religious networking is more important than a preacher having a pulpit.

Traveling Preacher Larry Scott: The Success of a Preacher without a Pulpit

Traveling preacher Larry Scott exists within an intricate and complex Charismatic informal networking scene. He frequently travels to guest preach throughout the Caribbean and USA, including many US cities like Seattle and Chicago. He owns a sports shop called Scott's Sports and Awards selling sports uniforms and trophies located near the center of the capital city Castries in the Gros Islet neighborhood just off Micoud Street. Scott makes a middle-class living from the profits of his sports shop. Of course, he also receives donations from tithes offered during his guest preaching services.

Scott does not own or lead a church, nor does he want the stresses involved in pastoring a congregation. Most importantly, Scott believes that his calling involves healing churches and congregations in distress, not pastoring churches. As Scott states, "I have turned down many opportunities, up to just recently. I just keep turning (down) opportunities to be a pastor of a church. I didn't understand it when God called me. He said to me, 'I want to go out and clean the churches.' That was confusing. How can you go and clean churches? In my mind, everyone in the church are born again Christian, and so I how can I go clean churches?" Serving as "cleaner" healing church problems allows Scott to enjoy independence while also using his abilities to travel as a guest preacher at local, regional, and international churches. Of course, traveling as a guest preacher throughout the Caribbean and USA does not just happen. Rather, in order to become a traveling Pentecostal pastor, it takes creative networking strategies with other religious leaders from the world beyond St. Lucia.

Scott's Charismatic-Institutional Networking Strategies

Scott's CIN involves the use of his special skills—discernment and deliverance—to establish connections with religious leaders of large institutions. As Scott puts it, "Because my area of ministry, the Lord has called me to the area of healing and deliverance. Pray for sick people, pray for people with problems, and you know, people who are possessed and all that kind of thing. That's my calling. That's what I do." His Charismatic ability or spirit gift of "discernment" involves figuring out the ailments that inflict individuals and churches, while "deliverance" refers to his power to heal people and churches of their problems. This expertise requires the ability to determine the source of an individual's suffering without it being directly stated to them. Scott explains:

I've never been asked to explain it. I don't know if I can explain it. If I'm going to pray for you, I don't need you to tell me what to pray for. I will tell you what you need prayer for. The Lord will just tell me what it is. I'm privy to His word. I will tell you things that you probably would be surprised to have me say it. So when I meet up with someone, most times, the Lord will let me know whom I'm dealing with and what I'm dealing with. I feel it deep down and the Lord will drop it in my spirit.

Once he discerns the problem, he cures it through the power of healing. Scott heals all kinds of problems, from physical, mental, or spiritual diseases to everyday life problems that plague us all. His power also includes the ability to solve the problems that might exist in a church. Churches sometimes struggle with internal division, dispirited congregations, low membership, and other issues that threaten the health and vitality of the group. It is believed that these problems often arise when demons take hold of the church and its congregation members, and perhaps its religious authority. Churches with problems invite Scott to determine what demonic forces plague the church and its people in order to fix the problem. Scott recalls one story where a church in the USA struggled with the forces of Obeah and witchcraft, "The pastor said to me, 'Brother, help me here. Help me understand what's happening here. There was a witch assigned to destroy the churches, a witch in the church. She was the pastor's right-hand woman. Everything the pastor wanted, she was to destroy. She'd be the destroyer of the church but then the Lord sent me there to explicitly destroy her." Of course, sociologically speaking, it does not matter if Scott actually possesses such supernatural gifts, rather it his ability to impart the perception to others that these gifts exist. His charisma lies in his ability to convince religious leaders and their congregation members of his supernatural qualities that serve to empower church leaders and their institutions. Scott's a religious man-of-action, a Pentecostal dynamo, and a mover and shaker with Holy Ghost mojo capable of discerning demonic spirits and casting them out of harm's way.

While Scott remains independent, he maintains a loose affiliation with large institutions like PAWI. The religious leaders of powerful institutions hire Scott as a Pentecostal medicine man to resolve problems beyond the control of the struggling church. CIN pastors like Scott employ their unique services as "religious freelancers" traveling around the Caribbean to guest preach at services with churches in need of his help. Of course, religious leaders fully host the guest preacher and offer tithes from the congregation members during church services. Scott frequently travels across Caribbean borders based on invitations from religious institutions abroad to fix problems and reinvigorate churches in danger of losing their Charismatic fire.

Scott uses his Charismatic qualities to network directly with institutions and frequently uses numerous institutions outside of PAWI to make connections, informal friendships, and official networks. Scott explains that he never introduces himself as a preacher. Rather, people become aware of his unique gifts from his guest preaching. The more he guest preaches, the more friends Scott establishes with religious leaders in St. Lucia and beyond. As Scott puts it, "As you go along preaching at various churches, you make friends, and your friends recommend you to other of their friends, and so that's the way it goes."

St. Lucia, like so many other English-speaking Caribbean islands, often hold large Christian revivals that bring together religious leaders and their followers from all over the region. This "revival networking" serves as a prime opportunity for religious leaders to learn of and meet with other religious leaders and establish connections beyond their borders. Scott explains the first steps toward developing his creative networking strategies, "Okay, the first step. There was a guy from America (referring to the United States) who came to St. Lucia to have some meetings in here leading to a big crusade for healing in our stadium." While Scott helped put together some of the equipment for the revival, he became acquainted with Francis "genetic salvation" Myles.[12] Together they decided to organize more crusades throughout the island for three days until Myles returned back to the USA. Scott explains how this began his path to establishing connections with religious leaders in both the USA and Caribbean, "So when we got back, we stayed in contact. He called me up and he said to me, but this is where my connections come in, 'I have arranged for you to preach for a friend of mine.'" Success as a healer gains recognition among other church leaders maximizing his opportunity to receive more invitations to guest preach. Scott explains how he continues to get booked for religious gigs across the Caribbean:

> I walked into a church in Dominica and preached for this guy in August. Later, based on an invitation from this man, I am having a national

conference on deliverance in St. Vincent as a mission on deliverance for three nights. The guy just called me two or three days ago, and booked me for this other conference. You know. Now, when you get there, other people hear you. Then they book you. He knows my area of calling. He knows what I'm involved in, so he wants to develop that in his church.

While Scott holds the credentials of a pastor, he relies largely on his Charismatic qualities and special skills to network with large institutions. Though lacking full access to resource-rich institutions, his loose religious affiliations and networking strategies allow Scott the ability to preach at churches in his own country and abroad, especially neighboring Caribbean islands. Even without a pulpit, CIN pastors like Scott use their innovative and creative strategies to influence their home countries and the Caribbean region beyond.

As some Pentecostal churches in the Caribbean and the USA struggle with internal conflict, bureaucratization, changes in church leadership, low membership, and lack of spiritual effervescence, it's Pentecostal dynamos with Holy Ghost mojo that travel to help churches experiencing dark times. Perhaps traveling religious "cleaners" like Scott help spark charisma in churches where the fire is slowly fading, thereby igniting revitalization and renewing church growth.

Is She Saved?

While standing inside Scott's Sports and Awards shop waiting to run errands with the traveling pastor, my phone vibrates with a message from home: my abuela is nearing her last breath. My father calls shortly thereafter stating that her death will come at any moment and that I should figure out a way home right away. Although we all knew her death was imminent, the realization of it hits at that moment. While staring to the ground, I say out loud and to no one in particular "My grandmother is going to die today" as my eyes begin to water. I look up to witness a young woman of about 22 with watering eyes looking straight at me with deep heartfelt compassion and understanding. Her lips quiver while she struggles to talk as tears of empathy fall from her big blinking innocent eyes. She finally asks, "Is she saved?"

I thought about her question, is my *abuela* saved? I knew exactly what the Pentecostals meant by those words but all I could think of is how my *abuela*—we call her Gaggi—how Gaggi made the ultimate sacrifices in her life to save those she loved. Gaggi possessed the bravery and strength to make tough decisions to save her family, making the greatest sacrifice a mother could make. She sent her children unaccompanied from these very Caribbean waters to a foreign country in hopes of saving them from a perceived danger due to a political coups d'état. I thought about Gaggi, deep down to the bones thought, about her unrelenting selflessness, endless devotion, self-sacrificing nature, gentle kindness, and layered wisdom as well as her ultimate sacrifice of temporarily losing her children to save them. I look at the young woman with the big brown watering eyes staring at me with hope, offer her a tender smile, and say with confidence, "Yes, my grandmother is saved." She lets out a deep sigh of relief along with more tears, saying, "She will be with God soon." This story reveals how some Pentecostals understand salvation and comfort themselves and others when death strikes.

BARBADOS

From the plane Barbados resembles a flattened green pancake with a coastal outline of narrow white sandy beaches giving way to breathtaking aqua-blue and green waters of the Caribbean and Atlantic. The expansive West Coast enjoys the calm Caribbean Sea where many European tourists lazily lounge away the hours over their rum served in coconuts while the Atlantic battered East coast boasts some of the best and most dangerous surfing in the Caribbean. The low rolling hills of Barbados, the easternmost island in the Lesser Antilles, compliments its coastlines draped around the geographically flat but culturally rich island. Barbados showcases a mixture of small but vibrant fishing towns like Oistins to its large and cosmopolitan capital city Bridgetown. Rapidly moving minibuses or route taxis[13] transport tourists and locals along the coasts, especially the western coast with its succession of tourist-intensive towns from Oistins in the south to the more northern town of Holetown, where the first English settlers arrived in 1627. The South coast runs into the even more tourist-intensive towns of Hastings, Worthing, St. Lawrence Gap, and Dover Beach catering to younger, usually European tourists, made evident with the rampant commercialism that pervades the area. The near empty and less traveled northern coast offers some hidden treasures and breathtaking scenes—including huge rock cliffs that hang over vicious Atlantic waves battering the coast. Barbados's tourist-intensive economy also depends on its sugar where its people ingest just as much cane as they do the Christian Bible.

Christians compose 95 % of the population while the other 5 %, including an estimated 1 % Rastafarian, are a mixture of everything from unaffiliated to "folk" religions.[14] Unlike St. Lucia where Catholics dominate the Christian population, Protestants compose a whopping 88 % of the Christian population in Barbados from Anglican (about 30 %) to Pentecostal (about 20 %) to Seventh-Day Adventists (about 6 %), among other groups. Despite a secular economy heavily dependent on entertaining, drinking, and reveling tourists, Barbados remains an overwhelmingly religious social world steeped in Christian beliefs.

If secularization dominates Western Europe and the northern part of the Americas, as the sociological scholarship suggests, the English-speaking Caribbean defies such secularization with religious influence continuing to permeate multiple spheres of social life—from politics to culture to academia. Leading religious scholar Jose Casanova[15] defines secularization in three ways that involve the (1) decline of religious beliefs and practices in modern society, (2) privatization of religion from public life as new institutions such as the state and economy shape history, and (3) institutional differentiation of the secular spheres (state, economy, science) from religion, or the emancipation of secular institutions from religious influence. While secular spaces exist in the tourist resorts and restaurants, the rest of Barbados pushes forward into modernity while resisting the forces of secularization, or the tendency to become "worldly."[16] As in much of the Caribbean world, religion and secular life sometimes jumble and coalesce in a postmodern stew while at other times they form sharp divisions diametrically opposed to one another. This division became immediately apparent when first landing in the Caribbean. First, let's meet PAWI pastor Michael Alleng of Barbados.

Pastor Michael Alleng of Arch Hall, Barbados

Pastor Michael Alleng stands tall and lanky at about six feet two inches, awkward but still somehow confidant. He heads the PAWI-affiliated Evening Light Pentecostal Church in Arch Hall, Barbados just outside of Holetown. This man is constantly busy, running a church, taking care of family, counseling married couples or couples planning to get married, holding church-related services, attending meetings, and counseling members of the church and community, among other things. Alleng combines ICN and IFN approaches to impact the Caribbean world locally and regionally. He networks with other religious leaders both inside and outside PAWI traveling to other churches in Barbados, the Caribbean, and the USA to guest preach. While Alleng uses his formal institutional connections with PAWI to establish connections within the organization, he uses his personal Charismatic abilities to network with religious leaders beyond the great Caribbean religious institution. He also spreads his influence throughout the Caribbean through speaking on local Christian radio stations including 97.5 and 90.1 FM. Perhaps most striking about Alleng, despite his more intrinsic personality and initial skepticism of outsiders, is his intellectual curiosity about Pentecostalism in the modern world and willingness to discuss ideas to an audience beyond his congregation. Although this intellectual curiosity and willingness to discuss Pentecostalism in the Caribbean eventually emerged after arriving to Barbados, initial contact revealed some of the sharp divisions between religious and secular worldviews.

Swimming Downstream: Religion and Academics in Barbados

While heading north on Errol Barrow Highway toward Holetown, Alleng wonders why an academic from the USA wants to conduct research on religion in Barbados and, more importantly, he also wonders about the religious persuasions of such a researcher. As we travel to a beach near an old Anglican Church where locals celebrate Father's Day, Alleng and I discuss the separation of church and state in the USA and Caribbean. In the Caribbean, he explains, religion retains a strong foothold in the lives of its people and institutions. While religion loses its stronghold in the shaping of world affairs, it remains vital to both private and public life in Barbados. Alleng's crinkled forehead and somewhat startled countenance show genuine concern and slight confusion when confronted with the political ideas of the separation of church and state, one that he considers a distinct USA problem that lies in the backwards thinking of many Americans. He finally questions my religious beliefs wondering about my state of salvation and relationship with God. He looks at me with surprise and disappointment when realizing that I'm not a born-again Christian. I explain that social scientists claiming to be born-again Christians in the USA find themselves to be "swimming upstream" in an academic world that frowns upon the blending religious belief and experience with social science research. Born-Again Christian academics, if not careful, find themselves marginalized among their more openly secular colleagues. Some academics might call out their religiously minded colleagues as out-of-their-mind "holy-rollers" removed from the world of rationality and logic. Making matters worse, many outsiders in and outside of academia link all born-again Christians to fundamentalist believers with homophobic and intolerant views toward gays and lesbians, beliefs in creationism and hell, and government control of women's decision-making processes in regard to birth control and abortion. Alleng believes that secularism in the USA shows evidence of a backward society lost in itself from the confusions associated with modernity. To Alleng, the USA is a dangerous and alienated world without God and direction. He points out how the Caribbean flips the coin on religion and secularization, including for academics and public intellectuals.

As opposed to their northern neighbors, born-again Christian professors and social scientists find themselves swimming decidedly downstream in the English-speaking Caribbean. Religious belonging actually serves to legitimate the credibility of social scientists in the Caribbean where the pursuit of academic knowledge and religious experience finds less tension. Alleng claims that a secular university professor or social scientist might actually be disregarded if not a born-again Christian. Alleng points to numerous academics he knows in Barbados and the Caribbean who openly discuss their born-again Christian persuasions and gain credibility as academics and public intellectuals for their religious beliefs. This is reminiscent of Weber's notion of trust in early American life where religious affiliation served as a form of credibility that allowed members of the community to establish trust networks and take out loans.[17] Weber discusses business life in the nineteenth- and early twentieth-century America where people used their affiliation with a Protestant church to gain legitimacy and secure credit of one's trustworthiness. While religion played a large role in fostering trust and legitimacy in the development of capitalism in the early modern USA, a strong relationship between religious belonging and trustworthiness persists in modern Caribbean life where Pentecostalism continues to make an impact in the region. To Alleng, religious belonging and affiliation gives one further credibility and legitimacy in everything from academics to economics. Unfortunately, at least initially, lack of religious credit increased Alleng's skepticism of an outsider wanting to understand the world of Pentecostal insiders.

Access to Pentecostalism in Barbados

Penetrating into the world of Pentecostalism in Barbados reveals how pastors and religious leaders balance institutionalization and charisma, negotiate internal and external adversity, struggle with church growth and power, and find strategies to use the forces of institutionalization against itself to return charisma to the movement. It also shows greater insight into the insider's perspective to understand Pentecostal attitudes toward homosexuals and "miraculous" healing as well as the professional temptations of the pastor. But gaining outsider access to Pentecostal insiders in Barbados, especially religious leaders within PAWI hierarchy, requires establishing at least some initial trust. Sometimes a bit of trust can be found in car rides that offer wild views of Atlantic battered coastlines and intense conversations between thinkers from different walks of life. Let's go on the Barbados drive.

We drive from Holetown to Speightsown along the Caribbean Sea to the northern city of Spring Hall and beyond reaching, yet again, the exact point where the Caribbean meets the Atlantic. We descend along the Atlantic coast where brave surfers take on the "soup bowl" and huge rock cliffs offer a view of pure beauty. We pass one of the world's last sugar windmills until finally reaching the town of Bathsheba that offers stunning ocean views of untamed waters along the island's east coast. Alleng and I zip and roar down the coastline as well as the interior of the island where remnants of the colonial past testify to the long history of the former slave colony that retains the resistance of the great Bussa.[18] Though Alleng dismisses research from a non-born again, perhaps it's the beautiful scenes of wild nature or the breathtaking views from high cliffs looking into the distant ocean that connect us at this moment to express our views about love and life and the power and struggles of the Pentecostal movement in the Caribbean and the world beyond.

Though at first skeptical to discuss issues related to Pentecostalism, Alleng finds it compelling to discuss a topic he finds both fascinating and deeply personal. We go back and forth on the struggles and triumphs of the movement, its successes and failures over the past hundred years, its resiliency to overcome the forces of modernization while it simultaneously finds itself in an increasingly precarious and vulnerable position. Suddenly he blares out with undeniable passion, "It's not that the (Pentecostal) Church has gotten too big, it's that it doesn't know how to handle getting too big and powerful." He immediately becomes silent and solemn, as if holding back his passions and emotions. Alleng stops the car, and turns his deep and penetrating eyes toward mine. He says, "Grab my hand, let's pray, let's pray."

Father, I have met Peter for the first time just today and he recently arrived in Barbados. He is a professor of sociology and from the United States, but you know everything about his life. He is a researcher studying the Charismatic movement in the Caribbean. I ask for you to touch him, meet him in a way that no man can meet him, and no church can meet him. Meet him in a way that no church can ever meet him. Touch him in a mighty way. Let the spirit of God cast the power of the Holy Spirit in the world that he is studying, in the world that he wants to understand and academically criticize. Let that Holy Spirit touch him, the Spirit of Christ. Just draw him, draw him in a way that will empower him, which this day is not something that he directs but that God directed, God initiated, and God induced. Put God in charge of everything. There's an objective witness that you can know and from which men can learn about you. Witness in his heart; touch him, open faith in his life. And God come in and, in this endeavor, in this pursuit, in this, what are father's wishes. Bring it to us in the place right now, in Jesus Christ, Amen.

This prayer asks God to empower me with the strength and knowledge to write a successful book properly representing the movement. Most important, it offers symbolic expression of initial trust and rapport, providing the path to gain access to Pentecostalism in Barbados. Following the prayer, Alleng stares at me for a few moments before explaining that this topic is of great interest to him, one in which he holds many opinions. We talk for days, along with others religious leaders and pastors, on issues related to Pentecostalism in the Caribbean, especially his concern on how the Charismatic movement is losing its fire, the charisma that sparked the original movement.

DOMINICA

Dominica sticks out of the Caribbean Sea like a rare jewel. The plane circles the high mountains of the island making even seasoned flight commuters squirm in their seat at the sight of the airship landing, or crashing into the mountains. The plane descends unevenly into the mountains, somehow navigating in between them into a tiny airstrip that looks like a thin piece of scotch tape. The rolling hills and towering mountains, thick rainforest and hot sulfur springs, the stunning waterfalls and bubbling lakes, and perhaps best of all, a Caribbean culture yet to be tainted by intensive formal international tourism, make this a magic island that impresses even the most jaded traveler. The plane lands in the Northwest part of the island near Londonberry Bay between the villages of Wesley and Marigot. The taxi to Dominica's capital Roseau takes about an hour from the airport. This Dominica taxi is a private minivan that shuttles people from the airport to anywhere on the 750 square kilometer island with a population of just over 72,000 people.

Like many other English-speaking Caribbean countries, Christians compose almost 95 % of the total population. The other 5 % largely consist of those identifying with either folk religions or other religions, including Rastafarian (1.3 %). Like St. Lucia, Catholics compose about 58 % of the total population while Protestants make up about 36 % of the overall population. Consistent with many islands in the region, Seventh-Day Adventist, Pentecostal, Baptist, Methodists, make up the majority of the Protestant population. But perhaps unlike other islands, religious tensions between the various Christian groups seem more pronounced here on the volcanic island, and ethnographic research found such heated tensions that presented challenges requiring some creative ethnographic networking strategies.

Ethnographic Pitfalls and Recovery in Dominica

Bishop Michael "Bill" Daniel, affectionately known in Dominica as Pastor Bill, is my initial contact in Dominica, a connection Apostle of Antigua established prior to my arrival. Pastor Bill serves as the president of the Dominica Association of Evangelical Churches, presiding Bishop of the PAWI Dominica District, member of the General Council of the PAWI, and the general Secretary of the PAWI Dominica District, among others positions and titles of distinction. He's also known to oppose gay and lesbian cruise ships entering Dominica.[19]

Pastor Bill heads People's Pentecostal Family Church located in the Goodwill neighborhood of Roseau about a 15-minute walk from the city center. Unfortunately, immediately upon entering the church to inquire about the pastor, I find out that Pastor Bill was struggling on his, as it later turned out, deathbed from colon cancer. After some convincing, the secretary provides new contacts with Evangelist Augustine and Pastor Cameron Robins. Robins, the acting Superintendent of PAWI in Dominica in place of Pastor Bill, becomes the new primary contact but finds little time in the next few days to meet. We agree to meet in the Northwestern village of Portsmouth, on the other side of the island, where a town meeting composed of religious leaders from both the Caribbean and the USA was to take place to bring unity to the divided church. Unfortunately, though I attend the entire meeting, Robins, after agreeing to meet, refuses to talk with me claiming that a non-born-again Christian does not have the right to write about the Charismatic movement. Unlike most Pentecostal leaders and pastors throughout the Caribbean, Cameron Robins seems uneasy, nervous, and skeptical about talking with me, as if concerned about any external scrutiny. He believes that only born-again Christians have the right to research and the ability to understand the Charismatic movement. He explains that if I'm not born-again, I can't write about the movement, any such writing, he says, is automatically disqualified.

As plans fall through to meet with Robins, it becomes necessary to make new connections. The first step is to establish contacts with the PAWI district central office in Roseau. Pastor Bill Daniel's brother Griffin Daniels, head pastor of Grand Bay Pentecostal Church, holds office hours and counseling services at the central office. The central office, located in the upstairs of a small building, is composed of a small front room with a secretary and small office for the head administrator. Griffin Daniels is a short and plump man with a nervous speech and awkward demeanor. Unimpressed with my contacts with Apostle in Antigua, Griffin Daniels dismisses any potential conversation refusing to talk or accepting any further conversations in the future.

Things do not fare much better with Evangelist Augustine. We first meet at Voice of Life Radio located in the small village of Loubiere just south of Roseau for prayer hour. Evangelist Augustine sits in a room taking prayer requests and testimonies that report the successes of past prayer requests from listeners calling in to the radio show. Understaffed, Evangelist Augustine asks for me to take prayer requests and testimonial reports. I work for an hour with four others answering phones and filling out two different forms, one for a prayer request and the other detailing a testimonial. After, we drive from the radio station to Roseau on the way to an afternoon prayer hour held in a rented small auditorium space called WAWU near the PAWI office.

While driving, Evangelist Augustine dismisses all questions and comments with what seems to be almost rehearsed and overstated Christian jargon that relies on gospel quotes. He spends most of the time lecturing me on the importance of becoming a born-again. Unlike most of the religious leaders and Pentecostal pastors encountered throughout the English-speaking Caribbean, Evangelist Augustine seems nervous and apprehensive. The afternoon prayer hour at WAWU involves worship and praise songs, testimonies, shouting, singing, and laying of hands with a focus on "deliverance." Like Robbins and Griffin Daniels, Evangelist Augustine is hesitant and cautious to discuss anything about the Charismatic movement in the Caribbean.

Almost ethnographically down and out in Dominica, the winds of fortune change amidst the lava craters and Boiling Lake in the "Nature Island of the Caribbean." At a neighborhood café, local celebrity radio Deejay Matt Peltier of Q95, after overhearing a conversation with an employee about my interest in religion in the Caribbean, strikes up a conversation with me about religion and politics in the Caribbean. Apparently, a recent scandal in Dominica broke out about the Catholic Church accepting a large amount of money from the government. The prime minister of Dominica recently made a $500,000 Eastern Caribbean dollars (about $185 USD) donation to the Catholic Church to restore a cathedral in Roseau. Deejay Matt invites me on his talk show to discuss religion and politics and offers a new contact for me to interview during my stay on the island.

The contact is a full gospel Charismatic Baptist pastor named Randy Rodney with strong ties to religious leaders in Dominica and throughout the Caribbean. We meet for about an hour and a half to discuss the various church denominations in Dominica, the conflicts and divisions among the Christian churches on the island, the role of religion and politics, among other topics related to the Christian churches. Randy Rodney wants to organize the established, Charismatic, and independent churches to reduce crime rates. He explains, as will be discussed below, how the Christian Churches come together and unite—despite its historical and ongoing division—when the church experiences external pressure and/or a common enemy. This supports the claims of many other church leaders throughout the Caribbean. As will be it is contradictorily the division in the Charismatic Christian church that simultaneously allows it to retain its charisma, among other things. Randy Rodney, a graduate of the University of West Indies in business, uses ICN and IFN strategies to make connections with other Christian religious groups, political and economic elites, and local celebrities like Deejay Matt to influence Dominican affairs. He's also starting the "Pastors National Fellowship" program to unite religious leaders of various Christian groups and currently runs a primary school near the capital Roseau.

Using "creative Charismatic ethnographic network" strategies, I establish contacts with other religious leaders and Pentecostal pastors on the island that opens the door to gain insight into the Charismatic movement in Dominica. While pastors like Cameron Robins shut the doors to outsiders, others like Pastor Jerry Comellas speaks more openly about the Charismatic movement stating, "I love the educational philosophical side of the church too" showing an interest to understand the movement from a spiritual and intellectual perspective. Dozens of interviews with religious leaders in and outside of Pentecostalism help understand the tensions that exist between various church groups with a long and ongoing division, the external pressures of the Charismatic church, and the divisions that exist within the Charismatic Christian church that simultaneously allows it to retain its charisma. The religious leaders on the island highlight some of the advantages of institutionalization and globalization, including how this process makes moving across borders easier with a common rhetoric that is generalized for all but particularized to none. Ethnographic observations from a town meeting in Portsmouth provide insight into how the large institutionally affiliated PAWI churches attempt to blend institutional and Charismatic forces and types of religious networking to better impact its communities. Research in Dominica also points the way to the problems of division in the Charismatic churches, especially as it relates to the Caribbean. In the end, perhaps church division is a necessary "evil" for, contradictorily, the survival and prosperity of the church.

The Charismatic Pentecostal Movement in St. Lucia, Barbados, and Dominica

Findings from St. Lucia, Barbados, and Dominica reveal important themes related to institutionalization that include a discussion on the (1) challenges of church growth and power, (2) external adversity and internal conflict, and (3) structural centralization and decentralization. The three themes that follow incorporate ethnographic research involving religious leaders and pastors from St. Lucia, Barbados, and Dominica.

Challenges of Church Growth and Power
Just as Bishop discussed the issues associated with the "Big Three" in Trinidad, the religious leaders of St. Lucia, Barbados, and Dominica understand the emerging role of the Charismatic movement in the political and economic affairs of the region, especially as CARICOM opens its private and public doors to the religious leaders of the Caribbean. The unanimous perspective of these religious leaders: Although

becoming powerful is necessary to create change, growth and power also threaten to undermine the movement. When discussing the problems of increased church growth and power in the Caribbean, nearly all of the religious leaders paraphrased the English historian, politician and writer John Dalberg-Acton's famous quote "Power tends to corrupt, and absolute power corrupts absolutely."[20] They understand the propensity for successful religious leaders and movements to join the political and economic elite as strength and power increases. While their views to understanding the problems associated with church growth and its solutions find some commonality, at other times their views vary as widely as their preaching styles.

For some, like Alleng, it's not the size of church growth that matters but rather the form growth takes. Alleng says, "It's not that the Charismatic church is getting too big, rather, it does not know how to handle getting too big and powerful." Alleng believes that it's a personal issue rather than a structural problem, pointing to religious leaders losing sight of the original intent of the Charismatic movement. Alleng argues:

> It's because of leadership who has lost sight of respect on leadership. You see that? So, it's not about bigness. We can have a massive church doing God's work. It's how leadership perceives and approaches their roles. It isn't a struggle to balance becoming big with allowing the spirit to flow freely. So, it has a lot to do with, not the bigness of church, but rather with what leadership does at that point.

Religious leaders nearly unanimously put the blame on the leadership within the Pentecostal movement. While losing vision is part of the problem, many hold that religious leaders must learn how to administer the people, especially learning to manage the gifts of God to better the people. Pentecostal preachers and leaders might retain personal charisma, but somehow forget, or lack the ability and skills to manage the office, especially when power becomes an issue. One religious leader explains:

> There's a lack of understanding on how to administer the gifts of God. Not a lack of charisma, but a lack of how to administer. The Bible isn't just about being gifted, it's so we can administer those gifts. There's an order that is not Roman Catholic in structure. That is a biblical order, that's how you manage a gift that is not controlled as order.

Others argue how difficult it is for religious leaders to minister large churches when compared to the smaller ones. Scott describes in detail the problems of administering to an increasingly large and growing church:

> They say the bigger the following, the bigger the problem. You know? The one with the smaller church, but you still calling from God, you know, whatever. But the one with the bigger church, don't forget, you have to minister to thousands. You've got to go to God and hear what is telling you for the thousands. But the one with the small little church with two people, yeah, God will tell you what to tell people. Guys like Stephen Andrews, in order to keep it up, they've got to be spending weeks and months in fasting, weeks and months alone seeking God, they need to be in the presence of God, they need to hear what God is saying because there you have a responsibility.

Scott uses the analogy of a parent having to feed children:

> I've got to feed one child, some guy gives me ten bucks and I can feed my child. But you cannot take a job that would pay ten bucks to feed your ten children. You know? It's going to take more. So the same way that in the physical; same it is in the spiritual. It's very hard. It's a difficult job. Once you are in there. You see, one step back, it looks glamorous. Oh boy, I would love to be that, but let me tell you, it's not easy. It's not easy.

Others warn that some religious leaders lose sight of the meaning behind leadership, often taking the role of a Lord rather than one who sacrifices for the benefit of others. One religious leader states:

> The church leader should not be a Lord, but rather should be a servant to everybody. As a matter of fact, the greatness of a leader is not measured by how many people you rule over, but the greatness of the sacrifice. This is where the idea falls back on leadership. Jesus has given us a blueprint of what leadership should be, so the reason why I see many of the problems happening with the church as it grows is because a lot of leadership is a wrong marker. Can I say that? They take their eyes off of the biblical.

The message that many religious leaders claim will ameliorate the problems of increased church growth and power is to remain a movement of the people, using grassroots, on-the-ground work, and to always be in touch with the everyday lives of the people. As Randy Rodney puts it:

I'm very opinionated as far as that's concerned. I am here to do my boss's work. And once I begin to compromise that position, I've lost my spine. I agree with you. Some churches will get very large, or I know the notion that some churches get very large, get very large again because they move in line with what's happening and not necessarily doing what God wants them to do. My position is as follows: our church is a people's church. This vision is the greatest church we can achieve. I want to be nothing but the pastor who's on the ground doing the work. I'm teaching people that this is what the church is about, on the ground, on the street, doing the work. And I've always said to them we must never get too weak to serve people because that's what we're called to do. And I love it.

Another religious leader echoes the importance of grassroots work within the Pentecostal movement, especially for its leaders:

One great pastor once said that he would never have a private jet if he has people in his church riding a bicycle to church. And I thought that was a very powerful position to take, because the temptation is great. Once people get to that place of power, they move to another place. And I felt that if many more people would take that position then we would still be doing what God wants us to. So my position is the church must be alive. The church can continue to be alive once the church remains true to its mandate and calling.

Arguing for a remaining committed to a grassroots orientation, many religious leaders argue for the importance of the church elite and its people to build unity through revivals. While they admit that church growth and power breed both the tendency for corruption and joining the political and economic elite, they hold that unity will bind the church together and create strength within the movement, one that brings an anointing and ability to defy the negative impacts of growth and power. As Jerry puts it:

Where there's unity, there's anointing. The bible says that when that unity among brothers is like the anointing that fell down Aaron's head and dripped down his beard, so we want the anointing because we really want to see an outpouring of God's spirit. We need not just a revival, but a great awakening.

Jerry, deeply reflective at the moment, discusses the importance for the church to maintain its focus on the ground, on the people that leaders must serve. Without that focus, he believes, the Charismatic church will be in trouble. Jerry explains:

And I think that when revival fires blow, or we say the wind of the spirit, that it's there for a time and it's there to embrace, but if we do not what we need to do, it's not just about 5-fold ministry. It's about getting our hands out there and helping people who are hurting and making a difference. And if we miss out on that, the winds just blow right by. That's what I think.

Unity, however, simultaneously creates internal conflicts. Interestingly, while revivals help unify the churches, so does external adversity from outside the Charismatic movements. Perceived enemies from the outside the Charismatic movement help bring together previously divided churches. As the divided churches unite to combat external threats, internal conflicts begin to emerge. The section below argues that these internal conflicts help maintain charisma within the Pentecostal movement as it continues push forward into history.

External Adversity and Internal Conflict
External adversity refers to the outside pressures that religious leaders of the Charismatic movement experience as the result of societal transformation, from political and economic to social and cultural transitions. These external pressures may derive from cultural shifts in public sentiment on sodomy laws, gay marriage, and abortion, political maneuvering to manipulate or shut out religious leaders, moral crisis and panics related to drugs and crime, cultural entrepreneurs with messages that go against the church, and political and economic leaders perceived as attempting to secularize the society, including the educational system, among other things. Internal conflict, on the other hand, involves divisions that exist from within the institution as well as those Charismatic churches inside and outside large institutions like PAWI. Internal conflicts stem from—just like many academic departments in a university—disagreements on doctrine, personality conflicts, competition for increasing membership size, vying for institutional power, institutional disobedience, legalism, and even jealousy and pride, among other things. While some religious leaders argue that what divides the church has little to do with doctrine and more about individual personality differences and competition, others urge that religious beliefs and church doctrine serve as the heart of the matter. As Randy Rodney puts it:

> Every denomination has its own tenets of beliefs. And the tenet of beliefs would represent the doctrinal position of that particular assembly. And one

person believes that and the other person does not believe that at all. In fact they're vehemently opposed to this. Many Baptists, for example, do not believe in speaking in tongues.

Another religious leader explains the sources of internal conflicts due to doctrinal disputes:

> Different religious groups in and out of the evangelical community were at odds because, doctrinally, they are different and they see each other as opponents, competitors. Over the last few years, some of us have been trying to change it.

External adversity and internal conflict help keep charisma alive within the institutionalized and institutionalizing Charismatic movement. While Poloma shows that revivals bring a resurgence of vitality to a movement,[21] revivals seem too few and far between. While Poloma argues that Pentecostalism needs revitalization where worship relates to religious vitality and serves as a form of institutional resistance,[22] I argue that external adversity remains much more consistent to put pressures—from political and economic to social and cultural transformations—on religious groups and leaders to unite and revitalize. External adversity operates to build unity among highly competitive and sometimes antagonistic religious leaders both within and outside of the Charismatic movements. As unity brings together potentially different religious leaders into the same social, cultural, and religious spaces, their sense of competition and antagonisms, create the conditions for increased charisma. This unity creates the condition of hyper-competition among Charismatic figures, one that actually revitalizes charisma from the humdrum of institutionalization. Ironically, it's the division within the Charismatic movements that helps to keep charisma alive.

The Charismatic church builds strength and develops a renewed sense of charisma when facing external adversity and internal conflict. External pressures involve hostility from both secular and non-secular individuals, groups, and institutions outside of the Charismatic movement. Pentecostal leaders view each external pressure as a common hostile enemy working against God and the mission of the church. Whenever the church is under pressure, the quality of conversion, conviction, and unity is stronger creating a more vibrant militant Charismatic church.

For example, Alleng explains that in Barbados, whenever the church is under pressure, the quality of conversion, conviction, and unity among his colleagues grows stronger. He explains that religious movements occur from external pressures using both historical and local examples. The church, he argues, needs something to stand behind, a cause to fight for, and a reason to have a call to arms. While slavery serves as a good historical example, he argues that external pressures in Dominica derive from large issues like human trafficking:

> Every great awakening happened when the church finally decided that there was some kind of social reform they wanted to make, and it's almost always slavery. I think in modern times, it would be human trafficking. I think maybe Dominica is going to be child abuse.

The church will unite together to stand up for just causes, and external pressures happen frequently. When it's not the big things causing problems, like gay marriage and human trafficking, it's the small things that call for big challenges bringing the divided churches together for common causes. Jerry points out how different churches in and out of the Charismatic movement at least temporarily united, in Dominica to stand up against a public performance by the Jamaican dancehall artist Leroy "Junior" Russell, otherwise known as Tommy Lee Sparta, who religious leaders in the Caribbean view as a Satanist. Jerry explains that, "The church was in uproar, they wanted to fight against him." Other religious leaders echo similar sentiments arguing that "They've [religious groups and leaders] gotta find something to unite on. If a church can unite on this, it doesn't matter who you are or what your denomination is, or your dogma or your theology, all that doesn't matter. This issue matters. And I think God wants us to recognize that too. The common cause joins people together. That's the only thing that we can take away from that division."

For religious leaders like Randy Rodney, crime serves as the main issue that unites the church, an issue that he takes personally. As he puts it:

> Well, we started the international committee on crime and violence and we planned to have a peace service and the committee decides to have the peace service at my church and other religious leaders served as the speakers in my church. Our particular organization is actually focused on bringing down the crime rate. And other Pentecostal leaders were the speakers. I shared the service, and that went pretty well, I thought. That's how we have started to build unity.

Other religious leaders hesitate to argue that divided churches unite over external adversity, but agree that a softening of the divisions occur that bring religious groups and their leaders together. One preacher puts it this way:

> There'll be a softening, if you like, of the antagonism that exists between and among preachers or priests. People become more centered. I do not see anything further than that. But certainly there is a move towards that direction [unity], there is a sense that people are beginning to soften up and say, you know what? You don't believe what I believe, however, I need to give him the respect that he functions with in order to carry out a goal.

External adversity can also derive from a growing educated public. Some religious leaders point to the great societal transformations taking place that impact their congregations. As many people in the Caribbean experience greater access to the Internet and social media as well as advanced educational opportunities, exposure to outside influences, and new ideas impact their worldviews. Expectations change and cultural attitudes shift in different and unexpected directions. One religious leader describes this process the following way:

> You can tell, when a congregation is well schooled, they don't get excited easily. They don't get as emotional. Today's congregation, in the Caribbean is a much more educated congregation than it was let's say twenty, thirty years ago. The people have gone to the university. They're more particular, they are more analytical, (and) they form different perspectives. The pastor and the preacher cannot be one-dimensional. He has to reinvent himself every weekend. He has to be able to assess whom he's preaching to very early. Even though they are the same people, from most of the same region, they now have different experiences and different situations.

Religious leaders unanimously see this as a more subtle but definite external pressure. Whatever impact education might have on the religious and spiritual effervescence of the congregation, exposure to social media and communication technology also exposes congregation members to other Charismatic leaders from around the world. What's more, a hyper-consumeristic world in an age of plurality further heightens levels of stimulation and expectations of fulfillment, spiritual, and physical. Religious leaders find this unanticipated consequence of modernity extremely challenging that both unites them to understand the changes of the new and emerging congregation while it also puts them in increased competition. Like Simmel's eccentric character that emerges from the urban dweller struggling to retain the subjective self from a cannibalizing objective culture, Charismatic leaders must become eccentric themselves to retain their distinct subjective self from a cannibalizing mass of religious charisma from powerful religious movements around the world. Now, religious leaders must become hyper-Charismatic to stand out above the Charismatic ordinary. As one experienced religious leader explains:

> The old pastors, the old preachers, they just got up and said, [shouting] "Jesus. Amen. Hallelujah." Now we have to find out what Jesus said, when Jesus said it, who he said it to, what kind of condition, and people need to hear that and they want to hear it, if you don't give it to them, they turn off. So, it's completely different. And again, it's what stimulates congregations in those small communities. It takes more to stimulate them, get them to their feet. They see all the televangelists and other mega-star preachers. That's what we got to deal with. Communities are always evolving and evolving and other things other than the church.

For Simmel, the major problem in modern life was for the individual to maintain the subjective self against the weight of an external, objective culture. Perhaps for the Pentecostal leaders it's the struggle to maintain charisma against the growing objective Charismatic religious world. This struggle to maintain individual charisma from getting swallowed up into the objective cannibalizing religious world keeps "eccentric" Charismatic religious leaders from the humdrum ordinary. Perhaps the fate of charisma for the institutionalized and institutionalizing Charismatic movement lies in this struggle of modern life. It's external adversity that also produces the eccentric religious actors that rise above the objective Charismatic ordinary, thus keeping charisma alive in the Pentecostal movement within the English-speaking Caribbean and allowing it to become a more formidable force in the shaping of local and regional affairs.

As religious leaders meet the demands that external adversities pose, including rising above the Charismatic ordinary, they must also deal with relative comparisons between local and regional religious groups as the churches begin to unite because of external adversity. In this postmodern religious catch-22, unity creates relative comparison between previously unfamiliar groups. As religious leaders from inside and outside the Charismatic movement unite, they begin to share similar spaces exposing themselves, their colleagues, and their congregations to new religious styles and ideas. As Randy Rodney began networking to unite with other religious leaders around the issues of crime, he found himself preaching at new churches and others preaching inside his church:

> Preachers begin to preach at other preacher's pulpits. In fact we have now started a pastor's fellowship, a national pastor's fellowship. And that encompasses pastors from all denominations. As we grow, we'll begin to see more of that. So I would preach a crusade for another church, and another preacher will be invited to mine. I'm having a function, in September, for example, I bring students together and bring pastors together and we have several pastors present and several pastors spring up from different churches.

One major religious leader puts it best explaining how today's religious leaders must have that extra something special:

> The average pastor today has got to be world savvy. And he's going to sing. And today, even how we preach, especially in the West Indian countries, it's hard. They [the congregation] just sit down and watch you. I've heard real good preaching, and the congregation, they say just one amen from beginning to end. They're just sitting down and watching. If you don't come extra special, they're not dealing with you.

While external adversity and internal conflict might help maintain charisma, it's not all sunshine and roses. Many religious leaders understand the challenges of realizing any meaningful unity. In fact, some argue that it's merely a dream:

> Actually, that's a dream. (Laughs) you correct. Sometimes I think about it, but it's a dream. Because to do that, right now, for example, the international committee on crime and violence, we're thinking of putting up a halfway house. And I have to finally say; I don't think we can do it. Let us find an organization that will do it for us and we'll support them. Because coming together is a hard job.

Others argue, especially in Dominica, how internal arguments prevent any meaningful social dialogue and community change from happening.

> They love the town meeting here to a fault, to a point where they [religious leaders] will get up and criticize one another. And you'll find that in the Caribbean there's a lot of legalism, meaning leaning more towards the law

in the bible rather than the grace in the bible, the letter instead of the spirit. So you see a lot of that. When I came and had to deal with the issues that the church is facing here, ran into a lot of that. A lot of people condemning one another, lot of people ridiculing, and so you cannot really have any successful outreach in the community if inwardly the church is attacking itself.

While the prognosis at times seems grim, religious leaders like Jerry maintain optimism stating, "This church has come a long way, but still has a ways to go. But they must be able to make disciples if it's going to be successful and they must be able to evangelize."

Structural Centralization and Decentralization
While the Charismatic movement continues to become institutionalized with the centralization of bureaucratic power among the elite, it also experiences the simultaneous process of decentralization. This institutional transformation involves both centralization and decentralization as power is simultaneously vertically concentrated and horizontally dispersed into many autonomous and semi-autonomous smaller cells under the umbrella of a large cell.

Alleng argues that this is one way that the Pentecostal Church best responds to both church growth and increased institutionalization. As the church grows, he believes, it should continue to decentralize into autonomous and semi-autonomous cells operating within a large cell. As Alleng puts it, "The way church should be governed as it covers greater territory, so as to not destroy charisma, but to maximum charisma, is to break the structure down to smaller units operating within a larger one." All of the religious leaders and pastors of St. Lucia, Barbados, and Dominica interviewed argue for such an approach to, yes, grow, but also to decentralize. Jerry explains, "Yeah. I think you gotta grow big and you gotta grow small at the same time. You've gotta maintain that small group structure, that fire of going on, of reaching out and not just for the sake of becoming institutional in a formal organization. For that reason, Assemblies of God never officially called itself a denomination. It's called a fellowship." Randy echoes a similar sentiment stating, "It [church growth and concentration of power] can produce tensions when you lose focus. I'm saying, it's my view that when you begin to grow, you should begin to decentralize."

Although the details vary for each church and religious institution, the goal is to disperse power among the congregation, to create roles and leadership within the church. Religious leaders and church pastors appoint members with various titles and roles to oversee church functions, study groups, prayer sessions, revivals, spiritual warfare meetings, and other important functions and rituals. What's more, they function semi-autonomously to allow for greater flexibility, free from the tight grips of institutional control. Randy Rodney, who serves as the head pastor of a large church, breaks down the details explaining how religious leaders and pastors follow the examples of others who devise similar strategies to decentralize:

> So multiply and disperse power. I know one religious leader on the island who did that. He appointed several different pastors at one time and kept appointing pastors. He broke up the church to a place where they set up for thousands, or whatever numbers the church was, to operate and meet in smaller groups. So it was like every twelfth man was a leader. They're doing the work on the ground. I took the concept from him and that is one of the reasons why just that our two hundred plus member congregation find themselves in thirty-one respective locations in different homes. Sometimes I just meet with them asking, "How are you? How's your husband? How are your children? How are you sending them to school? Let's pray for them. What else can we do?"

Another pastor creates semi-autonomous ministries that act nearly like independent churches within his church. This strategy can also apply to a single church or a few churches operating within an institution.

> I'm talking about the ministries. You have twelve different independent churches under your organization. There's a board and I'm the chairman of the board. I have six other people on the board, but I'm chairman, the Chief Executive Officer. I'm just using that word. But I'm the pastor. What I've done is I have structured a layered leadership. Each department is layered. So, our church is 215 [people], those layers of leaders, plus the board, constitutes a total of seventy-six people. Just think, that I have seventy-six people managing two hundred and fifteen. It becomes three to four for every one leader.

While this strategy of organization has the practical implications of reducing the workload of the head pastor of a large church, it also allows for the church to hold functions and services—from Bible studies to religious revivals and spiritual warfare ceremonies—separate from the more controlled, pastor-led church services. This keeps many church services and functions free from institutional control, and allows for new Charismatic leaders to emerge. One religious leader describes his strategy the following way:

Everybody comes to one place on Sunday. But there's a meeting on Tuesday, there's a meeting on Wednesday, depending on whatever day it is, there's a singles meeting, people meet, the men meet, the girls meet, and the boys meet. Keeps it small, keeps you from being a crazy busy man. So I try to go as lateral possible. Make sure everybody is getting involved and folks are doing what they want to do, how they want to do it, freely. We also have singles, you have youth, you have men, you have ladies, you have music, and you have whatever else, twice a month. From this hamlet, two or three families will come together in one location.

As this process of decentralization continues, church leaders, pastors, and emerging leadership begin to take on highly specialized roles, a "specialized charisma" that distinguishes religious leaders and pastors on an internally devised scale of Charismatic authenticity while also focusing attention on social change. Many of the Pentecostal pastors and leaders throughout the English-speaking Caribbean report their unique skill set, their "gifts" of the spirit that bring something new and important to the table. These skills range from business acumen to religious institutional leadership skills to counseling and advisors to spiritual gifts that include healing and discernment. As the church continues to experience processes of institutionalization, it does not necessarily imply homogenization. As one pastor explains:

Every minister now develops a different calling. There are some who work on the people, empower them and that kind of thing, but there are some ministers who are called to the government leaders and they would go to them and they would, you know, we all don't have the same gifts. We all are not lawyers, we all are not doctors, but whatever our calling. There are some ministers, when they come, they administer to leaders of the government. That's what they're called to. You know? They come to speak to the nation, not to the individual.

The specialization of spiritual labor works to keep charisma alive, except with pastors developing increasingly unique skill sets that distinguish themselves from the mass of pastors while also serving as an important use in the church and religious institutions. Religious leaders and pastors within the Charismatic movement in the English-speaking Caribbean not only take pride in these skill sets, but also develop important roles for both individual churches and larger institutions. While some pastors like Larry Scott of St. Lucia perform healing and deliverance for lay people, other religious leaders cater mainly to political leaders of their respective coun-tries. Some politicians develop skills that keep them on the ground grass-roots style with the people, while other religious leaders work closely with the political and economic elite, especially with the new and emerging role of various religious groups, including Charismatic Christian groups, with CARICOM. These pastors and religious leaders develop a specialization of labor that variously impacts different spheres of their social worlds—from politics to the economics to cultural and social institutions. This special-ization concentrates effort and focuses attention on specific tasks to bet-ter influence change within each institutional sphere. As religious leaders and pastors of the Caribbean find themselves within large and increasingly institutionalized churches, they disperse power within the congregation sowing the seeds necessary for new Charismatic leaders while also diversi-fying their labor to develop unique specialized charisma that focuses atten-tion on making social change throughout multiple spheres of social life.

Of course, most Pentecostal pastors, like Jared quoted below, believe that it is only God that will decide the fate of the Charismatic move-ment and its ability to resist the forces of institutionalization, remain Charismatic, and emerge as a stronger voice shaping the affairs of the region:

> If you study the ministry of the Holy Spirit, you learn that you never can tell what God will do. And so it's, a lot of times, it's that crisis forces you to recognize the importance of this Charismatic movement, that sometimes it seems that it's declining, and then something amazing happens again.

Conclusion

Research in St. Lucia, Barbados, and Dominica reveals three major insights about the Charismatic movement in the English-Speaking Caribbean, among other things. Religious leaders and pastors unanimously believe that it's not how much the church grows and becomes powerful, but rather how its leaders handle that growth. Rather, they must be able to change in order to meet the problems associated with power and institu-tionalization. Put differently the Charismatic movement must transform to better handle getting too big, powerful, and institutionalized. With growth and power comes increased external adversity, and this serves cha-risma and the vitality of the Charismatic movements well.

The Charismatic church builds strength and charisma when facing external pressures and hostility from a common enemy. Whenever the church is under pressure the quality of conversion, conviction, and unity is stronger. Increased adversity from the outside creates a vibrant militant Charismatic church. Ironically, it is the internal division of the church that allows it to maintain charisma. It is contradictorily the division in the Charismatic Christian church that simultaneously allows it to retain its charisma. Internal competition breeds charisma. Finally, as the church grows and centralizes, it experiences the simultaneous process of decentralization, forming many autonomous and semi-autonomous smaller cells under the umbrella of a large cell. This opens up the possibility for the church to remain grassroots oriented while also providing breeding grounds for the emergence of new Charismatic religious leaders. Perhaps it's some of these unanticipated consequences of advanced modernity where institutionalized social and religious movements, like Pentecostalism, recapture its charisma and vitality from the shackles of a stifling bureaucracy that joins the rank and file of power and orthodoxy. The Charismatic movement's capacity to defy the modern forces of rationality, even if unevenly and contradictorily, allows the church to retain its potential to make social change, and surprisingly, puts a big question mark on Weber's thesis of that horrid iron cage.

NOTES

1. Max Weber, "The Social Psychology of World Religions," in *From Max Weber: Essays in Sociology*, ed. and trans. Hans H. Gerth and C. Wright Mills (New York: Oxford University Press, 1946), 267–301.
2. Wolfgang Vondey, *Beyond Pentecostalism: The Crisis of Global Christianity and the Renewal of the Theological Agenda* (Grand Rapids, MI: William B. Eerdmans Publications, 2010).
3. Margaret Poloma, "The Symbolic Dilemma and the Future of Pentecostalism: Mysticism, Ritual, and Revival," in *The Future of Pentecostalism in the United States*, ed. Eric Patterson and Edmund Rybarczyk (Lanham, MD: Lexington Books, 2007), 105–122.
4. Max Weber, *The Protestant Ethic and the Spirit of Capitalism, Third Edition*, trans. Stephen Kalberg (Los Angeles: Roxbury Publishing Company, 2001).
5. Max Weber, "The Social Psychology of World Religions," in *From Max Weber: Essays in Sociology*, ed. and trans. Hans H. Gerth and C. Wright Mills (New York: Oxford University Press, 1946), 267–301.

6. C. Eric Lincoln and Lawrence Mamiya, *The Black Church in the African-American Experience* (Durham, NC: Duke University Press, 1990).
7. Thomas O'Dea and J. Milton Yinger, "Five Dilemmas of Institutionalization," *Journal for the Scientific Study of Religion* 1 (1961): 30–41.
8. Margaret M. Poloma, *The Assemblies of God at the Crossroads: Charisma and Institutional Dilemmas* (Knoxville, TN: University of Tennessee Press, 1989).
9. Margaret M. Poloma, *Main Street Mystics: The Toronto Blessing and Reviving Pentecostalism* (Walnut Creek, CA: Altamira Press, 2003).
10. Margaret M. Poloma and John Clifford Green, *The Assemblies of God Godly Love and the Revitalization of American Pentecostalism* (New York: New York University Press, 2010).
11. Peter Marina and Wilkerson, n.d.
12. Francis Myles claims that God showed him how to supernaturally change his DNA through what he calls "genetic salvation."
13. The wild and crowded bus from Dover Beach to Oistins ripped and roared along the east coast of Barbados. Bajan Buses resemble Mexican *collectivos* rather than a standard, boring American bus. Unlike the more erratic Mexican *collectivo*, the Baja bus follows a set and unalterable path. It's a minivan, much like the Trinidad Maxi-Taxi, with a sliding side door that opens and closes with passengers constantly entering and leaving the bus. The bus sits 14 people including the driver. Two people sit to the left of the driver (remember that the wheel is on the "correct" side of the car, unlike that of the USA), three people on the bench immediately behind the driver, and behind that bench another two benches that sit four people (one of those four seats on the last two benches opens and closes to make an extra seat for a fourth person). One man drives the bus while another man manages the bus, including seating people and collecting their money. Seating people involves pointing to people where they should, perhaps must, sit. This is much more difficult than appears at first glance. While some men might spend countless hours contemplating the butt of the woman, this man must fully comprehend the ass in all its dimensions, angles, shades, shapes, sizes, and its capacity for maneuverability. He must fit many asses into small spaces to maximize the profit of the bus route. Like a pimp, the more asses he moves, the more money the business makes. Therefore, he must not only understand the ass, but must also fully grasp the ass in all its complexity. He is an ass grasper. In a split second he must decide where each ass will fit, how it will fit between two different asses located on the same bench, and recognize the ability of an ass to make space sitting sideways or at an angle between two asses of various shapes and sizes. This man must fully and objectively know the ass, predict its

behavior, see patterns, and decide in an instant what ass belongs where and why. He must treat his profession as a sociologist—an entire subfield of an unknown but burgeoning discipline in Barbados to fully absorb all the complexities of the human bottom. The ass grasper must calculate all the asses on each of the four benches, make instant visual measurements of those leaving the bus, and observe asses coming from all dimensions walking toward the bus and—not knowing which ass will approach the bus first, must start calculating in his ever working mind a plan of action. When the asses finally approach the bus, he quickly shouts out, "You, over there (pointing to a space)," "You, get up and slide over. You, get on the next seat. You three, sit there in the back." And he must be accurate every time, no slip ups. The ass grasper is something to marvel at, his work underappreciated and underpaid.

14. Pew Research Center Forum on Religion & Public Life, *Pew-Templeton Global Religious Futures Project* (Washington, DC: Pew Research Center).

15. Jose Casanova, "Rethinking Secularization: A Global Comparative Perspective," *The Hedgehog Review* (2006); José Casanova, "Religion, the New Millennium, and Globalization," *Sociology of Religion* 62 (2001): 415–441; José Casanova, *Public Religions in the Modern World* (Chicago and London: The University of Chicago Press, 1994).

16. Casanova, 2006.

17. Max Weber, *The Protestant Ethic and the Spirit of Capitalism. Third Edition*, trans. Stephen Kalberg (Los Angeles: Roxbury Publishing Company, 2001).

18. Bussa led the largest slave rebellion in Barbadian history in 1816.

19. "Evangelical group tries to block gay cruises in Caribbean," *Associated Press*, 2006. Bishop Bill Daniel explains that he does not want Dominica portrayed as a gay tourist destination. He says, "We want the government to ensure that gay tourists do not come to the island and conduct themselves in any immoral way."

20. J.N. Figgis and R.V. Laurence, eds., *Historical Essays and Studies* (London: Macmillan, 1907), Letter to Bishop Mandell Creighton, April 5.

21. Margaret M. Poloma and John Clifford Green, *The Assemblies of God Godly Love and the Revitalization of American Pentecostalism* (New York: New York University Press, 2010).

22. Margaret M. Poloma, *Main Street Mystics: The Toronto Blessing and Reviving Pentecostalism* (Walnut Creek, CA: Altamira Press, 2003).

CHAPTER 7

St. Kitts and Montserrat

INTRODUCTION TO ST. KITTS

The plane above St. Kitts[1] offers a magnificent view of a small, 68-square-mile island that dwarfs in size compared to its Caribbean neighbors, but boasts tall mountains and picture-perfect beaches. The road from the airport near the capital of Basseterre hugs the coast and takes you through the entire island. Starting from the capital, the maxi-taxi style bus travels northwest through Brimstone Hill Fortress, Sandy Point Village, Newton Ground, St. Paul's, and finally to Dieppe Bay, the northernmost point of the island where the Caribbean meets the Atlantic. From Dieppe Bay, a short walk leads to a road where buses begin their travel of the Atlantic Coast side of the island in the east through the village of Sadler's, the plantation estate Ottley's, and the village of Cayon until finally reaching Basseterre. A taxi takes one to the more touristy and commercialized South Friar's Bay.

As in other Caribbean countries, St. Kitts unapologetically displays religion everywhere. Gospel hymns blare out from public schools onto the streets along with the sounds of religiously inspired school kids singing to the lyrics. "God is Good" is proudly displayed on public busses as well as on private taxicabs. Gospel music plays in the background of other public and private spaces, from the international airport to grocery stores. Jesus music blares in both private vehicles and public buses while religious slogans are written all over public walls as well as private homes and businesses. Perhaps if there is a God, he is alive and well in St. Kitts.

© The Author(s) 2016
P. Marina, *Chasing Religion in the Caribbean*,
DOI 10.1057/978-1-137-56100-8_7

The Caribbean, more than any place known in the world, in spite of what some country folks in the USA might say, is God's country. This chapter begins on the island of St. Kitts, providing insight into the challenges religious leaders from abroad face when taking over long-established local churches, a pastor's ongoing efforts to heal a paralyzed kid in a private home of a small village, and offers deeper analysis into how Charismatic leaders in the Caribbean understand the differences between physical/mental diseases and spiritual ones, including their views on homosexuality. Closer inspection into the world of PAWI leader Reverend Bartholomew showcases the struggle of a Pentecostal religious leader attempting to control a former PAWI-affiliated church from becoming independent, and potentially rogue. Heading to the small village of Sandy Point Town takes us to the world of Pastor Francis and his attempts to use his newly emerging gifts to heal a tragically paralyzed kid. The section on St. Kitts ends with a deeper look into some widely misunderstood perspectives of Charismatic leaders on the concept of disease and healing, which offers, for better or worse, a sociological understanding of their seemingly intolerant views on issues such as homosexuality and sin.

The second part of this chapter focuses on the island-country of Montserrat, widely believed to be the birthplace of the Pentecostalism in the Caribbean, to discuss the history of Pentecostalism on the island as well as insights into the highly regarded Caribbean scholar, politician, and PAWI leader Sir Howard Fergus on his views of the movement. The sections that follow discuss gender inequality within the movement as well as the struggles between charisma and institutionalization. The section concludes with some perspectives on hopes for the future, and some of that hope, among other things, involves the new generations of religious practitioners and their leaders.

Gaining Access to Religious Leaders in St. Kitts

Reverend Errol Bartholomew holds the prestigious position of General Administrator in PAWI's institutional hierarchy. Although Bartholomew is my initial contact to St. Kitts, all the contacts provided to reach him fail. Since he's new to the island, the contacts provided were yet to be updated. Bartholomew recently arrived to St. Kitts from Trinidad to serve as the acting pastor of the PAWI-affiliated church Christian Life Assemblies. In fact, Bartholomew arrived in St. Kitts only a month and a half prior to our visit. Word has it among the Pentecostal inner circle of religious leaders that the last pastor achieved some degree of wealth in St. Kitts and decided to move on to "greener" pastures in Florida. As a result, PAWI sent Bartholomew to temporarily lead the church until a new pastor could take over. Word also has it that Bartholomew currently struggles serving as the acting head pastor of the church.

The taxi from the airport drops me somewhere in the middle of the capital city of Basseterre. Lacking any useful contact information, I walk down the street into a random store to ask a clerk if she knows the location of Christian Life Assemblies. She points the way with the usual "up the road" directions common in the Caribbean. I go up and down the road eventually finding the church and knock on the door until someone finally answers. An older gentleman answers. His smile exposes teeth sticking out in many interesting directions. As I ask him how to locate Reverend Bartholomew, he looks at me with confusion, or perhaps aggravation. I plead my case for him to help me find the bishop. After some initial distrust, he calls the reverend on his phone, but to no avail. He asks his daughter to fetch the keys to the church van explaining how much responsibility he *used* to have in the church, though he proudly displays the church and van keys like they're the keys to the proverbial city. Once he finds out about my research, he opens up to reveal his sentiments about his old pastor while he shares his concerns about the new one.

This man serves as the custodian and all-around caretaker of the church. He's been a part of this church for many years and was close to the previous pastor. As we head toward the reverend's apartment in the southern part of the island, he talks openly about his concerns relating to the church, including what he explains as the dwindling numbers of church members. The custodian reports that church membership has been in steep decline during the transition, about a 20 % drop in the former 75-member congregation. He discusses problems associated with the transition to the new pastor. While he admits that he prefers the old pastor, who he says provided him a great deal of respect and responsibility, he also stresses that he has nothing personally against the new pastor. In frustration, the custodian indicates that he might soon give up his responsibilities if pushed stating, "All I can give is my best. If that is not good enough then I don't have to do anything."

After a few minutes of driving, the custodian explains that he believes, as others in the congregation also later shared, that pastor Bartholomew puts too much of a "stronghold" on the congregation, especially when it comes to making the church more of a PAWI church. He also believes that the pastor is too inflexible and rigid with the new congregation he inherited.

Although the church is a member of PAWI, the last pastor refused to conform to the rules and regulations of the organization. He ignored the doctrines, values, and principles of PAWI for many years. As a result, the church became completely estranged from PAWI. The job of the new pastor is to now put this church in line with PAWI and its institutional doctrines. The custodian explains Bartholomew spends a great deal of time preaching to the church about the principles, history, rules, and organization of PAWI, along with its structure and organization. This strong-arming, he urges, makes people feel uncomfortable as they struggle to learn the bureaucratic principles and procedures. This transition is not merely a change in pastors; it's an attempt to bring what became a largely independent church under the control of the larger PAWI institution.

We reach Bartholomew's apartment in a neighborhood called Bedrock and knock on the front door. A shirtless pastor wearing shorts opens his door in surprise and awkwardly invites us inside.

PAWI Church Assignments: New Pastors Taking Over Old Congregations

We sit on a sofa near a table with PAWI's constitution of rules, structures, and organization and a bookshelf with a copy of PAWI's published book *Ablaze* documenting the Pentecostal movement in the Caribbean. As I ask him about the books, he begins to explain that he uses them to educate the congregation on PAWI to make the church stronger within its organization. Bartholomew explains that there were some problems with the previous pastor who became too independent of PAWI; one of his purposes in taking over the church is to fix this. The problem, of course, lies in the struggle of an outsider taking over a church from the reigns of a beloved departing pastor and forcing an independent church to succumb to the rules and regulations of the highly institutionalized PAWI.

Bartholomew discusses the problems of taking over a church previously held by a longtime and beloved pastor, especially one that drifted away from its institutional underpinnings. He explains that when he took over the church and began introducing the congregation to PAWI's constitution, the members of the congregation would tell him, "Pastor, we never heard these things." He stresses the difficulty of taking over a church so isolated from PAWI and its inner workings, including preaching new PAWI approved messages.

Bartholomew explains that as the church moved away from PAWI, it also lost some of its independence falling into dire financial straits. According to him, the church became increasingly disorganized with problems running the daily operations. The church, he says, needs help, and help means putting it back within the power of PAWI.

Marina: So what are the challenges that come with takin' over a new church?

Bartholomew: (laughs) Well the issue with this church is that the pastor had not been active here for the work of PAWI.

Marina: What does that mean?

Bartholomew: Not participating in the conferences. He had not been aware of changes that were taking place just because in the organization we have new things you have to do. So he hadn't been keeping up for several of these changes, and the church became isolated.

Marina: From the inner-workings of PAWI?

Bartholomew: Yeah. So a lot of things that they should have known, they (the congregation) didn't know. For instance, changes have been made in the constitutional bylaws that we walk through in each conference. We have biannual conferences and we have a general conference where we bring all the changes as we come together.

Marina: So what are the challenges?

Bartholomew: So, the challenge of taking on a group like that ... it's more like, you have to have patience and dedication to help them through and become able to finance itself and run independently though under the umbrella of PAWI. But they got to learn about it, its constitution and rules.

Although starting a new church offers its own challenges, one of the advantages of starting from scratch is the ability to impart your own unique vision on the church at its inception. Bartholomew, a Trinidad native, was able to do that when he started a church in Port of Spain. In short, that church was *his* vision, or as Bartholomew puts it, "I became a pastor in one church I started and the vision of the church became my vision from the start, so there were no problems." Now the challenge is to figure out how to establish a new vision in an established church that has deviated from the institution, like teaching the proverbial old dog new tricks. While he admits new pastors who take over churches typically experience a "honeymoon" period, it's also a time to sow the seeds of the new vision. As Bartholomew explains:

I would say I'm on my honeymoon period. [We laugh.] The first two to six months is your honeymoon period because people are now getting to know you, people may tend to be nice to you, and all of that. And you don't want to go and shake everybody by the scruff of their necks, so you enjoy that nice period. But it's the honeymoon period that's the best period for you to share your vision. So for me, what I done coming in, I have simply decided I will not share what I want to do, but I ask them what they want to do. What they saw as priority for their mission at the church. What they saw the church becoming.'

The main approach, Bartholomew discusses, involves striking a balance between a leader imposing a vision on the church and allowing congregation members to have a voice in shaping their own vision for the church. Of course, all of this takes time. And just like any new leader taking over a position of authority, building trust and rapport with the congregation is key. As Bartholomew puts it:

I believe that as a new person, you have to share your vision. You have to do it over and over for maybe about two years before people begin to hear your vision. Because they don't know as members, if it's an autonomous church, they would have been exposed to a whole lot of other bad stuff. And because they are on the ground, if you come and impose your vision, it begins to become like resentment. So when I came through the door [at the new church], I said to [church] board, what would you like to see happen here?

The church board is the management committee of the church composed of some of its higher ranking and esteemed congregation members. Bartholomew explains that although the church claims to want to bring people together to better reflect the community, they have been estranged from PAWI for 30 years. As a result, he fears that the congregation has been exposed to bad habits, ideas, and behaviors. Simply, Bartholomew remains hesitant to allow the church free rein to adopt their own independent vision. He simply does not know what the congregation members have been exposed to. As a Trinidadian, he's also still uncertain about the culture of the church, much less the larger community. As Bartholomew points out, "They will have seen some things. I don't know this culture." While he claims to allow the voice of the congregation members to shape the church's vision, he also imparts his own stating, "So my strategy has been, don't bring my vision, but I want to try to mold new religious leaders. My vision is that every individual inside of here must become a minister, that's ministering somewhere, and that we will take the church outside to various communities to establish new churches."

Meanwhile, in order to establish his vision of creating new leaders, Bartholomew must teach them all about PAWI, including its institutional changes over the past three decades. He says part of the problem in getting the entire church congregation on board with PAWI relates to the divisions that existed within the church during the previous pastor's administration. Bartholomew explains that before his arrival, negative things were said about PAWI. The current congregation, he stresses, feels that PAWI abandoned them. But Bartholomew explains, something he reminds the congregation, that it's a two-way street and that the prior pastor was not reaching out to PAWI on their behalf. Bartholomew now wants to bring uniformity to the congregation, educate them on PAWI, and flesh out a shared vision.

Bartholomew unevenly negotiates the balance between congregational freedom and pastoral authority. Of course, if the pastor pushes the rules and regulations of PAWI too hard, the congregation will eventually dwindle to almost nothing and the pastor will lose legitimacy as both a head pastor and a religious leader within an institution. On the other hand, if Bartholomew, a high-ranking PAWI official, loses control of the congregation, he will lose credibility as an institutional authority within PAWI. That is, if the congregation becomes a rogue church, he loses credibility as both a Pentecostal pastor and a religious leader within a powerful institution. This challenge puts Bartholomew in a tenuous position as he continues to negotiate institutional authority with congregational agency.

The greatest problem related to Bartholomew's struggle is his attempt to assert institutional legitimacy over charisma authority, thus alienating a church congregation that once relied on the authority of charisma over institutionalization. The church moved away from institutionalization with a Charismatic pastor, now the attempt is to institutionalize a church congregation that became free of its grip. While the previous pastor may have taken his charisma with him to Florida, the congregation retains its charisma here in St. Kitts, and refuses to surrender it so easily to an institution. In order to prevent losing legitimacy as both a pastor of a church and a religious leader within an institution, perhaps Bartholomew must better negotiate charisma with institutional authority.

Other Challenges for Head Pastors within PAWI

Like in many relationships, money also becomes an issue. As the church declines in numbers and dollars, it needs financial help and outside support. But like the International Monetary Fund, that support will only happen if the potential rogue church succumbs to the power and domination of PAWI. Ironically for many church members, once they achieve some degree of financial autonomy after receiving help from PAWI, they must pay steep tithes to the organization and conform to its rules and vision. This puts the church in a difficult position as it faces the pressures to conform to a larger institution in order to remain alive, while at the same time, knowing that conforming to it might also create the type of division in the church that threatens to rip it apart. For now, at least, even those that reject PAWI, according to the reverend, still attend church regularly. As Bartholomew puts it, "We have had a few people comment that they don't wanna be part of PAWI, that they'll go to another church. But by and large, I have seen that even those who are against PAWI, who may have voiced that, I see them come to church." Bartholomew says optimistically, "Eventually, they will come around."

Of course, while institutionalization poses its own problems for a Charismatic movement and its vitality, it also makes spreading across religious and political boundaries much easier. Institutionalization provides Pentecostals with a common rhetoric and style easily transmissible to a large and varied audience. While institutionalized Pentecostalism "travels well across geographical and cultural space"[2] throughout the English-speaking Caribbean and beyond, its ability to continue making an impact on the region depends largely on how it meets the needs of a new, more educated, and cosmopolitan generation in a highly changing and increasingly reflexive culture.

One of the advantages for PAWI-affiliated Pentecostal pastors and leaders taking over new churches across the region is the shared rhetoric of the institution that preaches messages which communicate similar ideas. While institutionalization in the Charismatic movement increasingly threatens charisma, it certainly helps to spread the movement using the same, or at least very similar, rhetorical styles that convey a systematic and consistent message easily digestible to a wide variety of audiences, including the various cultures that exist throughout the English-speaking Caribbean. Further, as Reverend Nigel and I discussed in length back in St. Martin (see Chapter 4), many Pentecostal preachers remain isolated from the world outside their congregations.[3] Many Pentecostal pastors and leaders also lack a formal education from outside its closed religious institutions. While this makes it difficult for them to address the larger world outside of Christianity, including addressing many of the current debates on a global stage, it does allow them to appeal to many members of the Caribbean who also lack this type of exposure. This makes it easy for people to take over new churches using the same common rhetoric and consistent themes and messages. The only problem, one that Pentecostal leaders will eventually have to deal with in the near future, is that younger people in the Caribbean become increasingly exposed to more cosmopolitan views from both the highly appealing secular and religious worlds that offer alternative messages from the traditional Pentecostal rhetoric of their parents.

Although institutionalized Pentecostal practices and messages, as well as its particular forms and styles, have a high degree of transposability when moving across political boundaries, the movement must meet the cultural transformations of the future.[4] Perhaps Pentecostal preachers might make good use of a world outside their congregation and religious fundamental "theology" and venture into the world of the arts, social sciences, philosophy, and physics, and emerge as a new Charismatic voice better equipped with the ability to find its own voice in world affairs. While institutionalization might make it easier in the short run for Pentecostal pastors and religious leaders to take over churches, in the long term, the real challenge is finding new and Charismatic ways to keep the youth of a changing Caribbean culture active in the Pentecostal movement and part of the larger movement shaping its future direction.

Reverend Kenneth Francis

Reverend Kenneth Francis, a former maxi-taxi driver in Trinidad, serves as the head pastor of Abundant Life Assembly in Sandy Point Town, a small village that is also the second largest town in St. Kitts. Religious leaders describe him as a raw but genuine and affable man who likes to cook and eat. We talk for hours about his path to conversion and life of ministry and pastoralism, including his personal struggles along that journey. He's originally from Trinidad now heading a church in a small village that he believes is on the brink of a supernatural manifestation.

Francis discusses how becoming the head pastor of a church can be a lonely experience, especially since religious leaders have fewer people to confide in for advice and guidance. Pastors, of course, care for their flock, not the other way around. It's common for pastors to confide in only those who share an equal position in social class and status. As a result, according to Francis, pastors confide in other religious leaders of equal rank or, if they have a strong marriage, their wives. Francis explains that part of his path to becoming a Pentecostal pastor involved opening up honest relationships with people he could trust. It was a divorce that helped push him toward his original path to becoming a pastor, and it was a new marriage that solidified him as a leader with a strong woman he could confide in for everything, from the very beginning. As Francis puts it:

> Actually my second wife I had to confess all my secrets to. All. Everything. When we had just gotten married, our son wasn't born as yet. On one Sunday evening, well I know His (God) voice said, "You have to tell her. If you want me to clean you up, you gotta start." So one Sunday evenin' the voice of the Lord says, "Tell her now." Oh, Jesus. And I had that conversation exactly as I say it. "Lord? Now?" And he said, "Everything," and I said, "*Everything?*" I was amazed at how my wife responded.

While developing strong ties with his wife allowed Francis to learn the importance of honesty, and while this also helps to solve the problems of the loneliness of the pastor, what's most important is his belief that the experience of loneliness serves a larger purpose. It helps him develop Charismatic abilities, allowing him the type of deep introspection to develop his budding "supernatural" manifestations and new "gift" of prophecy. He believes that this gift can help change lives, like the life of the young man in the following tragic story.

Healing and Paralysis: Francis and the Paralyzed 17-Year-Old in Sandy Point Village

Not too long ago, on the Northwest coast of St. Kitts along the Caribbean in the small town of Sandy Point, a young man paralyzed from the neck down, lies helpless in bed riddled with bedsores and dripping with sweat from the stifling Caribbean heat. He slipped off a pole one day and into the wrong end of a pool in his village.

We walk into a small shack of a house and follow a narrow hallway that leads to a dark, undecorated small room with a tiny window, two single beds, and a medium-size fan to provide some relief to the heat.

Upon first glance of the young lad, Jeremy, it becomes clear that his body is not only paralyzed but also gruesomely mangled. His bones were so broken and disfigured that his limbs contort in the strangest, and what seems the most uncomfortable, ways. Although he retains full control of his mental faculties, the local school cannot accommodate his broken body. The diagnosis, of course, is that this 17-year-old boy will live out the rest of his days with a shattered and mangled body in this dark, plain, and hot room.

Francis, who visits Jeremy for about an hour every Thursday, starts with a prayer, asking for the boy to be relieved of his paralysis, then repeats, "We thank you, we thank you, we thank you." He stops the prayer to explain his process of healing. Francis says, "Usually, when I pray for him I use this cloth that represents one of the cloths that Jesus used to touch people and heal them. It's something I use when I pray for people. [While showing the colors and design of the cloth] All of this represents the scripture and the colors represent healing." Francis explains that he prays for the boy every week, but never knows when God will make a change, but he brings the cloth anyway. Francis explains:

I always come here expecting something. I see him walking [one day]; I expect something different. But it's a process. I really don't discourage him. ... Sometimes, you gotta build a friendship with people, a relationship with people. Sometimes I come out and we pray, then I talk sports with him and just lie with him, you know, be a friend, because he doesn't have a friend. He hardly sees friends, so I come and try to be the friend for him. Always hoping that one day, God does something Sometimes we pray and I ask him how he feeling, sometimes he feeling a warmness going through his body.

We talk about friendship and *fútbol* before getting into the serious matter at hand, to heal the young man of his horrible ailments.

Francis prays with feverish intensity as he places both hands on the boy's body from his head to his heart to his mangled arms and legs. The boy strains his face with his eyes shut, closed like a weightlifter finishing his last heavyset. Francis prays even more adamantly each time his hands touch a new part of the body, especially the parts most destroyed. The boy's eyes suddenly pop wide open as if in panic.

Jeremy's neck extends out while he struggles with some unknown force that puts a look of shock and bewilderment on his face. His body shakes and trembles, making peculiar jerking motions. Francis does not bellow out but rather mutters prayers under his breath, yet the words still manage to come out intelligibly, "Jesus, heal his body, Jesus, Jesus, give him relief and make this boy walk again. Jesus only your power can heal him." Francis continues to pray, touching the boy's body in key places and asking Jeremy to recite back a prayer as he goes. He prays with the pastor for a few minutes while gradually tempering down the strain in his face until it reaches a total halt. His body now lies motionless in complete despair.

The pastor says to me numerous times that he believes, and has seen in a vision, that this boy will walk again. He recognizes the frustration of the healing process, and the difficulties of never knowing when, or if, this boy will be healed. After the prayer, we all talk about the process of healing:

> Francis: It's difficult sometimes. You pray and nothing happens. You see others praying for people and they getting miraculously healed. All of that's part of the process.
>
> Marina: [*to Jeremy*] May I ask you your experiences with the pastor?
>
> Francis: [*to Jeremy*] He asking what you feel when we pray.
>
> Boy: Yeah, I feel like a hot feeling in my spine. Sometimes I feel when he puts his hands on me that something is happening. And sometimes I feel warm.
>
> Francis: The whole process is belief; it's not magic. In some people He [God] does it instantly, in some it's a process. Some people go through it partially, so as their faith grows, the healing is complete.

Francis holds the boy's hand as we close our eyes and sit in absolute silence. Francis continues to meet Jeremy every Thursday in hopes of him walking again one day.

While healing often involves physical ailments, it also includes the healing of sinister forces and the casting out of demons, ones that take on the appearance of physical and mental diseases.

Worldly versus Otherworldly Diseases: From Bipolar Disorder to Homosexuality

Some Pentecostal pastors and bishops take on leadership positions as moral entrepreneurs establishing moral crusades that attempt to prevent cruise ships with gays and lesbians from docking on their home islands, like former PAWI Bishop Pastor Bill in Dominica, among others. Admittedly, I always found Pentecostal views on homosexuality disturbing, especially among a group geared toward the biblical teachings of love and forgiveness. How can such a group claim to practice love, compassion, and humility—the virtues found in the Sermon on the Mount—rather than force and exaction when they seem so intolerant and hateful toward others with alternative sexual orientations? Although this in no way apologizes for Pentecostal views on homosexuality, the explanation below serves to understand their views regarding homosexuality, for better or worse.

Charismatic Christian religious leaders in the Caribbean explain the existence of two types of diseases: worldly and otherworldly. Worldly diseases involve the physical body and mind, or physical and mental illnesses. Otherworldly diseases involve the supernatural variety that deceptively takes on the appearance of a worldly disease but actually consists of a demonic possession. There is physical leukemia and spiritual leukemia; one needs a medical doctor to cure the former, and a preacher to cure the latter. There's mental schizophrenia and bipolar disorder and spiritual schizophrenia and bipolar disorder. In the case of a spiritual disease, a demon or evil spirit takes over a victim and manifests itself as a physical or mental disease. But of course, it is not physical or mental. This demonic trickery lasts while medical doctors and mental health specialists treat the victim. Doctors cannot treat a spiritual disease using western medicines or invasive surgeries intended to cure otherworldly problems, even if the spiritual sickness closely mimics a physical or mental one.

Most people seem to assume that Charismatic Christians attempt to use the supernatural powers of God to cure physical and mental diseases. Although Charismatic Christians will pray to deliver the individual from physical and mental sufferings, the vast majority uses the supernatural to cure not the physical or mental but rather spiritual diseases that manifests itself as a worldly disease. Demons, it is believed, make great liars, with grand illusions to make spiritual diseases appear as physical or mental. When medical doctors attempt to cure what they believe to be a physical disease, their treatments don't work. In fact, such attempts hide the true source of sickness and thereby keep the demon safe. No amount of science, medicine, or surgery can take the demon out of the body. The demon has problems when it is figured out that the sickness lies in the realm of the spiritual.

Charismatic Christian leaders do not try to cure physical diseases with solely spiritual weapons; that makes no sense. They say "Get a doctor, are you kidding me?" "You got Leukemia? Get a medical doctor man, you sick. Sorry, we will pray for you and that doctor." But if you have a spiritual disease that acts like a physical or mental one, a demon making it look like you got a physical disease, then what good is a doctor? It is like operating on the foot when the problem is the head; it accomplishes nothing except making new problems. If you have a spiritual disease, you need spiritual healing.

It is more likely the non-charismatic Christians, like many new age spiritualists in mainstream USA, will believe that supernatural forces and magical herbs alone will cure physical and mental diseases, not Charismatic Christians. Upon closer inspection, it is easy to understand the rationality behind their worldview, including their seemingly bigoted views on homosexuality.

Returning to the Rev's conversation on free will and the sociological concept of agency back in Barbuda (see Chapter 4), Pentecostal leaders believe humans possess free will. But the individual loses free will when demonically possessed, or at least free will becomes compromised and more limited. Pentecostal leaders claim to find discontent with the demon, not the victim. Homosexuals, they believe, lose their free will. They are forced into homosexuality that appears to be a worldly abnormality when in fact it is otherworldly, a supernatural possession. Freeing the inflicted is believed to cure homosexuals and return their free will and independence. Pentecostal leaders claim to love the individual but take issue with the demon denying the individual of free will and forcing homosexual behaviors against the will of the individual.

INTRODUCTION TO MONTSERRAT

Although the Pentecostal movement in the West Indies is headquartered in Trinidad & Tobago, its beginnings are credited to the small island nation-state of Montserrat.[5] While the initial seeds of the Pentecostal movement in the Caribbean were planted about two years before the Azusa Street revival, scholars and followers of Pentecostalism in Montserrat identify the first decade of the twentieth century as the very beginning of the Pentecostal movement in the Caribbean, some scholars say as early as 1907.[6] According to PAWI's unpublished book titled *Blazing the Trail*:

> It was not in Jamaica, in Barbados nor Antigua. Seemingly, God overlooked those islands and visited Montserrat, a tiny island of 39 square miles and certainly with a very small population and meager resources, for the initiation of the Pentecostal Ministry in the West Indies. ... Despite the apparent controversy about who started the Pentecostal work in Montserrat, all the records evidence that the work was launched sometime between 1909 and 1910 during or shortly after the Azuza Street Revival.[7]

Montserrat's impressive volcanoes offer symbolic representation of the supernatural underpinnings of a culture located in the heart of the Leeward Islands steeped in religious belief. Montserrat, respectively known as the Emerald Isle of the Caribbean and the Caribbean's Azusa Street, lies approximately 25 miles south of Antigua, closer than Antigua's sister island of Barbuda. Although debates continue on if the movement started in Montserrat, it's clear, at least, that PAWI started here. Either way, Montserrat played a strong role in establishing the Pentecostal movement in the region and facilitating its spread throughout the Caribbean.

This section proceeds with a history of the Pentecostal movement in Montserrat that includes insights into the preeminent historian and Pentecostal Caribbean scholar Sir Howard Fergus and his various views of the movement. Based on these insights, the section moves on to discuss gender inequality within the movement and the struggles between charisma and institutionalization. The section concludes with insights into the hopes for the future, leading to a discussion with budding religious leaders in the country and those visiting Montserrat from the surrounding islands who offer some surprising perspectives on the movement and its future.

Access to Religious Leaders in Montserrat

Although Bishop Meade is my initial contact in Montserrat, it's unclear if he's on or off island. It is also unclear where to find him, only a phone number was provided, and there's no answer. Fortunately, while waiting at the ferry to dock in Antigua for a boat to Montserrat, I ask a random woman sitting behind me if she knows Bishop Meade. Delightfully, she replies, "Why yes, he is my pastor." She tells me that he currently lives in the newly developed neighborhood of St. John's located just down Sweeney's Road from the capital city Brades. This woman just returned from Orlando to attend the 98th Annual International Assembly at the Church of God of Prophesy. Apparently, Bishop Meade also attended this meeting, though she is unsure if he was returning to Montserrat anytime soon. The woman explains that another one of my contacts, Pastor Abraham Riley, is now retired and no longer head of Faith Tabernacle Pentecostal Church, also located in Brades. Riley now resides in another new development located in a neighborhood called Lookout. Pastor Tony Allen now heads Faith Tabernacle Pentecostal Church. The woman also took time to discuss some important scholars' influential in the literature on religion and culture in Montserrat, including a man I would soon meet, Sir Howard Fergus, author of a book about PAWI called *Tongues on Fire*. Further, PAWI recently celebrated their 100-year anniversary in Montserrat, at the Faith Tabernacle Pentecostal Church.

Once in Montserrat, I jump in a taxi headed toward a guesthouse that turned out to be a perfect place to stay in this majestic volcanic country. David Lea, a white born-again Christian (and former hippie) from the USA, runs the guesthouse called Gingerbread Hill in St. Peters, along with his wife Clover and their son Noah. David also created the documentary series called *The Price of Paradise* recording the days leading up to the eruptions of the Soufriére Hills volcano that became active and eventually destroyed half the island, including Montserrat's Georgian era capital city of Plymouth. David decided to drive me around much of the island until eventually bringing me to meet Sir Howard Fergus.

Sir Howard Fergus

Sir Howard Archibald Fergus is a well-known writer, historian, academic, and teacher in the Caribbean and former Speaker and Acting Governor of Montserrat. He was born in a tiny village called Long Ground located in the southern part of Montserrat, now uninhabited and part of the exclusion zone due to volcanic activity. He attended universities in both the Caribbean and England, including the University of the West Indies and the Universities of Bristol and Manchester. Fergus previously worked as a teacher and Chief Education Officer, Speaker of the Legislative Council of Montserrat, as well as periodically serving as Acting Governor of the island since 1976. He also served on several constitutional and electoral committees. Although Fergus modestly says that he is an "average" academic, he explains:

> Sometimes I worked for government. I was also an educator. I was the chief education officer and the top person in the technical field of education, or officially the Director of Education. And then I went to the University of the West Indies to work in the Extramural Department, now called the School of Continuing Studies, or the Open Campus.

Sir Howard Fergus has published works from Montserrat history to books of poetry to books about volcanoes. One of his most recent works, *Tongues on Fire*, documents the history of the Pentecostal movement in

Montserrat. Fergus was the first person from Montserrat to be awarded the Order of the British Empire in recognition of his outstanding service to Montserrat and the Caribbean region. Finally, Sir Fergus currently serves in a leadership position in PAWI as General Executive.

Although Fergus is an academic and teacher, he has always remained a strong Pentecostal believer. In his own words:

> I was born to Pentecostal parents in a little village. And at that time, the church was kind of central to the village. There were two churches, one was Methodist and one was Pentecostal. But I grew up in the Pentecostal church and I went to Sunday school and children's meetings and all of that. But Pentecostals teach that your parents can't pass the thing on to you, that you have to receive Christ for yourself. And I got converted, I would say, at about age twenty-one. So I am a believer, and I have been a believer for decades.

Similar to the discussion with Pastor Alleng back in Barbados, Fergus explains how being a believer not only informs his scholarship but also gives it increased credibility in the Caribbean. The conversation illustrates the strong relationship between religious and academic legitimacy in the Caribbean.

> Marina: In your training, as you were being brought up and as you were going through the university, you were Pentecostal and a believer. Has that influenced your writing as a historian and a poet, and your academic work?
>
> Fergus: Yeah so my general answer to that is "yes." My faith, my religious experience would have informed my work, informed my work in some way. It's different here (the Caribbean).
>
> Marina: Are you considered even more legitimate as an academic if you're a believer, a Christian at least?
>
> Fergus: Um ... (short pause) ... yeah, I think so. I think so. Yeah, but certainly there's no negative attached to it in terms of how your work is regarded. I get requests to review books from people who are not into the church.

Perhaps it's his dedication to Montserrat, devotion to academic work, and university teaching as well as his faithfulness to Pentecostalism in a religious Caribbean country that has gained Fergus the credibility and high standing he achieved on the island and beyond. But Fergus is not the only well-respected academic in the Caribbean with strong religious convictions toward Charismatic Christianity. The discussion below shows how religious conviction provides some lagniappe legitimacy to people in positions of power in the Caribbean, from politicians to academics.

> Marina: Sure, sure. It almost seems as though, in many ways, being a man of God, or a religious person gives you a little bit more legitimacy in just about every area of life, including in academia.
> Fergus: It does, and it gives us some advantage because you have a following, you have some clout. I mean a chaplain's campaigning for election, and he was talking badly about a prominent Church of God prophecy pastor. When you go and talk against that guy, you are losing votes from his congregation. So, um, yes, it gives a kind of clout and legitimacy in politics.
> Marina: Yeah, like I said, it really struck me when it dawned that a born-again believer in the Caribbean as an academic gives them more legitimacy.
> Fergus: Yeah, because there's a guy who I succeeded as the General Executive of PAWI, he's a great historian, too. Alvin Thompson. And he's one of our good historians, and he's a staunch Pentecostal. Then there's a lawyer in Barbados, can't remember his name now, young guy, very good speaker who is Pentecostal. And, yeah, it's not as negative.

While politicians gaining legitimacy through religious belief is also common in the USA, finding it as an academic through religious conviction certainly differs from the Caribbean's northern neighbors. In fact, Alvin Thompson taught African and Caribbean History for over 40 years at the University of Guyana and the University of the West Indies. Thompson has published or edited five books with established presses from Routledge to the University of West Indies Press. He also served as the editor of the *Journal of Caribbean History* for over a decade. While of course not all Caribbean-born academics in the Caribbean gain extra legitimacy through strong religious convictions, it seems clear that being a born-again Christian does not carry the negative label it does for much of the mainstream USA, and may actually benefit one's academic standing.

The preeminent Caribbean scholar Fergus, widely considered an expert on the history of the Pentecostal Movement on the island, argues that religion serves as a powerful force throughout much of Montserrat, from social to political life. Now, it's not only the Anglican and Methodist church with a monopoly on power. According to Fergus, "The first colonists on Montserrat were fleeing religious persecution.[8] It was a Christian mission that served as the forerunner of the Pentecostal movement when it came to the island in the early twentieth century. Pentecostalism attracted some of the most marginalized inhabitants of Montserrat, beginning in the villages of Baker Hill and Cudjoe Head, proving most desirable to those people experiencing abuse from the colonials as well as poverty wage jobs in the post-emancipation era. As Fergus puts it, "The people were both poor and voiceless. Should we be surprised that radical Christianity appealed to them?"[9] Over time, the Pentecostal poor and voiceless increased their power and influence in Montserrat, like much of the English-speaking Caribbean. It was the up and coming Christian groups that paved the way from marginality to the ranks of power. As Fergus puts it:

> The charismatic movement in Montserrat is powerful. But there was once when churches like Pentecostal churches and Seventh Day Adventist churches were regarded as inferior to the Anglican Church and the Methodist Church and the Roman Catholic Church. It's only after a Seventh Day Adventist became chief minister (similar to a prime minister) of Montserrat in which these other churches came into greater prominence, and people got more recognition. Because you could have been slightly discriminated against if you belonged to a Pentecostal sect.

Fergus uses examples from his personal life as well as his experiences in national politics in Montserrat to illustrate how the Charismatic movement, including Pentecostalism, has gained new ground in recent history. He explains:

> My sister was educated but couldn't become a teacher because the schools were Methodist in orientation, and she belonged to a Pentecostal church. So religion interpenetrated life and culture and social life in negative ways as well. So there has been a change. There is a guy who is leading the opposition, and potentially could become the Premier of Montserrat. He is a Seventh Day Adventist. I was the longest speaker of Parliament in the common ground, the British Common Wealth of Nations, and I'm Pentecostal. So there has been a change.

As leaders from the more marginalized Christian groups rose to power among the established institutions, new opportunities arose for the followers of groups like the Seventh-Day Adventists and Pentecostals. Fergus explains how children of slavery in the Caribbean have three paths to social mobility—wealth, whiteness, or education. Now, Christian born-again believers from previously marginalized groups like Pentecostalism find that religious belonging increases the chances for upward mobility in multiple spheres of social life from politics to academia. As Fergus admits,

"Yes, religion is very important in social life, but some of the negatives have gotten really turned around. I've even acted as governor of this country from time to time."

While Pentecostalism is one source among others for upward mobility, the same cannot be said for sex and gender equality within the Pentecostal movement in the Caribbean, especially for its largest institution PAWI.

PAWI and Gender Inequality

It's interesting that so many women find empowerment in a religious group that generally marginalizes them within structures of institutional power. Currently, PAWI has few women occupying high-ranking positions within its institution. It's also interesting that this happens on an island where women actually started the Pentecostal movement in the Caribbean. According to the Caribbean Pentecostal scholar Fergus, the once staunch Roman Catholic Sister Laurencina Joseph, was led by the "Holy Spirit" to travel from St. Croix to Montserrat in 1904 (two years before the Azusa Street revival) to establish religious meetings emphasizing conversion. After her initial visit, she returned to Montserrat with her husband and rented buildings to hold services that eventually produced many new converts. Fergus explains that many of these people converted from other mainline churches, especially the Methodist Church. These services became a full-blown missionary sparking revivals that would challenge the large denominations on the island, leading these established churches to label Pentecostalism as unorthodox and bordering on the heretical. It was women like Sister Laurencina Joseph who stood up against power to help spark the global Pentecostal movement in the Caribbean.

Although most PAWI religious leaders object to women serving in high ranks of the institution, people like PAWI's General Executive Member-at-Large Howard Fergus fight for increasing gender equality within the organization. Fergus explains, "I've been fighting, for instance, a woman cannot have the top job in PAWI. And I've tried to change that." Fergus finds resistance to gender equality not only from men but also some of the women who object, based on some biblical interpretation, that women should remain subordinate to men. Fergus says in near disbelief, "And even some of the women don't support me." As Pentecostal scholars have long pointed out, the Azusa Street revival started as a radically egalitarian movement where men and women as well as blacks and whites alike contributed to its spark and spread. The irony, of course, is that a woman founded the Pentecostal movement in the Caribbean, and once it became fully institutionalized in the form of PAWI, women are denied equal access to its high ranks. Suffice it to say, PAWI and other religious leaders of the Pentecostal movement in the Caribbean have a long way to go in achieving social justice and equality for women, the very people who birthed a movement that has given its male leaders wealth and social mobility. Now perhaps it is time for PAWI and other Pentecostal leaders to make it right and give women the positions of power they are owed.

Charisma and Institutionalization in Montserrat

Just like Weber's description of church membership and financial credit in nineteenth-century USA, membership in PAWI provides religious pastors and leaders added credentials to their religious resume, a form of social and religious capital. Fergus explains that being a part of PAWI gives churches and pastors that are part of PAWI established credit and name as opposed to just being on their own. As I have argued throughout this book, a movement that relies on credit over charisma for legitimacy can lose its mojo. Fergus asserts, however, the revivals might just be enough to keep charisma alive from its more disenchanting institutional qualities. Agreeing that a tension exists between charisma and institutionalization, Fergus explains:

> Yeah, I would question that, because there's a word called revivement. You can have revivals where people can recognize that the fire is dying out. The whole idea is that the fire shouldn't die out. But like everything else, you have periods. And I think there'll be lulls, everything human, even love. I think it's one of the slow periods today, but PAWI's alive and well. And I've loved to death, like the Americans say, I've never loved someone to death.

While Fergus believes they will not love the Pentecostal movement to death, and that revivals offer the best hope for the future, he also points out the importance of keeping charisma alive. The best hope for charisma, he suggests, is to invest in the emerging religious leaders of the movement. Just like in the sport cricket, investing in the budding talent is tantamount to the future, or as Fergus puts it, "You know they always want to invest in younger players in Cricket. In cricket, you have to invest in the younger players and make them good. Say okay, let us work on our youngsters emerging as leaders in Pentecostalism." That's exactly where we now turn. This chapter ends with a conversation that provides some insight into the perspectives of two new and emerging leaders of the Pentecostal movement in the Caribbean today.

Lunchtime with Religious Leaders of Montserrat and Beyond

After running errands with David Lea, he drops me off to a community meeting about the importance of leadership at Faith Tabernacle Pentecostal Church where I meet a woman named Josepha Fenton who, after hearing about my research on the Charismatic movement in the Caribbean, invites me to a private dinner party with religious leaders visiting Montserrat from the surrounding islands. Ms. Fenton, whose grandparents were part of the original Pentecostal movement in Montserrat, lives in a beautiful house on a volcanic mountain overlooking the island's landscape. She's a woman of strength and pride, and an ardent born-again Christian with close ties to the movement and its leaders.

Apostle Dexter Laurence and Pastor Allen attend this rather elaborate lunch with their wives and children. These up-and-coming pastors are part of the new crop of budding religious leaders within the Pentecostal movement. Pastor Tony Allen now heads Faith Tabernacle Pentecostal Church in Brades. Pastor Laurence, originally from Trinidad, is visiting Montserrat from Antigua where he heads a church in the countryside. He's also a gospel musician and a singer and songwriter with his own social media sites and YouTube videos. The conversation begins as both Allen and Laurence discuss the importance of staying relevant within the church and having to always reinvent themselves. We start talking about some of the changes happening in Caribbean culture and the emergence of a new generation with access to new forms of social media and modes of communication that opens the Caribbean world to cultures and ideas from all over the world. Our conversation quickly moves to how the Pentecostal movement, and its newly emerging leaders, responds to the demands of a rapidly transforming Caribbean world.

Laurence explains how the budding leaders of the Pentecostal movement, and the Charismatic movement in general, need to navigate the difficult terrain of making changes with a transforming culture while also keeping fixed some of the major beliefs and traditions of the past. He states, "I was saying last night, don't conform to everything. You will lose yourself. But there are some standards that are set that you have to go by." I ask, "How do you balance that, though? As someone who wants to be highly unique, yet you're still part of an institution and its rigidity. How do you balance that as a pastor?" Speaking for Pentecostal leaders, Laurence explains that, "Our foundation is the Bible. And that's the difference between what we see as Christians, and somebody else." Laurence quickly seems to take a much stauncher stance, especially when discussing how much of mainstream society increasingly grows more "tolerant" of alternative lifestyles, like, for example, homosexual ones. While he says that we must adhere strictly to Christian values, I respond, "I would say that I have Christian values. I believe in social justice and have a sense of morality. My cultural lens doesn't conflict with the Bible. To me, someone who's gay, that would not go against the teachings of Jesus. Jesus would say no, you're all my brothers and sisters. Don't judge them." Laurence believes that lines must be drawn; standards must be kept in place to ensure that we live according to Christian standards. He replies, "My argument and my response would be, it's either you're all in, or you're all out. And there's no middle passage when it comes to biblical interpretation and the application of the scripture to your life. So you can't refer to scripture as a good way among other ways. My perspective is that it [homosexuality] is evil, there's no other way around it." As the conversation grows more passionate on both sides, we begin to enjoy a discussion turned into a debate. The excerpt below captures some of this animated discussion:

Marina: How many churches have been saying that? How long has the Christian church since its inception been saying that? And how long has that created a division in the church. There are so many different interpretations of religious reality.

Laurence: Jesus said that he didn't come to bring peace. He came to bring a sword. You're really talking about philosophical positions that you're going to hold to what you know, but I have agreed to do what I know is right, and that concept that you're expressing? It's becoming very widespread.

Marina: One thing I'm worried about with the charismatic movement is that it seems that the pastors, both the young ones and the older ones, have been preaching to their choir too long. You're not hearing outside perspectives so much.

Laurence: I understand that, and I think for too long, we have not positioned ourselves to have intellectual debates on issues that we believe in and our way of life in terms of how it conflicts or confronts with general perspectives and positions. Instead, in the past, it was "if you believe what I believe, that's good. If you don't believe what I believe, let's move away. ... I think we're becoming wiser, and realizing that, at the end of the day, it's the message that changes people. But sometimes it's not our job to change anybody. Just tell them the truth. Let them make their own decisions."

Marina: How does condemning people allow them to make their own decisions? All you are doing is alienating people from the message.

Laurence: Once we start comparing life, and you can't do that by always standing up with a microphone in your hand. Life must interact with life. So Peter must meet Dexter (Gestures to himself) and Vanessa (Gesturing to one of the wives sitting at the table). Vanessa must meet with Dexter and Vanessa's background and Vanessa's present, you know, interacts with Dexter's background and Dexter's present, and our outlook of life presently and where we're going tomorrow, those things must converge.

Marina: Histories, geographies and cultures come together.

Laurence: Must converge, and I'm guaranteeing you, that at the end, you're going to see God. I shouldn't be where I am. Look at me, talking to you. You're a doctor.

Marina: Well I could say the same thing; you're a man of God. Look at me talking to you! I'm the one that should be humble, right?

Laurence: You're out there lecturing to all kinds of people. I came from nowhere. And some might say, well that's a legitimate argument for what you believe. It's bigger than that. It's about God taking nothing and turning it into something powerful.

Woman at the table: Well Pastor, I would say that everyone comes from somewhere. Ain't nobody that come from nowhere.

Marina: Will the Pentecostals continue preaching to their congregation or do they want to open up? And if they're gonna open up, how do you deal with people from these various cultural lenses?

Laurence: That's the deception because that's not the bigger problem. The bigger problem is the soul. This Earth is gonna pass away. The only thing that transitions beyond here, according to scripture, is your soul and my soul. And that's the most important thing. And you're going to have to face the reality of what position your soul is in. I think your point is accurate, but inaccurate in terms of your attitude towards certain things. For instance, I don't have a very aggressive attitude towards homosexuals. I don't. I see right, I know right, I know wrong. I don't necessarily share in the argument that they are destined to be doomed.

While the topic remains on homosexuality and sin in general, Laurence explains that there needs to be a separation from living morally and immorally, because the Pentecostal Church and religion in general is about transformation. He talks with conviction about how, in order to preach transformation, it is just as important to preach the major issues that need to be addressed. At the same time, Laurence understands the importance of reaching out to both a larger audience and a changing generation of youths with exposure to views that counter mainstream Caribbean social and religious life. He says, "This doesn't mean that I can't understand the life that you speak of. It's a part of what I need to address. Let's go back to the original topic. If I am to be relevant, then I must understand the thought that runs in society concerning this perspective on life, and this perspective on my take on life." He compares the diversity of Trinidad to that of some of the other Caribbean islands stating, "I have found, contrary to Trinidad, that in the smaller islands—Montserrat, Antigua, St. Kitts—there's a heavy lacking of appreciation for diversity and different ways of life." Laurence explains that Trinidadians have to contend with many more cultures and religions than the smaller islands. He pauses for a moment, reflects, and states. "But I'm glad that we had this talk because the church had this philosophy of remaining closed. ... well I would say still has ... that if it's wrong, we should stay away from it."

As an emerging leader in the Caribbean Pentecostal movement, both Allen and Laurence believe that, though the institution matters, it's the individuals within it that matter most. They explain it's the individuals, including the religious leaders that operate on the ground, who interact with others and intersect with the world of everyday life. Laurence draws on the importance of teaching, and using the "pay it forward" approach in spreading the message and making an impact on the world. He says, "As pastor, as a teacher, my perspective is, I teach you so that you will go and teach him. It's the power of a real relationship." He explains that individual relationships are stronger than the power of an institution, or even mass indoctrination. The most important lesson for a new and emerging religious leader, Laurence urges, is to foster and tailor strong relationships. Further, he wants to increase the exposure of his church congregation to outside perspectives. The point is to confront the world, not hide from it. He puts it this way, "So right now, I'm culturing my church to become very interactive with society. Don't run! Like when other people come to challenge our religious thinking, where you suppose we go? We go inside! We hide! No, don't do those things! Put your stuff out there to the test. Go talk to the Rastafarian." The cultural transformation occurring in the Caribbean, and the widespread exposure of people to ideas and perspectives that counter traditional thought, we all agree, is inevitable. The challenge, both Allen and Laurence agree, is to confront that world directly and respond to it. They must, as they say, stay relevant in the world or become irrelevant to it. Laurence and Allen discuss the importance of younger pastors and religious leaders keeping up with the changing culture, from social media and new modes of communication to the changing perspectives and alternative views of the world, or else they become like the old man on the donkey, being passed up by all the cars and bikes.

As our conversation ends, we both share that our respective positions in life, he as a pastor and me as a professor, are driven by an overwhelming intellectual curiosity and passionate desire to bring change and social justice to this world. Though we belong within institutions, both bureaucratic and in many ways irrational, we agree that our ability to help people think critically about the world will, we hope, improve it in some way. This section concludes with Laurence's final comments below:

> I love to have conversations with people about faith, about God, and about our way of life, but when you do that, people know when you are pushing them away. They know. So you can't influence anybody without giving them an opportunity to express themselves. Because they want to know that you view their lives as legitimate as well. Because when you just diss them, and you just push them aside, you're telling them that you're just full of nonsense. ... Well you can't be that arrogant. My take on Christianity is [that] not everybody wants it. Not everybody believes that it's the best thing since sliced bread. I have work to do. I have to convince people that this thing is real and that it can work. ... This is a day when people want to know why. They don't want to know, just know. They want to know why. So you tell me that God loves me? Tell me why. You're trying to tell me that I should not do XYZ? Tell me why? Don't just tell me that I shouldn't, tell me why. And that's what we've got to engage people on.

Conclusion

Charismatic churches experience a transition in pastoral leadership all the time. Sometimes pastors retire or leave to conduct missionary work abroad. At other times, pastors may leave to take on new congregations, or head to "greener" pastures like Florida, as in the case of the pastor in St. Kitts. Sometimes a pastor's transition into a congregation occurs smoothly, without much problem. Other times, when new pastors attempt to take over independent and Charismatic churches using institutional authority, the transition proves difficult and wrought with challenges. One of the most defining aspects of the human condition is the remarkable capacity to resist structural subordination and authoritative control, especially when that control is perceived as too forced, oppressive, or unjust. It is human agency that allows for such subversion of power and dominance. Similarly, Charismatic Pentecostal congregations resist losing independence and succumbing to institutional control.

St. Kitt's Christian Life Assemblies serves as a prime example of what happens when religious leaders attempt to force the institutionalization of a Charismatic church. Unfortunately, PAWI placed Bartholomew in a tenuous position where he must tame a church and force it to accept institutional control. But the church does not accept this and may turn against the institution and its leaders. The challenge now for Bartholomew, if he wants to retain legitimacy as a church pastor and institutional authority, is to find a way to negotiate charisma with the goals of the institution to force this potentially rogue church into its control.

Many of the religious leaders and pastors of the Caribbean reported experiencing loneliness due to their high social positions in society. Pastors are highly regarded in Caribbean life with expectations to serve as role models and examples of how the righteous live. While these religious leaders and pastors make connections with other religious leaders to, in part, seek advice and guidance, it also helps them to build strong networks with other religious leaders throughout the Caribbean region. For Charismatic Christian leaders, the practicality of reaching out to others of equal status also helps build strong networks of support that help to spread the Charismatic movement throughout the region. For others, like Francis, loneliness turns them inward, helping them to develop supernatural skills to, for example, heal those in pain and suffering from tragic accidents.

Pentecostal leaders in the English-speaking Caribbean believe that physical and mental illnesses need western medical treatment while spiritual diseases necessitate supernatural cures. This also applies to their perceptions of homosexuality, widely viewed as a disease among Caribbean Charismatic leaders, and its need for a supernatural cure. While this might not change how many mainstream people view Pentecostals as being intolerant homophobic bigots, it does indicate that their views are not founded on hatred. At least, for better or worse, they claim to love the individual but hate the demon inflicting the victim. Perhaps time will change their views on issues such as homosexuality, among others.

It may not be the younger generation of Pentecostal leaders that transition toward an ever-changing culture. Sir Howard Fergus, a long-established historian and PAWI leader, pushes for change within the movement to make changes toward gender equality. This chapter documented how the Caribbean Pentecostal movement began in Montserrat with the pioneering work of Sister Laurencina Joseph. The irony, of course, is that women are denied equal access to power and upward mobility within a Pentecostal movement they helped ignite. The elder Pentecostal scholar Sir Howard

Fergus hopes to change some of these traditional biases to help pave the way for a Pentecostal movement to meet the demands of the times, including creating gender equality. The jury is still out on some of the younger budding religious leaders of the Pentecostal movement in the Caribbean who recognize the changing culture, and participate in its social media and more "hip" urban ways, while also holding strong to traditional notions regarding issues such as homosexuality. The question remains how these emerging religious leaders will deal with the traditional and more fundamentalist views of the movement regarding alternative lifestyles and values in a changing Caribbean culture with an emerging generation of youths increasingly exposed to cosmopolitan global views. Perhaps dealing with this very issue will shape what charisma looks like in the Charismatic movement as it pushes toward the future.

NOTES

1. St. Kitts is one of the islands in the dual island nation-state of St. Kitts and Nevis.
2. Thomas   Csordas,   "Introduction: Modalities   of   Transnational Transcendence," *Anthropological Theory 7* (2007): 259–272.
3. I find this similar to many professors outside their classrooms.
4. Marleen de Witte, "Religious Media, Mobile Spirits: Publicity and Secrecy in African Pentecostalism and Traditional Religion," in *Traveling Spirits: Migrants, Markets and Mobilities*, ed. Gertrud Hüwelmeier and Kristine Krause (Routledge, 2010).
5. Sir Howard Fergus, *Tongues on Fire: A History of the Pentecostal Movement of Montserrat* (Brades, Montserrat: Pentecostal Assemblies of the West Indies, 2011).
6. *Ibid.*
7. Unpublished work. Clara Emanuel and Edrys N. Joseph, *Blazing the Trail— Seventy Years of Faithful Witness* (1943–2013), History of the District of Antigua and Barbuda with St. Kitts and Nevis Member of Pentecostal Assemblies of the West Indies (PAWI).
8. The data taken on the history of Pentecostalism in Montserrat and its growing power on the island are taken from my interview with Sir Howard Fergus and his book *Tongues on Fire: A History of the Pentecostal Movement of Montserrat.*
9. Fergus, 2011, 12.

CHAPTER 8

Summary and Final Thoughts

This book began with an opening scene describing Bishop Bradford's attempt, after 15 years of preparation, to unify the once divided Christian churches of Antigua, with the hopes of eventually uniting the entire English-speaking Caribbean. Many leaders of the evangelical, established, and independent churches agreed, at least verbally, to put aside their differences and unite as one to become a stronger force shaping the region's affairs. The conversation presented below conducted toward the end of the research captures insight into the views of one of the top executives of PAWI regarding church unity.

> Marina: I'm asking about Bradford and his attempt to unite the evangelical, established and independent churches. On October of 2013, they all verbally agreed and they hugged and shook hands and this and that and I was like ok, where do you go from here?
>
> PAWI Leader: I hate to say it, but it's a symbolic act with no meat. Frankly, from my perspective, that's why I don't get involved. It's a lot of symbolism without significance.
>
> Marina: So what's the point of that then?
>
> PAWI Leader: Well, you know, from a strictly ministerial perspective, you have to do something, especially if nothing is being done. You have to be with your consciousness. And if something is laid upon your heart to do, I don't have a problem with somebody doing it. It is not always in the fulfillment of what you're dealing with when you look at the entire construct of the vision, the practically of it is going to be left out. Where I sit, I like to be

© The Author(s) 2016   209
P. Marina, *Chasing Religion in the Caribbean*,
DOI 10.1057/978-1-137-56100-8_8

real and for me, it is something that should be encouraged, but, in terms of it happening, I don't think so.

Marina: He says he has a vision from God that churches in Antigua will unite, they're gonna put away their long division and that they're gonna come together.

PAWI Leader: He has come to my home. He's come to Barbuda to promote it. I've never been involved.

Marina: But is it happening? Can you see if the churches are uniting?

PAWI Leader: No, the churches are not uniting. The churches are more divided than ever. I'm being frank with you. We have our own churches. And we have our differences. Big differences. It will take much more to unite all the evangelical churches. And I know of all these evangelical churches that have their own internal differences as well. So to once a year, especially somebody who comes from outside once a year to promote it, that is not going to be anything but tokenism. I'm not saying it shouldn't it happen, I'm just saying that it is not going to happen. [laughs]

Marina: W.hat makes you so certain?

PAWI Leader: It's going to mean that Pentecostals become Baptists and Baptists become Pentecostals. It's going to mean that everything I know about you, is going to be deleted from my mind, [laughs] you know what I mean? Everything, every harsh word was never said. Stuff like that. {He continues as we board a public bus}

That ain't going to happen. That's not going to happen. And people keep on fussing over stuff like that and whether you're Pentecostal, Baptist, Nazarene, or whatever. These are issues that we all fight with among ourselves and most of that fight is not settled now. It's only when people reach a bursting point that they say what they have to say right now.

It seems that most of the religious leaders agree that unity would be positive, though a nearly impossible goal to achieve. While much of the Charismatic movement involves miraculous healing, spiritual warfare, and speaking in tongues, it is also extremely pragmatic when it comes to catering to the needs of their local congregations. Given its pragmatic approach to solve everyday problems in the community, it's a wonder why practical religious leaders would engage in untenable practices. In other words, why simply go through the motions of uniting the churches when such an outcome is perceived as impossible? When I ask the relevance of going through the motions, the PAWI leader explains it this way:

Everybody wants it. Everybody wants to see it happen but the will to make it happen is a different thing. [There are] a lot of different reasons why it is not going to happen. Doctrinally, to unite, everybody means that that they have put aside all the theology that we have learned over time and all of the orthodoxy and different practical nuances of all the individuality. It's not going to happen.

One issue that prevents unity from happening involves the problem defining the concept of unity. Charismatic leaders frequently reference the word without any clear agreement on, or even understanding of, what "unity" actually implies. The PAWI leader explains that unity is a nebulous term without any clear meaning. Certainly, without a core concept to agree upon, any implementation of unity remains futile. As the PAWI leader puts it, "What is unity? What is it that we really want when we say unity? Are we saying that we want one church, to be good brothers and sisters? What is it that you're really saying when you say you want unity? It has to be spelled out for us and then fleshed out." The PAWI leader admits that, sometimes, Charismatic leaders use vague and ambiguous terms that can often be misleading. He says:

That's how we talk. I'm very practical and frank with how I say and view things. I don't like preaching all the bull and saying stuff. That's why I don't get involved because I would say something that would throw everything overboard. I don't want that. That's not my intention. But I just want us to have a clear understanding, but I would be misconstrued as being rebellious, non-cooperative or divisive.

While many Charismatic leaders claim that divisions within and between the various churches derive from theological differences, others argue that theology is the excuse to cover up for personality differences between religious leaders and pastors within the Pentecostal movement, especially when sharing the same PAWI umbrella. As we depart the bus to go shopping, the PAWI leader discusses how personality differences among church leaders serve as the main obstacle standing in the way of unity. He adamantly expresses, "Its not doctrine. It's not really doctrine. Doctrine is an excuse. It's personality, plain and simple. It's not doctrine. I mean we can solve the doctrine problem easily, if our personalities don't get in the way." One of the main reasons for the personality differences, besides the fact that some folks just don't get along, is the level of competition from Charismatic rock star religious leaders and those who want to become one. Many of these religious leaders, though outwardly expressing humility, develop a sense of self-importance and grandeur, especially when so many people perceive them as anointed by the Almighty himself. In fact, the PAWI leader believes that it's naïve to expect unity from men with such big personalities. And let's face it, it takes big personalities to become mega-preachers like Stephen Andrews or even preachers of small churches who build a congregational following from the ground up, with little to no resources. The PAWI leader explains that, "You have a whole sort of high-strung ministers who God has anointed and you think that we all are going to mesh together and we going to stay cool?" When big personalities concentrate within a single institution like PAWI, they clash and competition becomes the order of the day. The PAWI leader uses Apostle [Stephen Andrews] as an example of a religious leader who incurs the jealousy of others for his successes. What's more, Apostle achieved wealth and fame while being a foreigner to Antigua. The PAWI leader candidly explains:

> Take again for example, Apostle, he has gone ahead and built his wonderful church. People hate the man for that. I mean you have the same opportunity like him; you were there, in the same environment, you know? Why you [other PAWI leaders who had to give Apostle approval to build his multi-million dollar church] allow him to do it if you're going to be vexed with him? You know, that's my issue. He is able, even as a Trinidadian, to come to Antigua and to do something as significant as that. All right? You, with all your own little personal hang-ups, you're still down in the dumps and still can't do anything because of the same stupidity. You hear people say oh, he's too manipulative because he's able to manipulate rich people into building stuff for him. You hear them say as well he is, he is, an authoritarian, the guy sets goals and if you don't like it, you're out. Not too nice things are said. Instead you learn from, if anything, learn from him how he is able to do it, [instead] you go criticize the man, doesn't make sense.

This PAWI leader goes so far as to say that religious leaders and pastors with large egos, even if necessary for the service of God, also grow insecure in a world where so many Charismatic leaders impress thousands of people. He explains, "I tell people all the time, pastors are the most insecure people in the world. We don't feel good when we see another brother progress beyond us and want to know why and the best thing to do is competing with him and show others that we are of the same anointing." It seems, at least the perception exists among religious leaders, that church unity is nearly impossible, though desirable. Or is it?

I decided to present my theory to the PAWI leader that, ironically, the division in the church and the feelings of competition that keep religious leaders and pastors from uniting actually keep charisma alive in the Pentecostal movement. He responds admitting that competition and division is good for the movement, but not for the individual, stating, "What? Exactly! It's not a bad thing, I agree with you, it's not a bad thing in a sense for the movement itself, but you could view it as a bad thing for the individual if you're insecure." While religious leaders of PAWI seem to agree with my idea that internal division helps keep the vitality of charisma alive in the Pentecostal movement, a point that will be summarized below, the Charismatic movement does seem to achieve new and unprecedented levels of importance in the Caribbean. Though not necessarily connected, perhaps Bradford's vision of the Christian churches becoming a more powerful force in shaping the political and economic affairs of the region is becoming a reality.

As reported in Chapter 5 on Trinidad, religion, especially the Charismatic churches, are joining CARICOM and becoming part of the established power structure in the English-speaking Caribbean. The Charismatic movement is now crossing into unchartered territory, especially as it becomes a stronger force in shaping the political and economic affairs of the region. Although the Charismatic movement is currently making headway in shaping the English-speaking Caribbean, its ability to make an impact on the region depends on the themes developed throughout this book, including the five major themes summarized below.

BRIEF COMMENTS ON MAJOR THEMES AND FINDINGS

One of the major themes in this book involved how religious leaders of the Charismatic movement network and spread throughout the English-speaking Caribbean region. Chapter 4 on Antigua developed a typology on the types of transnational religious networking in the Caribbean that include (1) ICN, (2) IFN, (3) CIN, and (4) CFN. These typologies show the various ways Pentecostal pastors and leaders develop transnational religious networks to both impact their local communities and spread throughout the Caribbean. While the mega-preacher Apostle Stephen Andrews uses CIN strategies to impact his local community in Antigua while also spreading throughout the Caribbean, Matthew Noyce employs CFN approaches. Discussed below, unlike my past arguments that institutionalization means the death of charisma in the USA, the argument does not hold in the English-speaking Caribbean.

The CIN and CFN approaches, respectively, Apostle and his highly institutionalized church as well as Noyce and his small independent church, demonstrate useful strategies to make an impact on their local communities and spread across the Caribbean. These types of strategies serve as the best hope for the Charismatic movement in the Caribbean to balance the forces of charisma with institutional rationality. While the highly institutional Apostle retains his charisma while operating within an institution, Noyce develops his own while free from the shackles of an institutional bureaucracy. Both pastors have become influential in the local community and the Caribbean community beyond the borders of Antigua. Pastor Bartholomew, perhaps at the behest of PAWI, uses the IFN approach to assert power and legitimacy within the local community. The result, so far, has led to a congregation resisting institutional subordination. The PAWI church, in its attempt to control what became an independent church, might very well lose it. More attempts to use IFN strategies will likely lead to similar results.

Another theme relates to how the Pentecostal church handles increased growth as it continues to expand into the future. As many of the religious leaders shared, such as Alleng in Barbados and Bishop in Trinidad, Charismatic leaders within the movement need to be wary of "Mr. Big" while also "scratching where it itches" (see Chapter 5 on Trinidad) to solve the real pains of the people as well as to better serve their local community and resist joining the rank and file of the economic and political elite. The ability of these Charismatic leaders to keep true to their grassroots orientation and their resistance to power and authority will do well for the vitality of charisma as the Charismatic movement takes on an increased role in CARICOM, including the political and economic affairs of the region. The vitality of charisma offers the best hope for the Charismatic movement to retain its grassroots orientation to empower the Caribbean people, and impact the local and broader regional community.

A third theme relates to the simultaneous centralization and decentralization of the Charismatic church as it continues to grow and expand within the region. As Dominica Pastor Randy Rodney and others pointed out, while Charismatic churches continue to grow and centralize, they decentralize into many semi-autonomous smaller cells under the umbrella of a larger cell. This simultaneous process of centralization and decentralization allows the church to grow and institutionalize while also creating many smaller and potentially Charismatic semi-autonomous groups that maintains the potential for Charismatic vitality while also creating the conditions for the emergence of new and budding Charismatic religious leaders.

Another theme involves how the Pentecostal movement balances charisma and institutionalization as it pushes toward a postmodern world. While the four types of transnational religious networking demonstrate the balance between these tensions, so do the concepts of the

"Bureaucrasaurus" and "Charismaticrats" developed in Chapter 5. In short, the world of rules, procedures, and dogma lead to the drab, dim world of iron-cage rationality that defies both the human spirit and the very force behind the Pentecostal movement. My ethnographic chase in the Caribbean revealed both types of religious leaders within the Pentecostal movement, though the "charismaticrats" seem to somehow prevail. I'm not convinced charisma in the Caribbean Pentecostal movement will fade into obscurity; the will of the Caribbean people seems too strong. Perhaps the Caribbean people have yet to fall into the trap of Western rationality and excessive consumerism that removes people from their culture.

A fifth theme involves the internal division within the church as well as the external pressures it experiences from outsiders. One of the findings presented in this book argues that both the internal divisions and the external pressures of the church help keep charisma alive. The divisions within and between the Charismatic Christian churches might prevent the church from uniting into one powerful force, but it also breeds competition within the church where religious leaders and pastors must constantly distinguish themselves on an internally devised scale of authenticity that produces new and exaggerated forms of charisma. At the same time, the Charismatic church builds strength and charisma when facing external pressures and hostility from a common enemy adverse to the movement. Increased adversity from the outside creates a vibrant militant Charismatic church. Whenever the church is under pressure, the various churches begin to unite, enhancing the quality of conversion and conviction. The internal divisions and external pressures create a dialectical process for church groups that keep the vitality of charisma strong for the Pentecostal movement. External pressure makes unity stronger while simultaneously creating relative comparison groups between the once divided Charismatic churches that serves to enhance their levels of competition and division, which in turn, recreates the conditions necessary for increased charisma.

ON THE CONCEPTS OF CHARISMATIC CHRISTIAN INTOLERANCE AND POVERTY PIMPING

The sections on Barbados (Chapter 6) and St. Kitts (Chapter 7) tried to present a humanizing view of how Charismatic leaders in the English-speaking Caribbean view controversial issues such as homosexuality without trying to apologize for them. The purpose of these discussions was simply to provide deeper insight into how religious leaders in the Charismatic movement understand controversial social issues. These chapters also shed light into how Charismatic leaders easily blend old world miracles with modern rational thought in a postmodern world. They simply distinguish physical and mental illnesses from spiritual ones. In the case of a physical or cognitive disease, Western medicine serves as the best remedy. But in a world where spirits and demons still impact the physical world, spiritual diseases remain possible. Demons have the power to penetrate a victim and reproduce the symptoms of both physical and mental diseases. That's why, it is believed, sometimes the attempts of Western medicine to cure the sick fails. Western medical doctors simply misdiagnose the problem, part of their limitations with a strictly scientific view of the world. In this sense, Charismatic leaders are broader and more open-minded to other possibilities beyond scientific rationality. Put simply, diagnose a problem as physical or spiritual and treat according to the correct diagnosis.

Many outsiders believe that the leaders of Charismatic groups manipulate the poor, promising wealth and prosperity to the hopeful while taking advantage of their vulnerability. There's no doubt that some of this exists, though this was not personally observed in the research conducted for this book. I must admit my own sense of uneasiness when pastors like Apostle of Antigua and Bishop of Trinidad promise wealth in "doubles" to a largely poor congregation seeking comfort and empowerment. Further, my feelings of the Charismatic movement brought a sense of both fascination and disquiet toward a movement that at once denounces alternative lifestyles and promises wealth to the poor while simultaneously retaining charisma from the shackles of institutionalization and empowering its people to become more than the structural expectations imposed upon them allow. I frowned at their stubborn persistence to uncritically hold on to orthodox views of the world while marveling wondrously at their overwhelming desire to devote themselves to their local community. They simultaneously show the ability to develop extreme forms of self-importance while also showing a remarkable capacity for altruism—from the selflessness of Francis and the paralyzed kid to Noyce's unrelenting passion to serve his community to Apostle's unwavering devotion to change the Caribbean region to empower its people, even if he becomes rich in the process. In the end, of course, the reader decides if these Charismatic leaders pimp the poor or conduct noble lives.

The Future of the Charismatic Church in the English-speaking Caribbean

In my previous work[1] on the Charismatic movement in the USA, I argued that while charisma is dying in the large institutionalized church, it remains alive in the small non-institutionally or loosely affiliated church that is better situated to balance charisma with modern rationality. In other words, charisma remains in small churches and fades to obscurity in large institutionally affiliated churches in the USA. This theory does not apply to the English-speaking Caribbean where charisma remains alive in both the large institutionally affiliated and small institutionally unaffiliated churches. Further, the future for charisma remains promising when the leaders of the Charismatic movement employ ICN and CIN strategies that balance charisma with institutionalization. The question remains how charisma retains its potential in the English-speaking Caribbean, just south of where much research provides evidence that the future is dim for its neighbors in the north.

Perhaps the Caribbean people are too magical, or maybe too innocent or not innocent enough—the "advanced" civilizations of the world spilled too much blood and built a society from slavery. Maybe they are too smart, or perhaps saved from the iron cage of Western technocratic and bureaucratic (ir)rationality that dominates "freedom" in the postmodern "democracy" of the USA. Maybe it's just that the USA is too tainted, perhaps it started when we began taming the free Western frontier and its "savages." Perhaps we in the USA tamed everything and attempted to put the world—including God—in *our* image. Maybe our attempt to try and control the world has made us lose control of it, though we never actually had any control, God knows. Perhaps we lost all legitimacy, maybe the USA is no longer God's country; perhaps it never was. Maybe the USA has lost legitimacy to both God and man. Perhaps it's ironic that the colonized world of the Caribbean keeps its charisma while the "advanced" worlds of the north and west destroy themselves with their Western industrial progress and their inverted ideas of the enlightenment. To my knowledge, it's impossible to prove the existence of God, but if I were a betting man, I'd put my wager on belief in God(s) over this perverted economic and political system that oppresses the vast majority of humans on this planet.

The answer as to why charisma continues to resist going "gently into that good night" might have to do with the years of cultural resistance that developed in a region that endured everything from the savagery of slavery to modern-day postcolonialism where Western political and economic elite, including the USA, continue to control the Caribbean. The people have yet to become fully immersed into the materialistic culture and hyper-consumerism of the privileged West. Caribbean culture—including and better said especially the Charismatic movement—is a creative response to the collectively experienced problems embedded in the social structure presented in a late-modern and postcolonial world. Further, the people remain intimately connected to their land and the culture that is part of that land. Even Charismatic Christianity itself mixes and coalesces in highly complex and fascinating ways with African religious influences and Caribbean religious traditions, such as Obeah, that emerged from the experience of slavery. The people remain tied to a land they built from slavery and a culture that allowed them to survive it, and perhaps charisma now emerges as a powerful force and important weapon to keep the people from falling into submission. Here in the Caribbean, the chase ends with a perspective that, at least for now, the vitality of charisma remains a force of power for the Charismatic movement and the people of the Caribbean. While the purposeful attempts to unify the Christian Churches in the Caribbean is a noble endeavor, the dialectical process of external pressures and internal divisions keep the vitality of charisma alive in the Caribbean, as well as allowing for the potential of the movement to emerge as a new and powerful voice as it joins the political and economic elite of the region.

NOTE

1. Peter Marina, *Getting the Holy Ghost: Urban Ethnography in a Brooklyn Pentecostal Tongue-Speaking Church* (Lanham, MD: Lexington Books, 2014).

CHAPTER 9

Epilogue: Haiti

Two large cows lie dead just outside a Vodou temple in the backyard of a neighborhood shack about 10 kilometers from Port-au-Prince in the small village of Bon Repos. A man hacks away at their body parts over blood-drenched concrete near piles of guts and intestine. The villagers stand in place staring at me strangely as I walk toward the *houngan*, or Vodou male priest, sitting in front of the *ounfò*, or Vodou temple. The temple is the size of a large garage with a mud floor and displays props and background music that provide a festive, even family-oriented, atmosphere. Immediately upon entering the room, one sees a space for the food and cake and another section with an altar. Today's event reveals the syncretic nature of Vodou as it blends both Catholic and Voodoo traditions in its celebration of the Epiphany, or *Les Trois Rois* (Three King's Cake Festival). On January 6, Vodou practitioners and Catholics commemorate the arrival of the Three Kings to Bethlehem to pay homage to the biblical Jesus. Observers of this celebration can celebrate a Vodou *lwa* or a Catholic Saint, and often both without any contradiction.[1] I place a bottle of Rhum Barbancourt as my offering on the table decorated with Christmas lights.

The altar appears as a staggered shelf, like a staircase. The tools of the Vodou worshipper's trades, from oils and candles to strange brews and bottles, sit on each landing. On the top step, two human skulls sit on either side of a totem with a man's hat resting upon it directly beneath a small, plastic hanging skeleton. On both sides of the temple sit rows of chairs

© The Author(s) 2016
P. Marina, *Chasing Religion in the Caribbean*,
DOI 10.1057/978-1-137-56100-8_9

around a large empty space allowing for the free movement of people to perform various rituals, ceremonies, and dances. While some men sport attire from jeans and t-shirts, other men wear slacks and button-down shirts, while still others adorn white linen clothes. The women wear more elaborate and decorative clothes of various colors. Some of the women dress in dark violet quadrille or karabela dresses with magenta trim and matching head scarves while others wear a slightly different style of quadrille or karabela dress, only the skirt and sleeves are ruffled and multicolored with a matching head tie.

At first, nothing seems to be happening. It's just hours and hours of drumming, smoking, drinking, eating, singing, chanting, and dancing. The *batterie*, or drum set, consists of the Segon, Boula, and Manman drums used to attract the attention of the spirits, called *Loas*, which serve as personal guides to Vodou practitioners hoping to get possessed. (Similar to—but not the same as—the Pentecostal's "getting the holy ghost.") The participants of the ceremony hope to become mounted by the *lwa*, becoming fully possessed by the spirit. After many hours, into the late hours of the night, a spirit finally enters a woman who takes on the characteristics of the *lwa*.

In the distant background, the rara drums make that Haitian beat that combines the sounds of Africa and a culture of resistance from Caribbean slavery as the spirit enters the large and colorfully dressed woman. She holds a stick, making frequent strange hiccup-like yelping noises while sporadically shrugging her shoulders, as if experiencing little electric shocks in her back as she sits calmly in her chair. But the mood is anything but calm. Someone stands next to her with a bucket holding what seems to be oil, though it could be water. Her right leg bounces up and down while the ceremony participants begin to approach this *lwa*-possessed woman, including the *houngan*.

As each of the participants approach, they make a 360-degree circle one way and another the other way before going to their knees at the feet of the woman. Some kiss her feet while others hug her and still others offer a kiss on both cheeks. She rubs oil on their faces, chants, inspects their bodies, and embraces each of the participants who approach her for what seems to be some type of healing or empowerment. The responses from each participant making contact with the possessed woman vary in intensity. Some people simply perform the ritual like the mundane practice of a Catholic receiving communion from a priest, while others react as if a bolt of lightning strikes them, causing them to fly backward and fall to the ground or upon unsuspecting audience members. Sometimes the possessed woman takes off a woman's headscarf to rub oil on her; at other times she simply rubs oils on their hands and extends them out before rubbing the face and finally giving them a long embrace. Meanwhile, as the possessed woman tends to reach of the ceremony participants, the crowd wildly dances and chants to the drumbeat of the hot nights where *lwa* spirits roam.

Hours later, after more rum, drumming, and dancing, another *lwa* spirit mounts another participant. The man wears a large straw hat with a green scarf wrapped around it in a bow, a white tank top shirt with a red sash wrapped around him from the right shoulder to the left underarm, and jeans with a green scarf as a belt. He now holds the same stick as the previously possessed woman, but instead dances with it challenging members of the audience to take it from him. Like a sports player showboating after a score, he dances with the stick making provocative gestures thrusting his hips back and forth while holding the stick horizontally with both hands. First he grabs a portly man who wrestles for the stick with the possessed for a few seconds only to be thrown off the stick and shocked backward as if from some seemingly supernatural force. The possessed man takes turns picking members of the crowd to overpower him. He approaches both women and men, shakes hands, hugs and embraces, and finally pulls them toward the available space to wrestle for the stick. As this happens, the participants continue to dance and chant, while still observing the spectacle of the possessed man wrestling others for the stick between each new challenge, the possessed man dances wildly and occasionally shouts "ahhhhaaa" and "heyyyyyy" while moving through the crowd selecting one ceremony participant after another.

It is believed that those possessed in a Vodou ritual take on the qualities and characteristic of the *lwa*.[2] This man seems to imitate and ritually enact the characteristics of an *lwa* associated with fire. Members of the audience pour rum on the floor and light it with a match. The man yelps and dances with the stick around the fire, inspecting it, touching it with the stick, and flirting with the possibility of jumping on it. He seems somewhat hesitant, but continues dancing and shouting out, until finally requesting that the fire rise higher. They pour more rum on the floor igniting the fire. The possessed man yelps out again before jumping into the flames and dances circles around it until nearly falling down. He regroups, and jumps on the fire again to stomp and twirl on the flames, spinning around three times before collapsing to the floor.

While Vodou ceremonies and celebrations reveal the syncretic nature of Vodou religious practices, so do the religious worlds of all of Hispañiola, evident in the everyday religious practices of both Dominican Vudú and Haitian Vodou. But it's Haiti's great religious pilgrimage to Saut d'Eau and its enchanting waterfalls that best showcase a religious cocktail composed of a variety of global religious practices.

SAUT D'EAU PILGRIMAGE

While weeks immersed in the cultural life of the Dominican Republic revealed a syncretic religious world where *Caballos* engage a Dominican Vudú, or *Las21 Divisiones*, that blends various Afro-Caribbean and African religions (Benin and Yoruba), Haitian Vodou, and Taino Indian religious practices with Catholicism, the long journey to Haiti showcased an equally syncretic but much stricter and highly structured version of Vodou religious practices.

We travel north from Port-au-Prince to the town of Mirebalais and head east through the Artibonite Valley eventually reaching the tiny village of Bonheur near the sacred waterfalls of Saut d'Eau where thousands of Haitians make religious pilgrimages to participate in both Vodou and Catholic rituals and festivities. Two Spanish-speaking photojournalists, a Haitian chauffer, and I pay 50 gourdes to enter into the site. We head past a gate and down long winding steps where two magnificent waterfalls represent the "Bon Dieu," or the serpent spirit Vodou *Lwa* Damballah, believed to have created all the waters on the earth, and his rainbow goddess wife, Ayido Weda.[3] Many of those making the pilgrimage believe that the Virgin Mary once made an appearance here, which led to the creation of the Catholic Church of Our Lady of Mount Carmel, or what Vodou practitioners associate with the *Lwa* Erzulie Dantor (or Erzulie Freda). The pilgrimage to Saut d'Eau best showcases the syncretic nature of Haitian religious practices where some Haitians participate in the Catholic mass and parade a statue of the Virgin Mary in Ville-Bonheur while other Haitians engage in various Vodou practices from communal bathing to devotional ceremonies at the waterfalls. Many, of course, unproblematically participate in both Vodou and Catholic rituals and ceremonies.

As the gushing power of the waterfall crashes upon the rocks, the mist of the water rises and sparkles in the sunlight producing a rainbow as if Ayido Weda were watching over those calling out in her name. Many of the women and men bathe topless in the water holding broken *kwi*, or cut halves of hollowed-out gourd bowls that can also be used to hold sage, oils, Vieux Labbé special rum, a picture of what looks like Virgin Mary, matches, and other objects important to the religious and spiritual practices that take place during the three-day pilgrimage beginning on July 16.

The Catholic and Vodou practitioners at times collectively engage in the most intense and frantic forms of communal prayer that involve shouting, dancing, singing, and chanting. At other times, while still occupying the same collective space, they engage in the most personal and solemn acts of prayer in individual solitude. Sometimes, as one person breaks out in a chant while looking up at the great waterfall, others follow suit and collectively chant together until suddenly returning to highly individualistic acts such as scrubbing each body part with soap and sage.

A panoramic view from a large hill overlooking the waterfalls reveals a wide-open communal space with dozens of radically separate, ever shifting, and highly fluid scenes that somehow remain intimately interconnected. As the great waterfall crashes from the high heavens, some people lift their arms into it while others stand and shout at it from a distance. Others bathe while holy men and women rub sage all over their bodies, some get possessed and crumble to the ground while others keep them from submerging into the water. Some people sit naked in solitude as the water washes over their bodies as others dance and revel to rara bands that resemble the second lining brass band musicians of Haiti's sister city New Orleans. Some stand on the edge of rocks in the middle of the water with hands lifted in the air and eyes closed feeling the power and energy of this great and magical place.

A woman with large bare breasts extends her arms out toward the great waterfall. She holds a gourd bucket in one hand and a plastic container in another while frantically shouting as if making demands to the great spirits. A few feet away young men in their twenties dance and sing, falling all over the slippery rocks while embracing each other and drinking rum from small bottles as they heed to the energy of the waterfalls. Another beautiful woman lies in the shallow part of the waterfall with eyes closed as the flowing water passes over her naked body. Another woman in a crowd seems to lose control shouting hysterically as others try to calm her. A thin shirtless man rubs soap and sage all over his head and body, making sure to scrub seemingly every inch of it. Meanwhile, a group of unruly young men following a second line of musicians mock the religious devotees and sacred traditions of the pilgrimage and they dance and splash water and wrestle with each other in the middle of all the commotion.

A small crowd makes their way up the rocks of the waterfall to one of the many small makeshift Vodou altars nestled near the base of a rocky wall underneath the cascading falls. Candles with waxy bases are planted in the stone's divots as plastic bowls and hollowed-out gourds hold offerings that include pieces of rope, rum, cigarettes, and plastic soda bottles. Spots of soot speckle the stone's surface, as does ash from burned herbs. A woman dressed in a dark violet karabela dress and headscarf presides over the altar while others observe. Still others, both Catholics and Vodou practitioners, wait their turn at the altar.

About 30 feet away, near another section of the waterfall, a wide-eyed woman takes a cigarette lighter to her skin and eye as if nothing causes her pain. She looks at me and briefly rubs her body on me until moving back and putting a lit cigarette in her eye. Others look on in delight and awe believing, it seems, that this woman holds supernatural ability. A few feet away, at one of the dozens of altars in the semi-dry area to the side of the waterfall, people gather together playing rara music, chanting, and singing as they light candles and drink rum. The scene seems chaotic yet subdued as throngs of people line the path to the falls while on the sloped sides, groups of people gather in prayer circles, chanting and singing, rattling colorful gourds, and waving multicolored fabrics in the air. One larger group of mostly men stands over a pile of brightly decorated bowls, hats, and clothing while singing together and locking arms. Almost everyone wears a straw hat or baseball cap. The women are scantily clad wearing little more than skirt slips and bras. Tossed britches can be found all over the place. Next to a group of women, a man stoically sits behind a makeshift stone altar, its craggy surface covered in melted wax and burnt and burning candles. At some altars, Catholic and Vodou men and women of power and prestige preside as others seek guidance. At other altars, people merely reflect in solitude while drinking rum and giving candle offerings.

The highly fluid and dynamic syncretic nature of religion in the non-English-speaking part of the Caribbean helps to understand some of the great structural transformations of our times. Haitian Vodou, Dominican Vudú, and Cuban Santería serve as prime examples of how processes of globalization hasten the development of various religious traditions mixing and merging into a spiritual cocktail that takes on unique forms as they settle into new and ever-changing cultural conditions, especially cultures that develop in response to colonial and postcolonial conditions. In an uncertain postmodern world riven in contradictions and inequalities, religion takes on new shapes that, perhaps surprisingly, develop into new and emerging roles that challenge existing institutions of power. Understanding how Charismatic religions, Vodou, and Santería will shape the future of postmodernity will require perhaps another chase, but one in the Spanish and Creole-speaking Caribbean world.

NOTES

1. R. Murray Thomas, *Roots of Haiti's Vodou-Christian Faith: African and Catholic Origins* (Santa Barbara, CA: Praeger, an imprint of ABC-CLIO, LLC, 2014).
2. *Ibid.*
3. Joseph Carlson, *Voodoo Killers: Slavery, Sorcery and the Supernatural* (Futura Publications, 2011); Leslie Gérald Desmangles, *The Faces of the Gods: Vodou and Roman Catholicism in Haiti* (Chapel Hill, NC: University of North Carolina Press, 1992).
4. T. Tweed, *Crossing and Dwelling: A Theory of Religion* (Cambridge, MA: Harvard University Press, 2006), 54.
5. Michele de Certeau and Steven Rendall, *The Practice of Everyday Life* (Berkeley: University of California Press, 1984), 12.
6. M. Kusenbach, "Street Phenomenology: The Go-along as Ethnographic Research Tool." *Ethnography* 4 (2003): 455–485.
7. R.M. Carpiano, "Come Take a Walk With Me: The 'Go-Along' Interview as a Novel Method for Studying the Implications of Place for Health and Well-Being," *Health & Place* 15 (2009): 263–272.
8. D. Conquergood, "Performance Studies: Interventions and Radical Research," *The Drama Review* 46 (1984).
9. R. Aunger, "On Ethnography: Story-Telling or Science," *Current Anthropology* 36 (1995): 97–130.
10. G.N. Schiller, "Transnational Social Fields and Imperialism: Bringing a Theory of Power to Transnational Studies," *Anthropological Theory* 5 (2005): 439–461; V. Mazzucato, "Bridging Boundaries with a Transnational Research Approach: A Simultaneous Matched Sample Methodology," in *A Multi-Sited Ethnography: Theory, Praxis and Locality in Contemporary Social Research*, ed. Mark-Anthony Falzon (Aldershot, Hants, England, and Burlington, VT: Ashgate, 2009).
11. Mazzucato, 2009, 215–232; Peggy Levitt and Nina Glick Schiller, "Conceptualizing Simultaneity: A Transnational Social Field Perspective on Society," *International Migration Review* 38 (2004): 1002–1039; and Schiller, 2005.
12. Jock Young, *The Criminological Imagination* (Cambridge: Polity, 2011).
13. Young, 2011. For a good description on the use of reflexivity similar to this, see Jock Young's comments in *The Criminological Imagination* on Philippe Bourgois's *In Search of Respect*.

Appendix: Go-Along Ethnography in the English-Speaking Caribbean

Drawing from Tweed's[4] geographical concept of theory as a travel itinerary and religion as a set of spatial practices and "organic-cultural flows that intensify joy and confront suffering by drawing on human and superhuman forces to make homes and cross boundaries," this project moves past the hard world of maps and demographic monographs of researchers who chart the quantitative spread of religions.

Taking seriously the assertion of Michele de Certeau[5] that "what maps cut up, the story cuts across," this research uses creative types of ethnographic styles from the *go-along ethnographic approach* (see Chapter 3) to travel the soft, malleable, and bending spaces with those engaged in religious networking as their actions occur in lived time and space. Following Kusenbach,[6] this ethnographic approach accounts for the "invisible, transcendent, and reflexive aspects of lived experience," and is well suited to explore "environmental perception, spatial practices, biographies, social architecture, and social realms" with phenomenological insight that allows space for individual perceptions of religious leaders on what is going on while it is happening. Go-along ethnography requires the researcher to not just participate in the actions of the observed, but also participate in daily activities and routines, adventurous or mundane, in order to better understand the inner workings of a community or network of individuals.[7] It is a creative way to delve deeper into a group of people, more than traditional qualitative methods make possible. It requires full immersion into the lives of church leaders.

P. Marina, *Chasing Religion in the Caribbean*,
DOI 10.1057/978-1-137-56100-8

This research approach captures religious transnational stories in action navigating between official, objective, and abstract forms of knowledge and the practical, embodied, and popular forms of knowledge that require getting first-hand phenomenological insight into events as they are immediately experienced.[8] This methodological situationalism places human behavior in the context of space and time well suited to transnational studies.[9] Richly textured ethnographic studies of this type meet the demands of studying multiple interconnected field sites that result from transnational networks.[10] The increasing use of transnational ethnography today is a testament to the methods' unique sensitivity to the contextuality of transnational networks, practices, and identities that—through diverse narratives and storytelling—provide direct access to personal knowledges that result in the production of multiple nuanced accounts of everyday life and practices in a multisited transnational context.[11]

This go-along style chases religion from remote rural villages to large metropolitan centers to seaside towns throughout the Caribbean. The chase uses various forms of public and private transportation—from Haiti's moto taxis to Trinidad's maxi taxis—to travel with Caribbean religious leaders in 10 countries and 12 islands as they develop and maintain their religious networks throughout the region. Gaining entrée into culturally and socially difficult-to-access research sites requires tactics beyond methodological approaches found in many mainstream social science textbooks. Instead, the research approach depends on making personal connections and establishing genuine friendships with religious leaders beyond the "rapport" traditionally used to solicit interviews with strangers. This allows the researcher to enter into the private circles of religious leaders and gain access to the Charismatic networks they use to transnationalize religion throughout the Caribbean.

CHARISMATIC ETHNOGRAPHY IN THE CHARISMATIC CARIBBEAN

Just as religious leaders of Charismatic movements rely on their charisma to establish networks and cross political borders, this research relies on "Charismatic ethnographic networking" to gain access into the private lives of transnationalizing religious leaders. Of course, this presents a challenge considering many religious leaders in the English-speaking Caribbean are understandably cautious of outsiders, especially non-black religious skeptics lacking any direct ties to the region. Academics from the

West, especially non-believers, may not be considered legitimate scholars and professors. How is it possible, some of these religious leaders wonder, that one can be a respected academic without being a born-again Christian? As a Cuban-American university professor and admitted religious skeptic, the challenge becomes greater. Relying on my own institutional legitimacy and established credentials to gain access into the private circles of religious leaders, while fully aware of Western mainstream secular society's negative view of Charismatic Christians, was not enough. Further, many of these religious leaders are now part of the Caribbean's power structure, with access to the most powerful political and economic elite. As many ethnographic researchers know, it is far easier to study those in lower socio-economic positions than it is to study those above. As a result, this research relies on finding creative ways to find access into the worlds of religious leaders in both high and low places.

THE CHARISMATIC ETHNOGRAPHER

Sometimes you have to put down the notebook, toss the pre-established questions, rip up the questionnaire, forget the fake introductions, and establish actual relationships. The goal is to become fully embedded, as well as possible, within the authentic culture of the Caribbean. This requires becoming a Charismatic ethnographer.

The research quest often turns into a personal obsession, an insatiable desire to answer a question. Unpredictable things happen, and the journey involves surprising findings. Ethnographic research moves to the flow of social life, revels in its contradictions, and seeks to find the unexpected. It requires relying on your wit more than methodological doctrine and developing a "thinking on your feet" mentality. Textbook methods won't get you to the Promised Land. There is no guidebook or rules or tactics; just like in life, the study of it follows no rubric.

Ethnographic charisma involves living like a local, sharing ideas and passions, laughs and tears, joys and sufferings as well as debating controversial topics, eating local foods and drinks, as well as exposing one's own personal vulnerabilities, especially when expecting others to do the same. Ethnography involves calling people out on their posturing and masquerading and to admit your own. This type of research involves seeing and feeling—deep down in your bones feeling—the world of others. We understand the objective world through subjective experiences while simultaneously making sense of the subjective world by locating experience within objective institutions of power and ideology. Researchers gain access to the lives of others when they confront and share together life's many tribulations and curiosities. It's the Charismatic ethnographer who naturally connects to human beings through sharing of the human condition. The Charismatic ethnographer realizes the limitations of the social scientist having a privileged claim on authority or knowledge. There is no hubris of privilege, no academic authority, no pretenses, no arrogance. We don't sit in fancy ivory towers.

Charismatic ethnographers challenge their own culture while also challenging the culture of others. And research participants appreciate the opportunity to challenge the world of the ethnographer. Some religious leaders in the Caribbean question how a religious skeptic could secure a university position without the legitimacy of belonging to a religious group. Unlike the USA and much of the Western world, professors in the English-speaking Caribbean gain credibility in the wider community through their faith in the Christian God. In the Caribbean, the non-Caribbean researcher cannot rely upon their university position. Charismatic ethnographers rely on the personal connections they make with others while conducting research. Sometimes the best ethnographic approach involves talking to people like you would in your local bar. People learn a great deal listening to others, learning what makes them tick, discovering their joys and fears, and sharing in the human experience. It's about making genuine connections and sharing a moment of life together.

Whether elite "big fish" religious leaders or the pastors of small storefront churches, some of the research relationships develop into long-lasting relationships beyond "rapport." Going-along with religious leaders facilitates the development of these relationships while shadowing them in both their mundane and exciting moments of the day. This provides unusual insight into the world of Charismatic Christianity beyond the limitations of most research to gain behind-the-scenes access into the thinking of religious leaders as they perform religious activities from preaching to exorcisms. Much of this ethnographic odyssey involves a roller coaster of highly surprising and unexpected events that require methodological improvisation beyond the surface of social life and into the private and public spaces of religious life. And the sociological study of religious life is an endlessly fascinating venture into a complex and layered world fraught with surprises.

TAKING THE BLOOD OUT OF THE BULL

Taking a page out of the great criminologist Jock Young's—the notorious scoundrel to mainstream "lock 'em up" criminology—critical views on the humdrum sociological description of crime, the ethnographic descriptions throughout the following chapters avoid the use of dry, academic text to bring to life the fascinating world of religious life through the use of visual text. In his critical analysis on the state of criminology today, Jock Young notices the tendency of many criminologists and sociologists to take the thrilling topic of crime—with all its seductions—and turn it into a lifeless academic text of variables interacting with other variables, completely devoid of culture and creativity. These scholars develop the uncanny ability to transform the spice and thrill of social life to an odorless world of mundane blandness. Young wonders how topics such as crime and transgression, a world of drug dealers and takers, sex workers, police snitches, drug robbers, and thrill seekers, could become so "humdrum." This tendency of the social scientist to take the deviance out of deviancy or turn gold to gravel, what Young calls the "Anti-Midas touch," is in no way limited to the study of crime.[12] This criticism can apply equally well to numerous disciplines and subfields, including the sociological study of religion.

Imagine the religious scholar in the lab coat knocking on church doors and conducting surveys in small Caribbean villages with questionnaires asking religious leaders and their adherents: "How often do you attend church? On a scale of one to ten how religious are you? How much do you believe in the demons you exorcise?" Rather, the study of religious life gains greater insight moving beyond such questions, eschewing any attempt to explain the fascinating world of the supernatural using checked boxes and statistical formulae. It's a forced attempt to paint a clear portrait of religious reality. Young uses the analogy of artistic paintings to compare two alternative ways of representing social life. The first painting depicts realistic art that captures an image, like a fruit basket, as accurately as a photograph. This is the stuff of the orthodox sociologist providing a clear-cut, neat, and almost sanitized view of the world lacking contradictions. The other painting blurs and contradicts; the images have a dizzying, almost vertiginous effect on the viewer. The image, far from aesthetically pleasing, still titillates the eye with its fascinating depiction of a world riven in contradiction. The Charismatic ethnographer savors this world.

Chasing Religion in the Caribbean involves Charismatic ethnography in a sociological study of religion that takes into account this world that goes far beyond what meets the eye. It is here in the thrilling and mundane world of cultural life where we enter to understand religious life in its many nuances and complexities. This is the central task of this book and its methodological underpinning.

ETHNOGRAPHIC REFLEXIVITY IN THE STUDY OF CHARISMATIC CHRISTIANITY IN THE CARIBBEAN

Reflexive ethnography challenges the sacredness of Holy Ghost Science (see Chapter 3). Reflexive ethnography refuses to take the blood out of the bull. It admits the inherently subjective dimensions of the research process and the impact it has on the world the researcher enters. Reflexive ethnography strives for both the objective forms of knowledge while understanding the subjective experiences of both the researcher and researched. Ethnography attempts to place the subjective individual within the objective structures of power and ideology operating within a particular historical moment. Reflexive ethnography requires a deep understanding of the limits placed upon the ethnographer's observation by his or her position. It acknowledges the social world with a multitude of interpretations from a seemingly endless variety of lenses that can offer multiple accounts of a single event. Ethnographic reflexivity reveals the positivist, scientific dimension of ethnography and its inherent subjective and interpretive literary quality.

Ethnographic reflexivity involves developing rich narratives and biography, and in the context of the present study, a history of Afro-Caribbean slavery and resistance set in the cultural context of a highly unequal tourist-intensive postcolonial economy and the promise of the Western neo-liberal success while living in so-called second- and third-world spaces largely ignored in world affairs. The main characters struggle with living at and near poverty during uncertain times while finding empowerment in religious belief. The actors struggle with the challenges of everyday life, and—denied political, social, and cultural capital—find alternative forms of capital and empowerment. They create a subcultural world that both empowers and entraps them within conservative political and cultural views that serve as further obstacles to liberation. At times the characters express their vulnerabilities, struggle with spiritual issues, doubt their spiritual capabilities, confess their perceived sins, and consider whether their own roles exploit or help the poor. The characters reflect upon me as I reflect on them. They wonder why a secular non-black "crazy" academic wants to "rough it" throughout the non-tourist Caribbean world to study them, and they take pity on me for refusing salvation. I frown at their uncritical religious views, staunch conservatism, and highly judgmental attitudes. I reexamine my own stubborn secular views and euro-centric system of "objective" knowledge and science that dominates the world of social science and academia to try to understand their world of miracles, demonic possessions and exorcisms, tongue-speaking, and spiritual warfare. I wonder how they maintain charisma and enchantment in a world that increasingly denies it, while they wonder why I can't see the truth of their God through their eyes.[13] But in the end, we share the most intimate aspects of our lives to better understand the powerful religious world in Caribbean life.

INDEX

© The Author(s) 2016
P. Marina, *Chasing Religion in the Caribbean*,
DOI 10.1057/978-1-137-56100-8

INDEX 237

decentralization, 54, 55, 109, 149,
      163, 173, 175, 177, 214
demonic blasé attitude, 116
demonic forces, 4, 53, 80, 127,
      144n4, 151
demonic law, 16
demonic possession(s), 15, 17, 63,
      81, 233
demonic spirits, 3, 4, 151
disease, 4, 17, 37, 80, 81, 122, 151,
      182, 192–4, 207, 216
divided Christian churches, 1, 44, 45,
      52, 54, 64, 209
division in the church, 188, 203, 212
Dominica, 30, 40, 42, 44, 54, 67, 75,
      77n19, 108, 139, 147–77,
      179n19, 192, 214, 222, 224

E
early pentecostal movement, 34, 36–8
emerging leader (s), 54, 175, 201, 202
English Harbour, 112n3
ethnographic it, 53, 70–5
ethnographic pitfalls and recovery, 160–3
ethnographic reflexivity, 232, 233
ethnography, 53, 61n85, 63–75,
      112n5, 120, 225n10, 227–9, 232
evangelical movement, 1
evil spirits, 3, 8, 72, 80, 81
exorcism, 8–11, 13, 15, 21, 44, 53,
      63, 68, 79, 86, 87, 112n2, 113,
      117, 118, 120, 230, 233
exorcism scene, 21, 117
extended transnational religious
      organization, 51
external adversity, 54, 149, 157, 163,
      167, 168, 170–2, 176
external adversity and internal conflict,
      54, 149, 157, 163, 167, 168,
      170–2, 176
external pressure(s), 55, 110, 144,
      163, 167–9, 177, 215, 218

F
Family Focus, 121, 130
Fenton, Josepha, 202
Fieldnotes, 113
formal institutionalization, 123
Formal Organizational Structure,
      PAWI, 41–3
Francis, Kenneth (Reverend),
      108, 189
free will, 39, 89, 109–11, 144, 194
Future of the Charismatic
      Church, 217

G
Gaggi, 153, 154
Gaining entrée, 69, 228
Gay marriage, 140, 167, 169
gender inequality, 54, 182, 195, 200
generational curse, 85
gift (s), 23, 34, 36, 54, 55n3, 81, 82,
      106, 150–2, 164, 175, 182, 190
global religious networking, 64, 149
Go-along ethnography, 120–1, 227
Goffman, Erving, 68, 74
Gospel music, 181, 202
grasper, 178n13
Grazian, David, 71

H
Haiti, 30, 44, 67, 139, 219–25,
      225n1, 225n3, 228
Hard numbers (Charismatic
      Christianity), 23–32, 88
healing, 33, 34, 37, 54, 55n8, 56n9,
      67, 80, 86, 106, 120, 150–2,
      158, 175, 182, 190–2, 194,
      210, 220
healing and paralysis, 190–2
Hebden, Ellen, 38, 59n53
hell, 8, 15, 64, 66, 72, 77n22, 83,
      114, 132, 157

scientific knowledge, 80, 157, 230–3
Scott, Larry (traveling preacher), 108,
     149–53, 165, 175
scratch where it itches, 142
secularization, 4, 155, 157, 179n15
Seymour, William, 33, 34
Simmel, Georg, 116, 144n2, 171
simultaneous process centralization
     and decentralization, 173,
     177, 214
Sin, 103
Sir Howard Fergus, 182, 195–200,
     207, 208n5, 208n8
slavery, 4, 5, 9, 15, 21, 85, 169, 199,
     217, 218, 220, 232
small institutionally unaffiliated
     church, 53, 217
small pentecostal church, 87, 93
Soca music, 88
social change, 7, 22, 23, 39, 49, 52,
     54, 148, 175–7
sociological imagination, 71
soft Caribbean, 65–6, 88
Soulful ethnography, 70–5
specialization of spiritual labor, 175
specialized charisma, 175–6
Spencer, Baldwin, 45, 91, 138
spirit, 5–7, 9, 10, 12–16, 18n2, 23,
     33, 34, 37, 39, 41, 55n3, 55n8,
     56n8, 56n12, 57n17, 59n51,
     59n57, 60n71, 73, 80, 84–6,
     125, 133, 148, 150, 151, 159,
     164, 167, 173, 175, 176, 177n4,
     179n17, 193, 200, 215, 220–2
spirit possession, 80
spiritual battles, 8, 115, 116
spiritual demons, 17
spiritual disease, 17, 81, 151, 193,
     194, 207, 216
spiritual empowerment, 36
spiritual forces, 3, 36, 37, 80
spiritual gift(s), 36, 56n8, 175

spiritual mosh pit, 83
spiritual warfare, 3, 87, 120, 174,
     210, 233
sprit of witchcraft, 13–15, 151
structural centralization and
     decentralization, 54, 163,
     173–6
supernatural forces, 1, 4, 5, 9, 15, 16,
     53, 117, 125, 194
supernatural gifts, 54, 151
supernatural healers, 17

T
themes, 53, 54, 55n6, 71, 89, 144n4,
     148, 149, 163, 189, 213–15
The Rev. *See* Henry Nigel
Thomas dictum, 8
tongue-speaking, 19n8, 33, 34, 36,
     39, 48, 61n85, 67, 76n14, 83,
     112n5, 120, 218n1, 233
Too big to control, 133
Toronto Blessing, 5, 19n9, 148,
     178n9, 179n22
Transnational Holy Ghost capital,
     49, 52
transnationalism, 19n11, 50, 51,
     57n21, 58n38
transnationalization, 50–2,
     61n81, 104
transnational religious connections,
     50, 60n73
transnational religious networking,
     22, 53, 104, 107, 213, 214
transnational religious networks,
     50, 51, 213
Traveling preachers, 148–50
Trinidad, 21, 30–2, 40, 42, 44, 53,
     55n2, 60n65, 67–9, 73, 75, 90,
     102, 108, 109, 111, 113–45,
     163, 178n13, 182, 185, 189,
     194, 202, 205, 213, 214, 216

The manufacturer's authorised representative in the EU is Springer
Nature Customer Service Centre GmbH, Europaplatz 3, 69115 Heidelberg,
Germany. If you have any concerns regarding our products, please
contact ProductSafety@springernature.com

Printed and bound by CPI Group (UK) Ltd, Croydon, CR0 4YY
23/04/2026
02095595-0004